S J Weslake
Stewart, BC
Oct 25/73

31/05/74

SUPERNATURE

BY LYALL WATSON

SUPERNATURE
THE OMNIVOROUS APE

SUPERNATURE

BY LYALL WATSON

ANCHOR PRESS/DOUBLEDAY

GARDEN CITY, NEW YORK

1973

ISBN: 0-385-00744-2
Library of Congress Catalog Card Number 72–92399
Copyright © 1973 by Lyall Watson

"The most beautiful experience we can have, is the mysterious."

ALBERT EINSTEIN, in *Living Philosophies*, 1931.

Contents

PART THREE: MIND

PART FOUR: TIME

Introduction

SCIENCE NO LONGER holds any absolute truths. Even the discipline of physics, whose laws once went unchallenged, has had to submit to the indignity of an Uncertainty Principle. In this climate of disbelief, we have begun to doubt even fundamental propositions, and the old distinction between natural and supernatural has become meaningless.

I find this tremendously exciting. The picture of science as a jigsaw puzzle, with a finite number of pieces that would one day all be slotted neatly into place, has never been appealing. Experience indicates that things are not like that at all. Every new development in the microscope reveals further minute detail in structures once thought to be indivisible. Each enlargement in the power of the telescope adds thousands of galaxies to a list already so long that it is meaningless to all but mathematicians. Even research into what once seemed to be simple behavior patterns has a way of going on forever.

Fifty years ago naturalists were content with the observation that bats catch moths. Then came the discovery that bats produce sounds inaudible to the human ear and use echoes to locate their prey. Now it appears that not only do moths have soundproofing, but that they have ears specifically designed to listen in to an approaching enemy transmitter. To counter this advance, bats developed an irregular flight path, which confused the moths until they in turn came up with an ultrasonic jamming device. But bats still catch moths, and it can only be a matter of time before research discovers the next development in this escalating drama of nature.

All the best science has soft edges, limits that are still obscure and extend without interruption into areas that are wholly inexplicable. On the fringe, between those things that we understand as normal occurrences and those that are completely paranormal and defy explanation, are a cluster of semi-normal phenomena. Between nature and the supernatural are a host of happenings that I choose to describe as Supernature. It is with these go-betweens that this book is concerned.

In the course of a fairly catholic education in most of the life sciences, there have been many moments when the syllabus brushed up against something strange, shied away, and tried to pretend that it hadn't happened. These loose ends have always worried me and have now accumulated to a point where I am forced to go back and attempt to pick some of them up and try to relate them to the rest of my experience. Viewed together, they begin to make some kind of sense, but I must emphasize that this is very much a beginning and in no way a definitive study. I am resigned to the fact that my synthesis goes so far beyond the bounds of established practice that many scientists will find it outrageous, while at the same time it does not go nearly far enough to satisfy believers in everything occult. This is what bridges are about. I hope that there can be some kind of meeting in the middle.

The supernatural is usually defined as that which is not explicable by the known forces of nature. Supernature knows no bounds. Too often we see only what we expect to see: our view of the world is restricted by the blinkers of our limited experience; but it need not be this way. Supernature is nature with all its flavors intact, waiting to be tasted. I offer it as a logical extension of the present state of science, as a solution to some of the problems with which traditional science cannot cope, and as an analgesic to modern man.

I hope that it will prove to be more than that. Few aspects of human behavior are so persistent as our need to believe in things unseen—and as a biologist, I find it hard to accept that this is purely fortuitous. The belief, or the strange things to which this belief is so stubbornly attached, must have real survival value, and I think that we are rapidly approaching a situation in which this value will become apparent. As man uses up the resources of the world, he is going to have to rely more and more on his own. Many of these are at the moment concealed in the occult—a word that simply means "secret knowledge" and is a very good description of something that we have known all along but have been hiding from ourselves.

This natural history of the supernatural is designed to extend the traditional five senses into areas where others have been operating undercover. It is an attempt to fit all of nature, the known and the unknown, into the body of Supernature and to show that, of all the faculties we possess, none is more important at this time than a wide-eyed sense of wonder.

LYALL WATSON, PH.D.
Ios, Greece, 1971.

Rationale

THE SUBJECT MATTER of most of this book is so controversial that I have felt it necessary to give detailed references to all my sources of information. These appear as numbers in the text, which refer to the bibliography. Most are papers published in reputable journals, and where I have myself not been able to check the findings, I have had to rely on the fact that most editors send material to expert referees before accepting it for final publication. Wherever possible, I have consulted the original source material and found that this paid huge dividends. A report in *Scientific American* of March 1965, for instance, under the title "Eyeless Vision Unmasked," claimed that Rosa Kuleshova was a fraud and that "peeking is easy, according to those who understand mentalist acts." Several books since that time have used this report as justification for dismissing the entire phenomenon, but reference to the original research shows that, despite the fact that she was once caught cheating very clumsily at a public performance, Kuleshova also possesses a talent that cannot reasonably be shrugged off in this cavalier fashion. I make no apology for heavy reliance at many points on publications such as the *Journal of the Society for Psychical Research* and the *Journal of Parapsychology*—they set standards of erudition and objectivity as high as any other academic publications.

Where no reference appears, the flights of fancy are my own.

SUPERNATURE

PART ONE

COSMOS

"I cannot believe that God plays dice with the cosmos."

ALBERT EINSTEIN, in the London *Observer*, 5 April 1964.

THERE IS LIFE on earth—one life, which embraces every animal and plant on the planet. Time has divided it up into several million parts, but each is an integral part of the whole. A rose is a rose, but it is also a robin and a rabbit. We are all of one flesh, drawn from the same crucible.

There are ninety-two chemical elements that occur in nature, but the same small selection of sixteen form the basis of all living matter. One of the sixteen, carbon, plays a central role because of its ability to form complex chains and rings that can be built into an immense number of compounds. And yet, from the thousands of possible combinations, just twenty amino acids are singled out as the units of construction for all proteins. Most significant of all, these proteins are produced in the right place at the right time by an ordered sequence of events governed by a code carried in just four molecules, called nucleotide bases. This is true whether the protein is destined to become a bacterium or a Bactrian camel. The instructions for all life are written in the same simple language.

The activities of life are governed by the second law of thermodynamics. This says that the natural state of matter is chaos and that all things tend to run down and become random and disordered. Living systems consist of highly organized matter; they create order out of disorder, but it is a constant battle against the process of disruption. Order is maintained by bringing in energy from outside to keep the system going. So biochemical systems exchange matter with their surroundings all the time, they are open, thermodynamic processes, as opposed to the closed, thermostatic structure of ordinary chemical reactions.

This is the secret of life. It means that there is a continuous communication not only between living things and their environment, but among all things living in that environment. An intricate web of interaction connects all life into one vast, self-maintaining system. Each part is related to every other part and we are all part of the whole, part of Supernature.

In this first section I want to look at some of the ways in which our life system is influenced by its environment.

Chapter One:

Cosmic Law and Order

CHAOS IS COMING. It is written in the laws of thermodynamics. Left to itself, everything tends to become more and more disorderly until the final and natural state of things is a completely random distribution of matter. Any kind of order, even that as simple as the arrangement of atoms in a molecule, is unnatural and happens only by chance encounters that reverse the general trend. These events are statistically unlikely, and the further combination of molecules into anything as highly organized as a living organism is wildly improbable. Life is a rare and unreasonable thing.

The continuance of life depends on the maintenance of an unstable situation. It is like a vehicle that can be kept on the road only by continual running repairs and by access to an endless supply of spare parts. Life draws its components from the environment. From the vast mass of chaotic probability flowing by, it extracts only the distinctive improbabilities, the little bits of order among the general confusion. Some of these it uses as a source of energy, which it obtains by the destructive process of digestion; from others, it gets the information it needs to ensure continued survival. This is the hardest part, extracting order from disorder, distinguishing those aspects of the environment that carry useful information from those which simply contribute to the over-all process of decay. Life manages to do this by a splendid sense of the incongruous.

The cosmos is a bedlam of noisy confusion. Everything in it is subjected to a constant bombardment by millions of conflicting electromagnetic and sound waves. Life protects itself from this turmoil by using sense organs, which are like narrow slits, letting in only a very limited range of frequencies. But sometimes even these are too much, so there is the additional barrier of a nervous system, which filters the input and sorts it out into "useful information" and "irrelevant noise." For instance, if a cat is exposed to a continuous electronic click, it hears and responds to the stimulus at first but is soon habituated to it and in the end effectively ignores the sound altogether. (87) An electrode implanted in the auditory nerve, leading from the inner ear to the brain, shows that, after a while, the nerve no longer even sends information about the clicks on to the brain; the regular stimulus has been classified as irrelevant background noise and discarded as a source of information. But as soon as it stops, the cat pricks up its ears and takes notice of this novel and therefore incongruous phenomenon. Sailors respond in the same way by waking suddenly from even the deepest sleep when the sound of their ship's engine changes pitch or ceases altogether.

We all have this ability to focus on certain stimuli and to ignore others. A good example is "cocktail party concentration," which enables us to tune in to the sound of just one person's voice among so many all saying similar things. (235) Even in our sleep, recordings of our brain waves show that we produce stronger reactions to the sound of our own names being spoken than we do to any other names. These are responses that we learn, but all life automatically sorts out environmental chaos in the same way and concentrates only on the improbable orderly events hidden in the prevailing disorder.

Living organisms select information from their surroundings, process it according to a program (in this case one that will ensure the best possible chance of survival), and supply an output of order (which is in turn a source of raw materials and information for other life). This is an accurate description of how a computer operates, so it is not surprising that a greater understanding of life should have come hand in hand with the recent development of computer systems. Computers operate on the basis of programmed information, which is supplied in accordance with a theory that describes information as a function of improbability, saying "the more improbable an event, the more information it conveys." (41) Returning to the metaphor of life as a vehicle, this means that we are bound to hear the improbable rattle in a new motorcar but hardly notice the much more probable rattle in an old one. The sound may be identical, but heard from the driver's seat of the old car, it is a part of the environment that carries very little useful information. In a system in which everything tends toward decay, another symptom of disorder is not at all improbable and in no way distinctive.

A single bright light on a moonless night in the desert is very conspicuous and obviously worth investigating, but even when surrounded by other lights, one will stand out if it flashes on and off or changes color. Hurtling through space on our planet, we are continually exposed to the forces of the cosmos. Most of these are fairly constant and make little conscious impression on us; we are no more aware of them than we are of the force of gravity that keeps us attached to our vehicle. It is only when the cosmic forces change or fluctuate like flashing lamps that they become conspicuous and acquire information and signal value. Many of these changes are cyclic, occurring again and again at more or less regular intervals, which gives life time to develop a specific sensitivity to the changes and a response to the information they convey.

I have said that life occurs by chance and that the probability of its occurring, and continuing, is infinitesimal. It is even more unlikely that this life could, in the comparatively short time it has existed on this planet, develop into more than a million distinct living forms—and these are only the tip of an enormous pyramid of past successes and failures. To believe that this took place only by chance, places a great strain on the credulity of even the most mechanistic biologists. The geneticist Waddington compares it to "throwing bricks together in heaps" in the hope that they would "arrange themselves into an inhabitable house." (334) I believe that chance did in fact play a large part in the process, but that its action was mediated by a pattern of information that lies half hidden in the cosmic chaos.

The cosmos itself is patternless, being a jumble of random and disordered events. Grey Walter, the discoverer of several basic rhythmic patterns in the brain, puts it perfectly: He says that the most significant thing about a pattern is that "you can remember it and compare it with another pattern. This is what distinguishes it from random events or chaos. For the notion of randomness . . . implies that disorder is beyond comparison; you cannot remember chaos or compare one chaos with another; there is no plural of the word." (335) Life makes patterns out of patternless disorder, but I suggest that life was itself made by a pattern and that this design is inherent in cosmic forces to which life was, and still is, exposed. These environmental influences are behind most of Supernature.

THE EARTH

Cosmic forces recur in cyclical patterns, to which life learns to respond. The strongest responses are naturally linked to the shortest cycles, those which produce the greatest number of changes in a given period of time. The most fundamental and familiar of all the changes to which life is subject are those produced by the movement of our earth about its axis.

We live on a distorted sphere that is not only slightly flattened at the poles but also a little pear-shaped, with a bulge in the Southern Hemisphere. The sphere spins from west to east at about a thousand miles an hour and travels around the sun at more than sixty times this speed, but both movements are influenced by its irregular shape. The time taken for the earth to complete one full revolution about its own axis is not only variable but also depends on which object in space is used as a reference point to decide when the turn is complete. If we choose the sun as our fixed point, one revolution, or one solar day, lasts 24.0 hours. The lunar day is 24.8 hours, and, measuring our rotation relative to one of the distant fixed stars, we get a sidereal day 23.9 hours long. For convenience, we base our calendars on the mean solar day— the average length of all solar days throughout the year, but this is an arbitrary selection and it seems that life itself is sensitive to all three cycles.

We say that there are only twenty-four hours in "the day," and yet we also divide the same period up into "the day" and "the night." This confusion of words leads to real confusion about the roles of day and night in biology, but the fact is that all life on earth is ultimately dependent on the sun, and so the problem boils down to the presence or absence of sunlight. One of the most traumatic changes that life can experience is the sudden and unexpected disappearance of the sun. On the rare occasions of total eclipse, living things are thrown into complete confusion. I have seen an eagle drop straight out of the sky to take refuge in the crown of a tree, and a foraging troop of baboons rush into the defensive formation they usually assume in response to a predator, neither species knowing quite which way to turn to meet this new and unexpected threat. Only man knows when to expect the next eclipse of the sun by our moon, but all life is tuned to the daily obliteration of sunlight by the movement of our own planet.

Light and dark alternate in a regular pattern that provides life with basic information. This pattern has been called the diurnal rhythm, but the length of the cycle, the relative amounts of light and dark, and an organism's response to light or the absence of light, all vary. So a new and less confusing name was coined in 1960 by Franz Halberg, a medical physiologist at the University of Minnesota. He combined two Latin roots to produce the word "circadian," meaning that which lasts about one day. (132) Circadian rhythms produced by the earth's movement can be seen in action in life at every level of complexity.

At the lowest level are a group of organisms to which both botanists and zoologists lay claim. These are tiny pieces of undivided protoplasm that have chlorophyll and use it like plants to make food from the sun, but also have a long, whip-shaped flagellum, which undulates underwater and moves them like animals in pursuit of the sun. If kept in the dark, they abandon botanical methods of food production and pick up particles of ready-made food, in the best zoological tradition. Typical of the group is a little green teardrop called *Euglena gracilis*, which lives in shallow freshwater pools. At one end of its thin elastic body, near the whip-shaped propeller, is a minute "eyespot" of dark pigment that is not itself responsive to light, but masks the real photosensitive granule lying at the base of the whip. When the eyespot covers the "eye," nothing happens, but when light falls on the granule, it starts the whip waving at about twelve beats each second and sends the organism spiraling out into the light.

Euglena comes to rest in the sunlight by positioning itself so that the granule is covered by the rakish eye patch. As the sun moves, so does *Euglena,* but gradually it begins to lose its sensitivity, and toward the end of the day it is a lot less active. If it remained mobile all day, chasing after every stray sunbeam, the organism would use energy as fast as it could produce it and have none left over for other processes or for sustaining itself during the night. So *Euglena* has not only developed a vital response to change in the environment but has also acted on the information provided by the regularity of these environmental changes. It has produced a mechanism for regulating its movement so that it operates at an optimal level, working quickly when movement is most necessary and phasing out as it becomes less important. The fact that this regulation is "built in" has been shown by its persistence in a population of *Euglena* that were kept in continuous darkness. Despite the total lack of light, all individuals became active and sensitive to light at the same time each day, a time when the sun they could not see was coming up, and they became insensitive when the light outside the laboratory began to fade. (250) Unable to make food from the sun, they took to feeding on particles in their environment, but they did this only during normal daylight hours, despite the fact that this food was available all the time. Even *Euglena,* with its solitary cell, follows an accurate circadian rhythm.

Our knowledge of the development of multicellular organisms from the first single cells is very limited, because they seldom left a fossil record, but it seems likely that all plant and animal life was derived from something rather like *Euglena*. In the course of evolution, cells destined to serve more specialized functions in complex organisms were modified a great deal, but most retained something of their early independence. Even man has single cells that can still leave his body altogether and live and move entirely on their own—on their way to fertilize an egg. If one cell is taken from the root of a plant such as the carrot, it can be kept alive in a nutrient solution and give rise to a whole new carrot plant. (310) We see living organisms as entities and tend to forget that they are intricate societies of single cells and that each of the components has a great deal in common with all the other cells, not only in that individual but in every other organism that ever lived. Alexander Pope recognized that "all are but parts of one stupendous whole, whose body nature is. . . ." (251)

Circadian rhythms exist in simple unicellular organisms without hormones or specialized nervous systems. In more complex, multicellular forms that do have these advantages, they occur in more intricate patterns and respond to more subtle environmental stimuli.

Of all the species drafted into service in our laboratories, few have contributed as much to our knowledge of life as a fruit fly called *Drosophila*. There are over a thousand species belonging to the genus, but the most popular conscript has been *Drosophila melanogaster*. This little fly with its wings spread is just the size of a letter "v" in this print, but in 1909 Morgan discovered that it had enormous chromosomes in the cells of its salivary glands, and the fly was soon surrounded by murmurous haunts of geneticists. Today almost every university in the world supports a culture of fruit flies, so it is not surprising that when biologists turned their attention to the study of natural rhythms, *Drosophila* was again called in to assist the scientists with their inquiries. The results were fascinating.

Small animals have a very large surface area in proportion to their mass. If, like the fruit fly, they live on land, they are faced with the problem of losing water from all parts of their surface, and have to find some way of conserving body fluids. Most insects solve the problem by growing a tough, waxy cuticle that resists desiccation. Adult *Drosophila* are protected in this way, but when the flies first emerge from their puparia, the bodies are still soft and their wings are folded into a delicate tangle of lace that can expand and stiffen only if moisture is available. So the flies all emerge at dawn, when the air is cool and humidity is high. Under natural conditions the pupa is probably aware of light and temperature and can time its emergence properly, but it does not need all these clues.

Colin Pittendrigh of Princeton University devised a set of elegant experiments that show how well *Drosophila* responds to even the smallest scraps of information. (248) He kept fruit-fly eggs in complete darkness under conditions of constant temperature and humidity. The eggs hatched, and the larvae grew, and pupated. Development took place as if normal inside the puparium, and the adult flies eventually emerged, but they broke out at random, following no circadian pattern at all. Pittendrigh then repeated the whole experiment with a second batch of eggs, but this time he allowed the larvae to see light for just one thousandth of a second, by firing an electronic flash at them once. At no other time in their lives were they ever exposed to light, and yet all the flies emerged from their puparia simultaneously.

The internal rhythms of the developing insects were synchronized by an incredibly subtle signal and continued to keep time for several days following the stimulus. Pittendrigh went on to show that the rhythm was circadian by giving the larvae a slightly longer exposure to light. Flies from these emerged together at a time that would have been sunrise if the time when the light went out was considered as sunset on some earlier evening. In other words, the flies started counting when darkness fell. It seems from these experiments that the rhythm is inherent in *Drosophila* and that the fly has only to be prodded very gently to get the cycle going and to keep it going. I am particularly impressed by the fact that emerging from a puparium is something that a fly does but once in its life; it has no chance to learn and practice this activity, and yet it operates on a 24-hour schedule. This natural rhythm must be instinctive, built into the memory of the insect's cells and waiting only to be tuned by the environment in order to produce a series of perfectly timed behavior patterns.

The cells themselves may house this clock, but Janet Harker at Cambridge University has shown that co-ordination between cells is achieved by chemical messengers that carry time signals. (135) Cockroaches generally suffer from a bad press, but they are excellent experimental animals. The common species *Periplaneta americana* becomes active soon after dark each day and scavenges continuously for five or six hours, but if one has its head cut off, it no longer shows this circadian rhythm of activity. Not surprising, perhaps; but in fact if the head is removed surgically and precautions are taken to keep the insect from bleeding to death, it survives for several weeks. A headless cockroach eventually starves to death, but while it lives, it continues to move in a random and desultory fashion.

Janet Harker found that she could give a cockroach back its sense of direction by a process of transfusion. All insects have very rudimentary circulatory systems, in which blood just washes around in the body cavity bathing the internal organs. One individual can be made to share its blood with another by simply cutting a hole in the body wall of each and connecting them together with a short glass tube. Harker solved the problem of differences of opinion by an ingenious if somewhat gruesome compromise. She strapped the blood donor upside down on the back of the headless cockroach and cut off the upper one's legs to prevent it kicking and up-setting the weird combination. Paired like this in parabiosis (which means living side by side) the double-bodied cock-roach with one head and one set of legs functioned almost normally. It once again showed the typical circadian rhythm with activity confined to the period immediately after dark. (137) Something in the blood of the donor passed through the glass tube and communicated rhythm to the legs of the disorganized, headless cockroach. The substance responsible seems to be a hormone produced in the insect's head. Harker made a series of surgical transplants, each involving one of the organs in the head, and found that the subesophageal ganglion (a tangle of nerves just below the mouth) was the source of the message. She discovered that if this ganglion was transferred to a headless cockroach, the insect developed a rhythm identical to that of the donor.

So, in the cockroach, the center that responds to natural cycles of light and dark has been located and can even be translocated. This is vital information, but Harker went on to turn up something even more interesting. (136) She kept one group of cockroaches on a normal schedule and put a second group on a reverse timetable, with lights burning all night and darkness during the day. The second lot soon adapted to this situation and became active during the artificial night, so their rhythms were always out of phase with the control group. A subesophageal ganglion could easily be transplanted from a member of one group to a headless individual in the other, and it would impose its own rhythm on the recipient; but if the second cockroach kept its own pacemaker as well, there was immediate trouble. The extra ganglion turned out to be a lethal weapon. Having two time-keepers sending out two completely different signals, the poor insect was thrown into turmoil. Its behavior became completely disorganized, and it soon developed acute stress symptoms, such as malignant tumors in the gut, and died.

This is a perfect demonstration of the importance of natural cycles in life; confusion of the cockroach rhythm kills the insect. Life keeps time, and it seems that the beat is an old one, determined mainly by the rotation of our own planet, which turns the sun on and off like some giant cosmic strobe light.

Life arose in the primordial broth by the action of sunlight on simple molecules. It is just possible, by stretching our knowledge of biochemistry, to envisage a situation in which life could arise in the absence of light, but it is difficult to see how it could continue to survive once it had consumed all the available food. Light waves carry both energy and information. It is no accident that the amount of energy contained in visible light is perfectly matched to the energy needed to carry out most chemical reactions. Electromagnetic radiation covers a vast range of possible frequencies, but both sunlight and life are confined to the same minute section of this spectrum, and it is difficult to avoid the conclusion that one is directly dependent on the other.

As various forms of life evolved on earth, the advantage went to those that were able to sense their environment and act on the information received. Because light covers considerable distances, it is probably the best source of information available, and of all cosmic forces, the best suited to sensing. The daily alteration between light and dark provides information on the earth's movement about its axis. And the fluctuation in the relative amounts of light and dark in each day tells of the earth's progress in its movement about the sun.

The axis of the spinning earth is tilted from the vertical, so as the planet travels on its orbital circuit, it presents each day a slightly different face to the sun. Twice in every year, the suns rays fall vertically on the equator and days and nights everywhere are exactly twelve hours long. At all other times either the North or the South Pole is angled toward our star and there is an imbalance between the amounts of light and dark that fall on places at various latitudes. The regular shift in this relationship provides organisms with information that helps them adjust to a yearly cycle of changes in the circadian rhythm. This sensitivity is called the circannual rhythm—that which lasts about one year.

It was discovered almost by accident by Kenneth Fisher in his work at the University of Toronto, on the golden-mantled ground squirrel *Citellus lateralis*. (244) Fisher kept these tiny high-altitude rodents in a windowless room at a constant temperature of $0°$ C and twelve hours of light each day. He found that they were active and healthy, with a body temperature of $37°$ C, until October; then their temperatures fell to $1°$ C and the squirrels went into their usual winter hibernation. And then, despite the lack of any changes in light or heat, they all woke up in April, were active all the summer, and went back into stupor the following autumn. In a second experiment, Fisher changed the temperature to a constant $35°$ C and found that this was warm enough to prevent the squirrels from becoming dormant, but they still gained weight in autumn and lost it slowly through the winter, just as though they were actually hibernating.

Sensitivity to an annual cycle has obvious advantages: It helps an organism to predict seasonal changes in its environment and to make the necessary allowances for them. A bird that spends its winters in the constant conditions of the tropics could use this sense to tell it when the time had come to return north for nesting. A mammal that stays behind through the northern winter profits from a sensitivity to annual changes by knowing when to lay in a store of food. Both animals are co-ordinated by photoperiodism—a sensitivity to the relative amounts of light and dark in every day.

The tiny pale-green plant lice, or aphids, that spend their summers busily plunging their mouth parts into plants and sucking out the juices, reproduce during the long days by a process of virgin birth in which no males are involved. (191) But when there is less than fourteen hours of daylight, as autumn approaches, they start reproducing sexually and lay eggs that last through the winter. Many other animals change their appearance, rather than their habits, and adopt a winter plumage. Dull-brown summer weasels turn into resplendent white winter ones that can find concealment in the snow. If a weasel is kept under extra artificial light in the autumn to extend its days, it never produces its camouflage coat, so, like the aphid, it depends entirely on the day length to tell it when winter approaches.

Visible light from the sun also acts on non-living matter, by agitating its molecules and producing heat. Temperature is nothing more than a measurement of the amount of energy a molecule develops by moving. At high temperatures, molecules have more energy, move faster, and bump into each other more often. This is why an increase in temperature speeds up the rate of most chemical reactions—hence the Bunsen burner applied to an experiment to get it going. Biochemical reactions are affected in the same way, and as long as the heat is not high enough to do any damage, the higher the temperature the greater the rate of metabolism. So, by their very structure, living organisms have a built-in sensitivity to temperature change, and as the changes are produced by sunlight, they follow the same 24-hour cycle as photoperiodism. Hans Kalmus at London University found that grasshopper eggs hatched at dawn every day if kept at

22° C, but that they hatched only at sunrise on every third day if kept at 11° C. (170)

Most cold-blooded animals are completely at the mercy of temperature fluctuations, which set the pace of their lives, but in mammals and birds it is often the activity that determines body temperature. Mice reach a temperature peak when their activity is greatest, around midnight, and are coolest in the heat of midday because that is the middle of their rest period. (18) So their temperatures follow a 24-hour cycle even though this is not imposed by the temperature of their surroundings. Some parasites take advantage of this phenomenon and set their clocks by the cycles of their hosts.

Malarial parasites invade red blood corpuscles, where they multiply until the cell can no longer withstand the pressure and bursts, releasing the offspring to seek out other corpuscles, where the same thing takes place again. If the parasites did this one at a time, they would have little effect on their host, but what happens is that all the malaria cells present in the body multiply at exactly the same time, and this simultaneous onslaught produces the classic symptoms of fever. Soon after noon the host begins to feel cold and starts shivering despite the fact that his skin feels hot to the touch; headache, backache, and vomiting follow and intensify throughout the afternoon until, at sunset, the body temperature shoots up as high as 42° C and he sweats profusely. It is biologically inefficient for a parasite to kill its host, but the *Plasmodium* that produces malaria fever takes this risk, because it is vital for its own survival that it should also come into contact with another kind of host. Man is home for the non-sexual stage of the parasite, but the sexual stages require the unique environment of the stomach of a female of a certain species of mosquito. To get there, they have to be sucked up by the insect as it bites the man, which is a complex situation requiring perfect timing, but it all works out splendidly via the fever. The parasites become active and reach sexual maturity in man's blood stream, producing a fever, which raises the host's temperature, produces sweating, and attracts the mosquito just after dark, when these nocturnal insects are most active.

Little or no light penetrates to the blood vessels, where the parasites live. Their environment has no marked photoperiod, but they are able to bring their cycle to a peak at dusk by following the pattern of their host's temperature rhythm. Man is active during the daylight hours; his temperature follows the pattern of activity, and the parasites follow the temperature. Night workers reverse their activity patterns and therefore have their fevers in the morning, confusing the parasites hopelessly and putting them completely out of step with their alternative hosts, the mosquitoes. (141)

In the same way that parasites set their clocks by the body temperature of their host, so all life can measure time by responding to temperature changes of the body of our host, this planet.

Extensions of the photoperiodic research on fruit flies and cockroaches show quite clearly that both these species also respond to what could be called thermoperiodism. In constant darkness flies emerge from their puparia shortly after the temperature cycle reaches its lowest point, which in nature would be just before the dawn. Temperature can act as a time signal. In fact it may do even more than that: it may be absolutely essential for survival. An American botanist has found that the leaves of tomato plants are damaged and die if kept under conditions of constant light and heat, but remain perfectly healthy if given a 24-hour cycle of temperature change. (150) In practice it does not matter whether the temperature goes up or down; any regular fluctuation between the limits of 10 and 30° C was found to be equally effective.

Piece by piece we are beginning to build up a picture of the way in which physiological rhythms respond to environmental cues. Life is adapted to the earth's movement by a circadian rhythm and to the earth's position in space by a circannual rhythm. Sometimes these daily and yearly cycles intertwine to produce patterns of exquisite sensitivity that make an organism responsive to every nuance in its environment. This is as it should be. As parasites on the skin of our planet, we can be truly successful only when we become aware of its pulse and learn to pace our lives to the rhythm of its deep, untroubled breathing.

Our host, however, is not alone. Earth in its turn is ruffled by the galactic winds of change and subject to forces brought to bear on it by an even wider environment. Inevitably these forces filter through to us, and life on earth learns to dance to the rhythm of other bodies. The most insistent beat comes, naturally, from our nearest neighbors.

THE MOON

When Isaac Newton was twenty-three years old and a student at Cambridge, he was forced to leave his college by the wave of bubonic plague that brought black death to most of England in 1665. While on this enforced holiday in the country, he saw an orblike apple fall to the earth and, in his own words, "began to think of gravitation as extending to the orb of the moon." These thoughts led to his universal theory of gravity, which says that every particle in the universe attracts every other particle with a force that depends on their masses and the distance between them. The earth attracts the moon strongly enough to hold it in orbit, and the moon is large enough and close enough to tug insistently at earth's mantle. The water on earth's surface behaves like a loose garment that can be pulled out from the body to fall back as earth turns away again. The moon circles the earth once every 27.3 days, rotating brazenly as she does so, to keep the same face turned always to us, but earth shows all its sides to the satellite once very 24.8 hours. This means that the waters of earth flow out toward the moon, and therefore bring high tide to any land that lies in that direction, forty-eight minutes later each day.

Every drop of water in the ocean responds to this force, and every living marine animal and plant is made aware of the rhythm. The lives of those that inhabit the margins of the sea depend entirely on this awareness. One very small flatworm, for instance, has entered into partnership with a green alga, and whenever the tide goes out, it must come up from the sand to expose its greenery to the sun. Rachel Carson took some of these animals into the laboratory and there described their conditioning to the tidal rhythm in her usual effortless and poetic way: "Twice each day *Convoluta* rises out of the sand in the bottom of the aquarium, into the light of the sun. And twice each day it sinks again into the soil. Without a brain, or what we would call a memory, or even any very clear perception, *Convoluta* continues to live out its life in this alien place, remembering, in every fibre of its small green body, the tidal rhythm of the distant sea." (66)

This is true of any tidal animal taken to a laboratory near the sea. For convenience' sake, most marine research units are established on the coast, but fortunately for science one indefatigable researcher into natural rhythms lives and works a thousand miles from the sea, in Evanston, Illinois. Frank Brown started working with oysters in 1954. He found that they had a marked tidal rhythm, opening their shells to feed at high tide and closing them to prevent damage and drying out during the ebb. In laboratory tanks they keep this strict rhythm going, so Brown decided to take some specimens home with him to Illinois to examine more closely. Evanston is a suburb of Chicago on the shore of Lake Michigan, but even here the oysters continued to remember the tidal rhythm of their home, on Long Island Sound, in Connecticut. Everything went well for two weeks, but on the fifteenth day Brown noticed that a slippage in the rhythm had occurred. The oysters were no longer opening and closing in harmony with the tide that washed their distant home and it seemed as though the experiment had gone wrong, but the fascinating thing was that the behavior of all the mollusks had altered in the same way and they were still keeping time with each other. Brown calculated the difference between the old rhythm and the new one and discovered that the oysters now opened up at the time the tide would have flooded Evanston —had the town been on the shore and not perched on the bank of a Great Lake 580 feet above sea level. (42)

Somehow the oysters realized that they had been moved one thousand miles to the west and were able to calculate, and apply a correction to, their tidal timetable. Brown at first suspected that the later times of sunrise and sunset might have given them the clues they needed, but he found that keeping oysters in dark containers from the moment they were collected in the sea, made no difference at all. It is true that there is no ocean tide near Chicago, but something we tend to forget is that the same gravitational force of the moon that acts on the ocean can also act on very much smaller bodies of water. The Hughes Aircraft Laboratory in California has developed a "tilt meter" so sensitive that it has been able to record lunar tides in a cup of tea. (165) The moon also draws away the envelope of air that surrounds the earth and produces regular daily atmospheric tides. Brown compared his oysters' new rhythm with the movements of the moon and found that most of them were opening when the moon was directly overhead in Evanston. This was the first piece of scientific evidence to show that even an organism living away from the ocean tides could be influenced by the passage of the moon.

These lunar rhythms are close enough to the solar day length to be included in the circadian classification of "about one day," but the moon also produces another rhythm, with a period of about one month. We see the moon because it reflects light from the sun, and the amount of moon we see depends on its position relative to the sun and ourselves. The traditional phases of the moon follow a cycle slightly longer than the lunar orbit—it is 29.5 days from one full moon to the next. Twice during this cycle, the sun and the moon are directly in line with the earth and the pull of their bodies is added together to produce higher tides than usual. These spring tides occur when the moon is full and again when we see the first thin sliver of the new moon setting. And twice each month, at the quarters of the moon, when the pull of the two heavenly bodies is opposed, we have much more moderate movements of water called the neap tides.

Marine organisms are greatly affected by this cycle. A small silver fish, the grunion *Leuresthes tenuis,* has made such a precise adjustment to the moon that its very survival depends on the precision of this response. I cannot improve on Rachel Carson's description: "Shortly after the full moon of the months from March to August, the grunion appear in the surf on the beaches of California. The tide reaches flood stage, slackens, hesitates, and begins to ebb. Now on these waves of the ebbing tide the fish begin to come in. Their bodies shimmer in the light of the moon as they are borne up the beach on the crest of a wave, they lie glittering on the wet sand for a perceptible moment of time, then fling themselves into the wash of the next wave and are carried back to sea." (66)

During that brief moment in the air, the grunion leave their eggs buried in the wet sand, where they will be undisturbed for two weeks because the waves will not come that high again until the next spring tide. When the sea does return, the development of the larvae is complete, and they wait only for the cool touch of the water to break out of the eggs and swim away through the surf.

Another marine form that responds to the lunar rhythm is the palolo *Eunice viridis,* a flat, hairy version of the earthworm that spends most of its time hunting for food among the crevices of coral reefs in the South Pacific. (74) It feeds itself but it mates by proxy, concentrating eggs or sperm into the hind part of its body, which it equips with an eyespot, breaks off, and sends up to the surface of the sea to conjugate with the similar portions of other anonymous parents. Although the worms never actually meet, the rendezvous of their private parts is perfectly arranged by the moon. At dawn on the day the moon reaches its last quarter in November each year, all the worms cast off their hindquarters, and the seas around the reefs of Samoa and Fiji run red with the masses of eggs. The local people respond to the same time signal and gather over the coral in fleets of canoes to celebrate the "great rising" and feast on its bounty.

The most dramatic examples of lunar periodicity come from animals that live in the sea, where the passage of the moon is accentuated by huge movements of water, but there is some evidence to show that it is not the tide so much as moonlight itself that acts as a signal. The light of the moon is three hundred thousand times less bright than that of the sun, and yet life is able to respond to this minute cosmic stimulus even through several fathoms of sea water. At the University of Freiburg they are working on the polychaete worm *Platynereis dumerilii,* which swarms to the surface of the sea around the last quarter of the moon. (140) This worm loses its rhythm, swarming at all phases of the moon, if kept under constant light in the laboratory. But if the usual bright light is supplemented on just two nights of the month with another light, brighter than the moon but still six thousand times less bright than the sun, the worms are aware of this addition, interpret it as the time of the full moon, and swarm exactly one week later. Or, if they are not physiologically prepared for breeding at that time, they wait for thirty-five days—to bring them to the same phase of the moon in the following month. This means that, in nature, the moon could be concealed by cloud for all but two nights and the worms would still be able to set their clocks by it. And even if the moon were to be covered completely during every single night in the month of swarming, they could still remember what happened the previous month and use this as the signal for timing their reproductive rendezvous on the surface.

Land animals are also influenced by the moon. Adult May flies live for only a few hours, during which time they have to find another fly, mate, and lay their eggs in water. In temperate climates these insects respond to clues of changing light and temperature, and all emerge together in enormous numbers that hang in gossamer ballets over quiet country pools on a few warm evenings in May. But in the tropics the climate is so constant that these cues are missing and the May flies have to find another timekeeper and even another month. Lake Victoria straddles the equator in Africa, and yet it has a very successful species of May fly, *Povilla adusta*, which solves its timing problem by emerging only at the full moon. (138)

The Luo people, who live along the lake, say that it is going to rain when they see the May flies swarming, and they could be right, because we are just beginning to discover that superstitions like these often conceal truths or half-truths based on old and sometimes sound observations.

We know, for instance, that the moon pulls on the earth's atmosphere as it passes, drawing it away and allowing it to flow back again like an oceanic tide. Receding tides of air never leave a continent gasping in the same way that a beach is exposed altogether on the ebb, but the depth of air above us changes constantly, alternately decreasing and increasing our barometric pressure. As with tides of water, not all parts of the planet are equally affected; there are locations, which have now been pinpointed, where unusually high and low air pressures prevail. These are factories that churn out cyclones and anti-cyclones, loaded with good or bad weather. Since the invention of the weather satellite, we have been able to produce accurate maps of these disturbances, and by studying the movement of warm and cold fronts, predict changes several days in advance. But even armed with this information, it was not until recently that our attention was drawn to the role played by the moon in producing these weather patterns.

The news broke in *Science* magazine in the form of two short papers published on facing pages of the same issue in 1962. The authors of the papers had been working completely independently, in the United States and Australia, both coming to the same conclusions but reluctant to publish their findings for fear of ridicule. Only when each discovered the existence of the other and learned that their findings had been confirmed, did they go to press—together, for mutual support, in the same magazine.

The American team collected data from 1,544 weather stations in North America that had been in continuous operation over the fifty years from 1900 through 1949. From this they extracted all rainfall figures and plotted the times of widespread rain against the lunar cycle. They got a strange pattern, which led them to this conclusion: "There is a marked tendency for extreme precipitation in North America to be recorded near the middle of the first and third weeks of the synodical month." Which means that heavy rain occurs more often on days after the full and the new moon. (36)

In Australia the meteorologists collected rainfall data from fifty weather stations for the period from 1901 to 1925 and found that the same patterns were true for the Southern Hemisphere. (1) Both sets of statistics seem sound and point to the conclusion that the moon does affect weather. We know that rain falls when enough dust, salt, or ice particles are present in a cloud for water vapor to condense around them and fall to the ground. This principle is used when "seeding" likely clouds with chemicals from rockets or airplanes to produce rain exactly where it is needed. A natural source of suitable particles is meteor dust, which falls at the rate of about a thousand tons each day on earth. (34) This could be the link between the moon and the weather, because two other independent teams have just come up with the discovery that the rate of meteor arrival at the edge of earth's atmosphere is greater at the times of full and new moon. (40)

Frank Brown, of oyster fame, has been working for twenty-five years on ways in which life can be influenced by remote environmental factors. Instead of testing these one at a time, he has tried to eliminate them altogether, and most of the time he has failed, but his failures succeed in giving us an astonishing picture of the sensitivity of life to the most subtle stimuli. One of his early experiments involved seaweed, carrots, potatoes, earthworms, and salamanders. He was interested in their cycles of activity and used as his measurement the amount of oxygen each consumed throughout the day. All his subjects produced splendid rhythms even when kept, like the oysters, in the dark at a constant temperature. Brown then tried to eliminate the influence of changing barometric pressure by designing an apparatus that equalized changes in barometric air pressure. His instruments told him that the pressure in the test chamber was constant, but his plants and animals continued to produce rhythms that told him they were still aware of changes going on outside. (43)

Brown now has a vast mass of data to show this phenomenon beyond reasonable doubt. His study on potatoes alone has gone on continuously for nine years and provides full metabolic data for more than a million hours of potato time. (47) The tubers "know" whether the moon has just appeared over the horizon, whether it is at its zenith, or whether it is setting. Brown says that "the similarity of changes such as these in metabolic rate with the time of lunar day can be plausibly explained only by saying that all are responding to a common physical fluctuation having a lunar period." This heretical notion, that the "constant conditions" (Brown always puts the words in quotes) referred to in thousands of painstaking laboratory studies might not be so uniform after all, has drawn a storm of criticism from biologists fighting a rearguard action for the old idea that nothing could touch animals kept under constant light, temperature, humidity, and pressure. But Brown continues to gather evidence to show that there are other, even more subtle factors that need to be taken into account.

One possible candidate is magnetism. We know that the earth's magnetic field changes slightly according to the positions of both the moon and the sun. Readings taken at Greenwich from 1916 to 1957 show that the geomagnetic field alters hourly in direct accordance with the solar day, the lunar day, and the lunar month. (190) So, if living things were sensitive to magnetism, they could follow the movements of both the moon and the sun even while confined in the "constant conditions" of laboratory dungeons. It seems that life does have this sensitivity.

If you look carefully into the surface layers of a freshwater pool, you are almost certain to see, rolling smoothly along through the water, a determined little green ball as big as this "o." This is *Volvox*, probably the most simple of all living organisms composed of a number of cells that show a common purpose, and almost certainly a direct and little-changed descendant of the first experimental union of the early single cells. For these reasons J. D. Palmer, an associate of Frank Brown at Evanston, chose *Volvox aureus* as his subject for an experiment with magnetic fields. (239) *Volvox*, whose name comes from the Latin for "rolling," is a photosynthetic plant, but one that moves rapidly and well by the co-ordinated beating of whip cells that stick out from the surface of the ball. Palmer confined his colony in a small glass corral with a long thin neck that pointed toward magnetic south; then, as the green balls came tumbling out, he noted the directions in which they traveled. He recorded the emergence of 6,916 *Volvox*, one third under natural conditions, one third with a bar magnet placed at the entrance so that it augmented the earth's field, and the final third with the magnet pointing east-west, at right angles to the field. The magnet provided a field thirty times stronger than the natural one—and the results were quite unequivocal.

With the magnet in line with the earth field, 43 per cent more *Volvox* than normal turned to the west. With the magnet lying across the field, there was an additional bias of 75 per cent. This shows that these organisms not only can detect a magnetic field but are aware of the direction of lines of force in that field. And the fact that *Volvox* is an archaic form shows that life's awareness of magnetism goes back a long way and is probably very deep-seated.

Brown pursued this study further with *Nassarius obsoleta*, a mud snail that slithers in rapidly moving herds over the mud flats on New England shores. He also confined them to a corral whose south-facing exit was wide enough to allow only one to emerge at a time—and recorded the movement of thirty-four thousand snails in this way. Some turned left, some right, and some continued straight ahead, depending on the time of day. In the morning, the tendency was to turn left, toward the east, and in the afternoon toward the west. Brown introduced a magnet with a strength only nine times that of the earth's field and found that, when this was in the same direction as the natural field, it made no difference—the snails continued to follow the sun. But when the magnet was at right angles to the natural field, they began to follow a lunar pattern. (46)

As the earth's cycle and its field are influenced both by sun and moon, it is not surprising to find that both also affect an animal's response to magnetism. *Nassarius* is adapted more to the solar rhythm, but in a later experiment with a more nocturnal species, Brown found that he could get clear-cut responses to the phases of the moon. He chose the planarian *Dugesia dorotocephala*, a very popular little freshwater flatworm about an inch long with an arrow-shaped head and an endearing squint. In the same test apparatus, the worm turned left, that is to the east, at new moon, and to the right when the moon was full. (45)

Since this work was done, there have been similar experiments with rats and mice that show some evidence of response to magnetic fields, and an old suggestion, that migrating birds may navigate along lines of the earth's field, has been revived and is being re-examined. The work on snails and worms shows that life has a clock-regulated capacity to orient itself in a weak magnetic field. This possession of both a living clock and a living compass fulfill the two essential prerequisites for any system of navigation.

THE SUN

Beyond earth's atmosphere, beyond even the orbit of the moon, lies space. By definition this is supposed to be empty, an interval separating things from each other, but instruments sent out to probe this space reveal that it is far from empty. The vacuum is filled with a variety of forces, many of which reach the earth and some of which affect life here. The most powerful of these forces come from the star we call our sun.

The sun is a dense mass of glowing matter a million times the volume of earth and in a permanent state of effervescence. Every second, four million tons of hydrogen are destroyed in incredible explosions that start somewhere near the core, where the temperature is 13 million degrees C, and send fountains of flame shooting thousands of miles out into space. In this continuous and unimaginable holocaust, atoms are split into streams of fast-moving electrons and protons that rush out into space as a solar wind that buffets all the planets in our system. Earth falls well inside the sun's "atmosphere" and is constantly exposed to the changes in its weather. Scattered over the face of the sun like acne are spots of even more violent activity that flare up from time to time. These are usually about the size of earth, and sometimes the rash spreads quickly and the sun erupts in a bout of bad weather that produces magnetic storms in our atmosphere as well.

We first notice these storms when they disrupt radio and television reception and produce the fantastic draperies of the aurora borealis, but we continue to feel their effects in changes they produce in our own weather. At times of sunspot activity there is a tendency for cyclones to form over the ocean and for anti-cyclones to develop over the land masses, producing bad weather at sea and fine conditions ashore. One of the ways in which the moon may influence weather is by deflecting the solar wind so that it hits the earth at a different angle or misses it altogether. The IMP-1 satellite of 1964 recorded fluctuations in magnetic field produced in this way. (225)

It would be possible to use sunspot activity as an aid to

weather forecasting were it not for the fact that it seems to vary from day to day in a completely random fashion, but there are regular cycles of activity covering much longer periods of time. In 1801 Sir John Herschel discovered an 11-year sunspot cycle, which has since been confirmed many times and found to correlate with the thickness of annual rings in trees, the level of Lake Victoria, the number of icebergs, the occurrence of drought and famine in India, and the great vintage years for Burgundy wines. All these variables are dependent on the weather, and it seems certain that this regular pattern of change is produced by cycles in the sun. An even more sensitive measure has recently been made available by the study of thin layers of fossil mud deposited on the bottoms of old lakes. These layers are called varves, and their thickness depends on the annual rate at which glaciers melt and therefore provides an indication of climate conditions. Microscopic measurement of varves going back as much as five hundred million years shows that, even in Pre-Cambrian times, there were cycles about eleven years long. (347)

Computer analysis of varves in New Mexico has turned up another, longer sun cycle as well. (7) The 11-year peaks grow higher and higher for about forty years and then fade away to complete an 80- or 90-year cycle. This rhythm has been delicately confirmed by the German botanist Schnelle, who collected dates for the first annual appearance of snowdrops in the Frankfurt region from 1870 to 1950, and found that they formed a smoothly curved pattern. (297) For the first forty years the flowers always appeared before the average date of February 23, but after 1910 they blossomed later and later until, in 1925, they were almost two months behind. Then the snowdrops began to reverse the trend, and in 1950 they were a full two months ahead of schedule again. There is a perfect statistical correlation between the snowdrop and sunspot cycles. (214) In years of great sunspot activity the flowers bloomed later, and in years of the quiet sun they appeared ahead of time. The numbers of earthquakes in Chile over the past century seem to have followed the same cycle. It seems that, overlying the short-term variations in climate, there is a world-wide uniformity of change and that this is very largely determined by regular magnetic storms in the sun.

These and other studies provide ample evidence of the electromagnetic influence of the sun and the way in which it is mediated by the moon and affects our weather. Life in turn is influenced by the weather, and so storms in the sun touch us indirectly, but there is at least one way in which all living things can be directly controlled by cosmic activity. The answer lies in some peculiar properties of water and is quite incredible, so I shall start with basic principles and approach it cautiously.

Every high school student knows that water is H_2O, a chemical compound of two simple elements. And yet scientific journals are full of articles arguing the merits of various theories on the structure of water—and we still do not understand exactly how it works. There are so many anomalies: water is one of the very few substances that are more dense in the liquid than the solid state, so ice floats; water is unique in that it is most dense a few degrees above its melting point, so that heating it up to $4°$ C from its melting point of $0°$ C causes it to contract even further; and water can act both as an acid and as a base, so that it actually reacts chemically with itself under certain conditions.

The clue to some of water's strange behavior lies with the hydrogen atom, which has only one electron to share with any other atom with which it combines. When it joins with oxygen to form molecules of water, each hydrogen atom is balanced between two oxygen atoms in what is called the "hydrogen bond"; but having only one electron to offer, the hydrogen atom can be attached firmly on only one side, so the bond is a weak one. Its strength is 10 per cent of that of most ordinary chemical bonds, so for water to exist at all, there have to be lots of bonds to hold it together. Liquid water is so intricately laced that it is almost a continuous structure, and one worker has gone so far as to describe a glass of water as a single molecule. (252) Ice is even more regular, and forms the most perfectly bonded hydrogen structure known. Its crystalline pattern is so very precise that it seems to persist into the liquid state, and though it looks clear, water contains short-lived regions of ice crystals that form and melt many millions of times every second. It is as though liquid water remembers the form of the ice from which it came by repeating the formula over and over again to itself, ready to change back again at a moment's notice. If one could take a photograph with a short enough exposure, it would probably show icelike areas even in a glass of hot water.

So water is tremendously flexible. The tenuous links between its atoms make it very fragile, and little external pressure is necessary to break the bonds and destroy or change its pattern. Biological reactions must occur quickly and take place with very little expenditure of energy, so a trigger substance such as water is the ideal go-between. In fact all living processes take place in an aqueous medium, and most of the body weight of every living organism (in man the figure is 65 per cent) is made up of water.

No scientist now doubts that water behaves like this inside a plant or an animal. As I intend to show that external, even cosmic, influences can change the form of water inside an organism, the next step in the argument is to demonstrate that water outside the body can be influenced in this way.

At the same time that Frank Brown was busy demonstrat-

ing the unconstancy of "constant conditions" in biological experiments, an Italian chemist was busy upsetting his contemporaries by showing that chemical properties were equally
inconsistent and changed from one hour to the next. Giorgio
Piccardi, Director of the Institute for Physical Chemistry in
Florence, has always been intrigued by the way in which
chemical reactions occasionally prove idiosyncratic and go
off in the wrong direction or refuse to take place at all. He
began his research with an experimental method for remov-
ing incrustations from industrial boilers. (246) Sometimes it
worked well and sometimes it did not. He suspected that outside influences might be affecting the reaction, and so he
tried enclosing the whole experiment in a thin copper sheet
and found that, with this in place, it always worked well.

Piccardi was interested in the forces that could influence a
reaction like this, and to find out more about them, he designed an experiment that would yield a large number of
observations over a long period of time. He chose a simple
reaction, the speed with which bismuth oxychloride (a col-
loid) forms a cloudy precipitate when poured into distilled
water. Three times a day, every day, he and his assistants
carried out this simple test until they had more than two
hundred thousand separate results. These have now been analyzed, together with results of a parallel series of tests made
at Brussells University. (63)

There were several kinds of change in the speed of precipitation over the ten-year period of the experiment. Short-
term, sudden changes, often lasting only a day or two, were
frequent, and all were connected with the sun. The reaction
always took place more quickly when there was a solar eruption and changes in the earth's magnetic field could be
measured. There were also long-term changes, and when
these were plotted on a graph, they formed a curve exactly
parallel to that for sunspot frequency in the 11-year cycle. As

a control, Piccardi did simultaneous experiments with the same solutions under the protection of a copper screen—and found that precipitation always took place at the normal speed when shielded from outside influence in this way.

So a chemical reaction taking place in water is influenced by cosmic activity, which means that either the chemical or the water is susceptible to electromagnetic radiation. All available evidence points to the water. Two other Italian chemists have found that they could alter the electrical conductivity of water simply by exposing it to a very small magnet. (32) And at the Atmospheric Research Center in Colorado a series of experiments is in progress that shows that water is very sensitive to electromagnetic fields. (102)

Piccardi takes the argument the last step along the way. In 1962 he said, "Water is sensitive to extremely delicate influences and is capable of adapting itself to the most varying circumstances to a degree attained by no other liquid. Perhaps it is even by means of water and the aqueous system that the external forces are able to react on living organisms." (247) This suggestion is nicely complemented by a recent demonstration which shows that water is particularly unstable, and therefore most valuable to life, between 35 and 40° C—the body temperature of most active animals. (205)

Which leaves us, I think, with the conclusion that there certainly are ways in which the sun, and other cosmic forces, can influence life.

OTHER FACTORS

Traveling with us in the solar system are eight other planets, all of which revolve the same way around the sun, in orbits that lie, with the exception of Pluto and Mercury, in the same plane as ours. We know that the planets influence each other, because Lowell in 1914 used previously unexplained aberrations in the movements of the inner eight to predict the existence of another planet. It was only in 1940 that Pluto was actually discovered.

In 1951 John Nelson was engaged by RCA in the United States to study factors that affect radio reception. By this time it was well known that sunspots are the major cause of interference, but RCA wanted to be able to predict disturbances in the atmosphere more accurately. Nelson studied records for poor reception dating back to 1932 and found, as expected, that they were closely linked to the occurrence of sunspots, but he also discovered something else: Sunspots, and therefore radio disturbances, both occurred when two or more planets were in line, at right angles, or arranged at 180° to the sun. (228) He worked first with Mars, Jupiter, and Saturn and found that, by computing their positions, he could predict the time of future large sunspot actions with 80 per cent accuracy. (229) In a later study he refined his method to include data from all the planets and improved his accuracy of prediction to an impressive 93 per cent. RCA was delighted, and so, of course, were the astrologists, because this was the first piece of hard scientific fact to show that we could be influenced in any way by the planets. What happens, it seems, is that the position of the planets influences, or is at least an indication of, the sun's magnetic field and that certain configurations coincide with strong sunspot activity—and we know that this in turn touches life here.

If the planets can affect the sun, then it seems reasonable to assume that they also affect the earth, which, with the exception of Mercury, is much closer to them. One night in 1955 an astronomer using a radio telescope in Maryland found a foreign body in his pictures of the Crab nebula. (106) On the following nights it was still there, but it had moved, which made him think immediately of a planet, so he pointed his antenna at Jupiter and found that it was sending out strong radio signals, both short and long wave, with the power of a billion watts. It has now been shown that Venus and Saturn are also powerful sources of radio waves. (278) At least part of the planetary effect may be due to the fact that each body leaves behind it in space a magnetospheric tail of disturbance like a long wake of disturbed water that takes time to settle. The tail that earth drags behind it may be more than five million miles long. (35) So, far from being insignificant specks in space, it seems that the planets are more like territorial animals that leave behind them powerful marks whose influence lingers on long after they themselves have passed by.

The universe does not end with the solar system. On a clear night we can see about three thousand other individual stars, many of them larger than our sun, and all of them part of a hundred billion that go to make up our disk-shaped Milky Way galaxy. Beyond this, scattered more or less uniformly through space, lie perhaps ten billion other galaxies of similar size. From all these sources come radiations of varying strength.

We know that certain stars emit radio waves all the time, while others send out powerful flares of radiation when they undergo violent changes. Some large young stars explode and, in the process of becoming supernovae, produce enormous quantities of cosmic energy. (319) The normal amount falling each year on the atmosphere of earth is about 0.03 roentgen, but during the time that life has been on earth it has been exposed at least once to a short, sharp dose of 2,000 roentgen, about four times to doses of over 1,000 roentgen, and perhaps ten times to 500 roentgen. The lethal dose for most laboratory animals is between 200 and 700 roentgen, but female mice can be completely sterilized by only 80 roentgen. So the explosion of supernovae has subjected the earth at least fifteen times to showers of radiation strong enough to kill most forms. Plant seeds are radiation resistant, and marine life would be protected to some extent by water as the land is by the blanket of air, but these bouts of high radiation could well have been a significant factor in the evolution of life. Even at lower levels, radiation from other suns than ours could have a strong influence on life here.

James Clerk Maxwell revolutionized physics in the middle of the nineteenth century with a set of laws describing all electric and magnetic phenomena. In one of these he proved that disturbances in conditions at one place could be carried across space to another place. He called his carriers electromagnetic waves and found that, no matter what the disturbance, all news of it traveled at the same speed—the speed of light. The electromagnetic spectrum includes X rays, light rays, and radio and television waves, and covers an enormous range, from waves longer than the diameter of the earth to waves so short that a billion strung together would barely cover a fingernail. All these are broadcast by the cosmos all the time. We are most responsive to light waves, which lie somewhere near the middle of the spectrum, but life seems also to be aware of radiation from the electromagnetic extremes.

Radioactive substances occur in nature, and in all of them nuclear changes take place that result in three kinds of radiation: Alpha rays can be stopped by a sheet of paper, beta rays can just about get through aluminum foil, but gamma rays travel across space with so much energy that they can penetrate even lead. Their wavelength is so short that they pass through matter like X rays that have been supercharged, so that even animals in the deepest caves or at the bottom of the ocean feel their effects. Frank Brown has tested his planarian worms for response to a very weak gamma radiation emitted by a sample of cesium 137. (44)

He found that worms were aware of the radiation and turned away from it, but only when they were moving north or south. They ignored the radiation, no matter where it came from, if they were swimming in any other direction. This shows that gamma rays can be a vector force that somehow indicates direction as well as intensity. The earth rotates from east to west, so any organism that behaves like these worms and responds to the field in only one direction, has a mechanism that can be used for navigation and for the recognition of all the important geophysical cycles.

At the other end of the usual electromagnetic spectrum are enormously long waves, recently detected by equipment designed to monitor variations in the magnetic field. Most waves are measured in cycles per second, but these are so huge that they take more than a second to pass by—which makes them more than 186,000 miles long, or more than twenty times the diameter of the earth. Some waves eight seconds long occur at night, particularly during displays of the aurora, and there are indications of a few as much as forty seconds, that is seven million miles, in length. (146) At the moment, we cannot even begin to guess at the possible significance of these signals; all we can do is record that such waves exist, that they traverse whole galaxies with little effort, and that, despite their very low field strength, life might be sensitive to them.

The entire universe hangs together, or comes apart, depending on your theoretical bias, by the most basic cosmic force of all, the force of gravity. Electromagnetic waves react only with electrical charges and currents, but gravity waves interact with all forms of matter. The amount of gravitational energy coming from the center of our galaxy is ten thousand times greater than the electromagnetic energy, but we still have trouble measuring it. (338) Gravitational waves from the cosmos have now been recorded, but nobody has yet been able to demonstrate that life is aware of them. The best evidence so far comes from a Swiss biologist working on little flying beetles with the interesting name of cockchafers. (296) He put swarms of the beetles into an opaque container and found that they responded to the invisible approach of a lump of lead outside. When lead weighing more than eighty pounds was moved closer to their container, the beetles gathered on the side farthest from it. They could not see the lead, and the experiment seems to have been designed to eliminate all other clues, so we must assume that these insects at least are aware, by change in gravity, of the distribution of masses around them. It is possible that the stronger gravitational fields produced by the sun and the moon could have similar effects on behavior.

So now we know this much:

Life arose by order out of chaos and maintains this order by collecting information from the cosmos. Cosmic forces bombard earth all the time, but the movement of celestial bodies and the movement of earth in relation to these bodies produces a pattern that provides useful information. Life is sensitive to this pattern because it contains water, which is unstable and easily influenced.

Which means that living things are involved in an open dialogue with the universe, a free exchange of information and influence that unites all life into one vast organism that is itself part of an even larger dynamic structure. There is no escaping the conclusion that the basic similarity in structure and function are ties that bind all life together and that man, for all his special features, is an integral part of this whole.

Chapter Two:

Man and the Cosmos

LIFE ON EARTH is like the bloom on a plum. In recent
years part of this delicate film of mold have got together and,
by massive communal efforts, managed to throw a few
tiny spores high enough off the surface to prevent their falling
back. To do this they had to be boosted to the escape velocity
of 17,500 miles an hour, which was a major undertaking, and
yet all this time the plum itself was hurtling along at four
times that speed.

We tend to forget that we are all space travelers. A hand-
ful of men, dogs, chimps, and germinating seeds have been
on extravehicular activity, but the rest of the biosphere has
had to stay aboard, where the ship's life systems can take
care of them. We are only just beginning to learn how important earth's rhythms are to our well-being. Today jet aircraft move numbers of people rapidly around from one time
zone to another, and like the cockroaches with extra ganglia,
they have foreign rhythms imposed on their own. These cause

considerable distress, because in common with all other living things we are influenced by the natural cycles produced by earth's rotation.

Human body temperature, for instance, is seldom exactly 37° C but follows a regular circadian pattern of change. Our temperature rises with the sun and goes on rising, along with the rate of heart beat and urine production, until all three reach a peak of activity in the early afternoon. Metabolism then gradually slows down until it falls to its lowest level of activity, at about four in the morning. It is no accident that this is the hour invariably chosen by secret police and security forces for the arrest and interrogation of suspects. Life is at its lowest ebb during the dogwatch just before dawn.

Midwives have always complained about the hours they are forced to keep by babies that insist on being born just before breakfast. Halberg, the physiologist who invented the word circadian, has also produced statistics that show that this is not just an old midwives' tale. (132) Labor pains begin twice as often at midnight as at noon, and the peak in births occurs at about four o'clock, just when the metabolic cycle hits its lowest trough and the mother is likely to be most relaxed.

To test the effect of light and dark on this cycle, Mary Lobban of the Medical Research Council in Britain took a group of student volunteers to the Spitzbergen Archipelago one summer. (197) The islands lie north of Norway, well inside the Arctic Circle, where there is continuous daylight from May until August. The volunteers were divided into two groups that lived in colonies on separate islands. All those in one colony were given wristwatches that ran slow; when these indicated that twenty-four hours had gone by, twenty-seven had actually elapsed. Those in the other colony had watches that ran fast, so that their 24-hour "days" were really only twenty-one hours long. The groups lived according to their separate schedules and were examined six times every day.

Body-temperature rhythms of volunteers in both groups quickly adjusted to the new schedules: Temperature fell to its lowest level during the sleeping period and was at its highest soon after rising. No matter whether the person was on a 21- or a 27-hour cycle, the rhythm followed the pattern of activity. It seems that man's temperature changes are quite independent of light and dark. The cycle of urine production took longer to acclimatize to the new schedules, but after three weeks all the volunteers were producing the greatest volumes of urine at the same time as they reached their temperature peak. This function, too, seems to be independent of light and tied more to the pattern of activity of the whole body, but Lobban fortunately took one further measurement of metabolism and this produced quite different results.

Among other vital trace elements, the human body contains about 150 grams of potassium. This is concentrated in cells such as the nerves, which carry signals by rapidly exchanging sodium and potassium through their surface membranes as they are stimulated. As the nerve recovers, after the impulse has passed, sodium is pushed out, potassium is taken back, and the cell is cocked, ready to fire again. Each time this exchange takes place, a little potassium is lost, and about three grams is excreted from the body each day. Normally, elimination of potassium follows a rhythmic pattern similar to that of body temperature and urine production, but at Spitzbergen it was found to be quite independent. All volunteers showed a cycle of potassium excretion, but the greatest amounts were being lost at regular intervals of twenty-four hours—actual hours, not hours as measured by their dishonest wristwatches. Follow-up studies on men at Arctic and Antarctic bases have shown that, even after two years away from the normal rhythms of day and night, 24-hour cycles of potassium excretion still persist.

It seems that, while gross responses of our organism are susceptible to short-term environmental changes, the basic activities of life, such as communication between separate cells, are controlled by deep-seated mechanisms that respond to the time pattern of the planet as a whole.

Man also has a natural tendency to respond to the annual cycle. Some workers have found that there is a circannual rhythm in body-weight change and in the frequency of manic-depressive attacks, but the most convincing evidence comes from our dates of birth. (244) In the Northern Hemisphere there are more children born in May and June than in November and December. The obvious explanation would seem to be that these children were conceived during August the previous year, when the parents were on their summer holidays and such things are more likely to happen. But there seems to be a more fundamental biological principle involved, because children born during May are, on the average, about two hundred grams heavier than those born in any other month. (118) This difference is caused by an annual rhythm in the production of hormones involved in pregnancy. We still have a breeding season.

The situation is of course reversed in the Southern Hemisphere. A study of twenty-one thousand army recruits in New Zealand showed that the taller men were all born between December and February, which are the midsummer months down under.

In both hemispheres, being born in the best months seems to carry a birthright of longer life and greater intelligence. Long life naturally depends on nutrition and health care and perhaps even hereditary factors, but the fact remains that in a comparatively homogenous area such as New England those born in March live an average of four years longer than those born in any other month. (269) The measurement of intelligence by IQ alone is suspect, but an analysis of seventeen thousand school children in New York showed that those born in May scored better at these tests than those born at any other time. (156) A similar survey of mentally deficient children in Ohio showed a different pattern, with most being born in the winter months of January and February. (179)

MAN AND MOON

The third basic rhythm of life, the lunar cycle, also appears in patterns of human birth times. The moon is so closely linked to birth that in some places it is even called "the great midwife." To test this possibility, the two doctors Menaker collected information on more than half a million births that occurred in New York hospitals between 1948 and 1957. This enormous sample showed a clear and statistically significant trend for more births to take place during the waning moon than the waxing moon, with a maximum just after the full moon and a clear minimum at new moon. Other studies, in Germany and in California with smaller samples, have found no such relationship, but it is worth bearing in mind that lunar influences differ in different geographic locations. Tides in the Bay of Fundy rise and fall over fifty incredible feet, while the difference between low and high tide in Tahiti is only a few inches. There is a connection between birth and tides. The times of births in communities living on the North Sea coast of Germany, show that an unusually large number occur just at the time of high tide. In other words, there is a sudden increase in births each day just when the moon is passing directly overhead. A similar relationship occurs in Cologne, which is on the same latitude but far from the sea, so it is not the tides themselves that control uterine contractions, but the moon that influences both.

The time of birth is of course directly connected to the time of conception, and this depends on the phase of the menstrual cycle. It has not escaped notice that the average length of the female cycle is almost identical to the period between two full moons. All the women in the world do not of course menstruate on the same day at the same phase of the moon, but it is difficult to believe that the similarity between the two cycles is purely coincidental. The great Swiss chemist Svante Arrhenius once recorded 11,807 menstrual periods. He found that there was a slight relationship to the lunar cycle: the onset of bleeding occurred more often during the waxing than the waning moon, with a peak on the evening before new moon. A recent German study of ten thousand menstruations also found a peak near the new moon. Other workers have found no such correlation, but it is possible that some confusion is caused by the method of measurement. We say that the menstrual cycle begins with the first day of bleeding, but this is just a convention: the uterine lining breaks down for three or four days and bleeding can become evident at any time during this process. The moment of ovulation, when the follicle bursts and discharges the egg, is a much more precise and important biological event and surveys made using this as the beginning of the cycle might show closer lunar connections.

The egg lives less than forty-eight hours, and unless a sperm reaches and fertilizes it during this time, it dies. So conception can occur only during this rather short period. Eugen Jonas of Czechoslovakia has discovered that the time of ovulation is connected with the moon, and that the ability of a mature woman to conceive coincides with the phase of the moon that prevailed when she was born. (284) He has set up a service in several eastern European countries that provides each woman with a chart based on her own lunar affinities. Used as a contraceptive measure, these charts have proved to be 98 per cent effective—which is as good as The Pill, and with no side effects. Of course the charts also give a woman notice of all those days in her life on which she can conceive, and they are now being used extensively to ensure fertilization as well as to avoid it.

Jonas had many critics among obstetricians, but it must be said in his defense that menstruation as a whole is such a paradoxical process that there is a great deal about it that we do not yet understand. It is unique in our bodies in that it involves the regular destruction of tissues in a normal healthy individual. George Corner of Princeton calls it "an unexplained turmoil in the otherwise co-ordinated process of uterine function." (306) Perhaps the paradox once owed much more to lunar influence, and the present range in the length of menstrual cycles from nineteen to thirty-seven days is just an indication of its growing independence of this cosmic influence. Two American Air Force scientists have recently shown that it is possible to influence the cycle with an artificial moon. They selected twenty women with a history of chronic menstrual irregularity and persuaded them to leave their bedroom lights on all night on the three days closest to ovulation. All the women menstruated exactly fourteen days later, so perhaps the moon still influences menstrual bleeding quite strongly. (88)

There is definitely a close connection between the moon and bleeding in general. Superstition has it that the moon controls blood flow in the same way that it controls the tides. When bloodletting was a customary form of medical treatment, it was always done when the moon was waning, for it was believed that it was too dangerous to let blood when the light was increasing and the tide beginning to flood. This superstition may be founded in fact. Edson Andrews of

Tallahassee reports that in a survey of over a thousand "bleeders"—patients needing unusual means of hemostasis on the operating table or having to be returned to the theater because of hemorrhaging—82 per cent of all the bleeding crises occurred between the first and last quarters of the moon, with a significant peak when the moon was full. Dr. Andrews ends his report with the comment: "These data have been so conclusive and convincing to me that I threaten to become a witch doctor and operate on dark nights only, saving the moonlit nights for romance." (155)

There is something about moonlit nights that affects a number of people in strange ways. The very word "lunacy" suggests a direct connection between the moon and madness; in fact this superstition is so widely believed that it was once even written into law. Two hundred years ago a distinction was made in English law between those who were "insane," meaning chronically and incurably psychotic, and those who were "lunatic" and therefore susceptible only to aberrations produced by the moon. Crimes committed at the full moon by those in the second category were considered more leniently by the courts. Superintendents of asylums have always feared the influence of the moon on "loony" inmates and canceled staff leave on nights when the moon was full. In the eighteenth century, patients were even beaten the day before full moon as a prophylactic against violence on their part the following night. Official violence of this kind is now thankfully outlawed, but much of the old moon lore lingers on. There could be something in it.

The American Institute of Medical Climatology has published a report on the effect of full moon on human behavior in which it records that crimes with strong psychotic motivation, such as arson, kleptomania, destructive driving, and homicidal alcoholism all show marked peaks when the moon is full and that cloudy nights are no protection against this trend. (155) Leonard Ravitz, a neurologist and psychiatric consultant, has discovered a direct physiological connection between man and moon, which could explain these correlations. (266) For many years he has been measuring the differences in electrical potential between the head and the chest of mental patients. He has also tested passers-by selected at random and found that all people show a cyclic pattern that changes from day to day and that the greatest differences between head and chest readings occur at full moon, particularly in mental patients. Ravitz suggests that, as the moon modifies earth's magnetic field, these changes precipitate crises in people whose mental balance is already rather precarious. "Whatever else we may be, we are all electric machines. Thus energy reserves may be mobilized by periodic universal factors (such as the forces behind the moon) which tend to aggravate maladjustments and conflicts already present."

Studies continue to be made on other possible physiological relations between man and the moon. It has been claimed that deaths caused by tuberculosis are most frequent seven days before full moon and that this may be linked to a lunar cycle in the pH content (the ratio of acid to alkali) in blood. (245) And a German physician reports correlations among lunar phases, pneumonia, the amount of uric acid in the blood, and even the time of death. (131)

The moon obviously affects man in many ways. The influence of lunar gravity is a direct effect, but where light is concerned, the moon is just a middleman basking in the reflected glory of the sun. So it is not surprising to find that man is even more strongly touched by the sun.

MAN AND SUN

The black death that drove Newton from his college and into a momentous discovery, swept England in 1665. Astro-

nomical records of the time show that this was a year of
intense sunspot activity, and studies of annual tree rings,
which are wider when the sun is disturbed, reveal that the
terrible plague of 1348 was also accompanied by an active
sun. (30) A Russian professor of history has been collecting
correlations of this kind for forty years, many of them spent
in Siberia for daring to suggest that major social changes
might be due more to sunspots than dialectical materialism.
(316) Tchijevsky claims that the great plagues, the diphtheria
and cholera outbreaks in Europe, the Russian typhus, and the
smallpox epidemics of Chicago all occurred at the peaks of
the sun's 11-year cycle. He also points out that in the century
1830 to 1930 there were Liberal governments in power in
England during sunspot peaks and that Conservatives were
elected only in quieter years.

This sounds incredible, but we know that behavior is
governed by physiology and we now have evidence that the
sun has a direct effect on some of our body chemistry.
Maki Takata of Toho University, in Japan, is the inventor of
the "Takata reaction," which measures the amount of al-
bumin in blood serum. This is supposed to be constant in
men and to vary with women according to the menstrual
cycle, but in 1938 every hospital that used his test reported
a sudden rise in level for both sexes. Takata started an
experiment with simultaneous measurements of the serum
from two men one hundred miles apart. Over a period of
four months, their curves of daily variation were exactly
parallel and Takata concluded that the phenomenon must be
world-wide and due to cosmic factors. (313)

Over a period of twenty years, Takata has been able to
show that the changes in blood serum occur mainly when
major sunspots are interfering with earth's magnetic field.
He made tests during the eclipses of 1941, 1943, and 1948 and
found that these inhibited his reaction as much as perform-

ing them in a mine shaft six hundred feet underground. (312) He also experimented on subjects in an aircraft at over thirty thousand feet and discovered that the reaction took place more strongly at heights where the atmosphere was too thin to provide effective protection from solar radiation. Recent Soviet work lends support to the idea that our blood is directly affected by the sun. (299) Over 120,000 tests were made on people in a Black Sea resort to measure the number of lymphocytes in their blood. These small cells normally make up between 20 and 25 per cent of man's white blood cells, but in years of great solar activity this proportion decreases. There was a big drop during the sunspot years of 1956 and 1957, and the number of people suffering from diseases caused by a lymphocyte deficiency actually doubled during the tremendous solar explosion of February 1956.

Other diseases directly affected by magnetic disturbance include thrombosis and tuberculosis. (280) On May 17, 1959, there were three very powerful solar flares. The next day twenty patients with heart attacks were admitted to a Black Sea hospital that normally deals with an average of two each day. Two French heart specialists have found that there is a very high correlation between the sun and myocardial infarctions (heart failure caused by blood clots). (253) They suggest that solar radiation promotes the formation of blood clots near the skin in people so predisposed and that these clots then produce fatal blockages in the coronary artery. Hemorrhage in the lungs of tubercular patients follows a similar pattern. (198) The most dangerous days are those in which the aurora borealis can be seen—that is, those days when strong solar radiation activity disturbs the atmosphere.

Many of the body's functions seem to be influenced by sun-induced changes in the earth's magnetic field. If this is so, one would expect to find that the nervous system, which depends almost entirely on electrical stimuli, would be the most affected. This seems to be the case. A study of 5,580 coal-mine accidents on the Ruhr shows that most occurred on the day following solar activity. (207) Studies of traffic accidents in Russia and in Germany show that these increase, by as much as four times the average, on days after the eruption of a solar flare. (249) A survey of 28,642 admissions to psychiatric hospitals in New York shows that there is a marked increase on days when the magnetic observatory reports strong activity. (109) This suggests that accidents may be due to a disturbance deeper than a simple decrease in reaction time. These results make it clear that man is, among other things, a remarkably sensitive living sundial.

THE PLANETS

Our sensitivity to the sun extends from light rays into the longer wavelengths of radio. We see the sun, we feel its warmth, and we respond to changes it produces in the earth's magnetic field. These changes affect radio reception in a pattern that, as Nelson has shown, can be predicted by the position of the planets. (229) The amount of change is small, but its effect is most marked on biochemical processes such as nerve activity. Even by drilling two holes in the trunk of a tree, one can measure variations in electrical potential that follow the movements of bodies in our solar system, so it is no surprise to find that the complex human organism is affected by the planets. (54)

Michel Gauquelin, of the Psychophysiological Laboratory at Strasbourg, was the first to quantify this effect. His twenty years of painstaking research are summarized in his excellent book *The Cosmic Clocks*. (119) In 1950 Gauquelin became interested in planetary rhythms and looked for possible correlations on earth. As our planet spins on its axis, the sun and the moon appear to move overhead, rising and setting in solar and lunar days whose length depends on our latitude and the time of year. The other planets travel across our horizon in the same way, producing Venusian and Martian days that are equally predictable. In Europe all local authorities record the exact moment of birth in official registers, so Gauquelin was able to collect this information and match it with the positions of planets computed from astronomical tables. (119) He selected 576 members of the French Academy of Medicine and found, to his astonishment, that an unusually large number of them were born when Mars and Saturn had just risen or reached their highest point in the sky. To check these findings, he took another sample of 508 famous physicians and got the same results. (120) There was a strong statistical correlation between the rise of these two planets at a child's moment of birth and his future success as a doctor.

Taken together, the two tests produce odds of ten million to one against this happening just by chance. For the first time in history a scientist had produced evidence that the planets actually influence, or indicate an influence, on our lives. This gives science a point of vital contact with the old beliefs of astrology.

Astrology is based upon the fundamental premise that celestial phenomena affect life and events here on earth. No scientist, and certainly no biologist familiar with the latest work on weather and natural rhythms, can deny that this premise is proved. Earth and its life are affected by the cosmos and there is room for argument only in the matter of degree. Astrologers make many claims that are still without foundation and may well be ill-conceived, but there is a growing body of evidence to show that some of it, at least, is true.

Michel Gauquelin continues to make the most important contributions in this field. Following his discovery of the link between Mars and medicine, he extended his studies to other professions and collected all the birthdates of famous Frenchmen he could find. (115) Once again there was an impressive correlation between the planets and professions. Famous doctors and scientists were born as Mars was coming over the horizon, while artists, painters, and musicians were seldom born at this time. Soldiers and politicians were born more frequently under the influence of a rising Jupiter, but babies born when this planet was in the ascendant seldom became scientists.

No famous French writer was born with Saturn in the ascendant, but not all relationships were so clear-cut. Gauquelin had to resort to statistical techniques to demonstrate correlations—and the use of these raises certain problems. We know that in the Northern Hemisphere the month with the highest birth rate is June and that the days in June are longer than in any other month. So, despite the fact that there are equal amounts of light and dark in any year, there is a greater chance that babies will be born in daylight. We also know that births follow a rhythmic pattern, with more babies being born in the morning than the afternoon, and this introduces yet another bias. Planets follow the same kind of motion as the sun, so the chances of a birth taking place in all hours of the planetary day are not equal. Gauquelin applied corrections for all these conditions before comparing his samples and assessing their significance. His statistics were examined in detail by Tornier, professor of mathematical theory in Berlin, who could find no fault with them, but another statistician suggested that the results merely reflected a national peculiarity of the French and that the same methods applied to other countries might produce different results.

Gauquelin was forced to do similar work in Italy, Germany, Holland, and Belgium until, three years later, he had twenty-

five thousand records. The results were the same. (116)
Scientists and doctors were positively linked with Mars and
Saturn; soldiers, politicians, and team athletes with Jupiter.
Writers', painters', and musicians' births were not linked to
the presence of any planet, but clearly avoided Mars and
Saturn, while scientists and doctors were negative on Jupiter.
Solo performers such as writers and long-distance runners
were much more markedly linked to the moon than to any
of the planets. This time three well-known statisticians, including Faverge, the professor of statistics at the Sorbonne,
studied the results and could find no fault with Gauquelin's
calculations or the methods he used to collect his data. A
control experiment was performed on people selected at
random, which yielded results strictly according to the laws
of chance.

One persistent critic of this work, though forced now to
admit rather reluctantly that the position of certain bodies
in our solar system has something to do with at least nine
different professions, dismisses the whole thing by declaring
that it is "the absurd expression of an absurd experience."
His emotional dislike of anything occult disguises the fact
that the work falls a long way short of showing astrology
to be a proven fact. It shows, beyond reasonable doubt, that
the position of the planets means something—the position,
and not the planets themselves. We still have to decide
whether the planets are acting directly on us or whether their
position is merely symbolic of some much larger cosmic pattern
of energy of which they, and we, are just a small part.

I want to return to this problem later, because, in a sense,
it does not really matter what the causal agent is. If an
astrologer can use the position of the planets as a reliable
key to interpreting and predicting the action of a cosmic
force, it makes no difference whether this force comes from
Andromeda or from a flying saucer. Electricity was discovered

and used very effectively a long time before anyone understood how it worked. What matters more at this moment is understanding the effect that the planets seem to have on us.

Firstly, we know that labor in pregnancy is more easily induced when the mother is relaxed at the lowest point of her circadian cycle. It has also been shown that there is a marked increase in births during magnetic storms, so it is possible that electromagnetic conditions at the time that a planet such as Mars comes over the horizon could bring on labor pains and induce birth to take place. (270) This would mean that only the mother was involved and that conditions at the moment of birth made no difference to the child at all, but it does not explain the link between the planet and the child's ultimate profession.

The second possibility is that the planet, or the prevailing conditions, modify the child at the moment of birth and determine its future in some way. This is of course the orthodox astrological attitude: the pattern of the heavens at the exact moment of birth impinges on the child and shapes its destiny. Most modern astrologers are by no means fixed in this rigid, rather awkward belief, and I must say that, as a biologist, I find it unsatisfactory. What, for instance, is the moment of birth? The average time taken for the birth of a first child, from the moment the head meets the pelvic floor until the last limb emerges, is two hours. During this time a planet can change its position altogether. Some astrologers measure life from the moment of the child's first cry, but it is difficult to see why this should be the significant moment. There are other, more critical, times in childbirth. The journey down the four-inch birth canal is probably the most dangerous we ever take, and at one point the child undergoes considerable trauma and discomfort, which might make it more than usually susceptible to outside influence. The pelvis rotates the baby's head into the best position for birth, and the softness of the skull bones, together with the space between them, allows it to pass without overt damage, but the uterus is shoving from behind with a force strong enough to break an obstetrician's finger. This could be the astrological moment, when the brain is tormented into a new kind of activity by the physical pressure on it and opens itself to cosmic influence. But this does not account for the normal lives of those born by Caesarean section, who, though deprived of the birth drama, still have their own unique destinies.

A stronger objection to the "moment of birth" theory comes from what we now know about the cosmic forces involved. The womb was once thought of as the living equivalent of that "constant condition" chamber much beloved of experimental zoologists, but belief in both must now be abandoned. The womb is certainly warm and comfortable, temperature and humidity controlled like a room in a Hilton hotel, but other conditions are not so uniform. A certain amount of light penetrates the thin, distended skin of the mother's stomach; every mother knows that a loud sound can frighten an unborn child and make it hammer on the walls of the womb in protest; and most radiation passes through the bodies of mother and child alike almost without pause. It is difficult to believe that electromagnetic forces from the environment influence a child only at the moment of birth, when it has been exposed to these forces throughout the period of gestation.

A far more likely theory is that the cosmic environment plays an important part at the moment of conception or soon afterward, when the raw materials of heredity are still sorting themselves out into the ultimate arrangement for the new individual. Even the smallest nudge at this time would be enough to alter the direction of development sufficient to produce a major effect on the end product. The amount of energy necessary to produce an effect increases as the embryo gets older, bigger, more complex, and less flexible. Most cosmic stimuli are fairly subtle, and it seems much more likely that they would act in the early stages of development than later on, at birth. Although the womb is by no means quiet, an embryo is cushioned from the environment and protected from some of its more obvious effects. In this relatively peaceful place, it is possible that the child learns to respond to signals that are masked from us by the barrage of stimuli outside. A hamster deprived in the laboratory of the sun, which once told him when to hibernate, learns to change up from nature to Supernature and responds instead to the more subtle rhythm of the moon passing by. An unborn child might well be more sensitive than its mother to delicate synchronizers from space and even use these cues to "decide" when to be born. The placenta and the fetus originate from the same cell, they are indeed the same flesh, so it is not unlikely that it is the child that gives the signal to the placenta that starts uterine contractions and begins the labors of birth. Which leaves us with the notion that cosmic forces could best influence man by acting at an early stage on the embryo to modify the blueprint in some way, and that the developing embryo remains in tune with the cosmos, perhaps even to the extent of setting the scene for its own first public appearance.

Gauquelin feels that the tendency for the baby to be born under a certain planet might be hereditary. To test this idea, he worked for more than five years on the birth data of several counties near Paris, collecting information on more than thirty thousand parents and their children. He plotted the positions of Venus, Mars, Jupiter, and Saturn for all the people involved and found overwhelming evidence that parents born when one of these planets was rising most often gave birth when the same planet was in the same position. Factors such as the sex of the parent, the sex of the child, the length of the pregnancy, and the number of previous children had no effect on the results; but the correlation was highest if both parents were born under the same planet. This idea is easily linked to the earlier one of the child itself setting the birth pace, by assuming that each individual carries a gene that makes him sensitive to a particular pattern of cosmic stimuli. We know that this is what happens in fruit flies, which unerringly emerge at dawn. Gauquelin concludes that a child's whole career depends on its genetic structure and that part of this determines when it will be born. He suggests that, by study of the position of the planets at birth, ". . . it seems possible to develop a forecast of the individual's future temperament and social behavior." (117)

Michel Gauquelin himself seems reluctant to admit it, but this is exactly what astrology claims to do. It is time that we had a closer look at astrology.

ASTROLOGY

For a start, we can discard the popular newspaper version of astrology altogether. Glib, all-embracing predictions, in which everyone born under Pisces will have a good day for making new plans, while another twelfth of the world's population will be busy meeting attractive strangers, have nothing to do with astrology. They are held in well-deserved contempt both by astrologers and by their critics. Perhaps the best approach to the real astrology is to examine the tools of the trade and see how they are used. The most basic instrument is the horoscope, which literally means a "view of the hour" and consists of a detailed and formal map of the heavens as they were at the exact place and at the precise time that the person was born. Every horoscope is different; if it is well drawn, with proper attention to detail, it can be almost as distinctive as a fingerprint.

There are five steps in the construction of a horoscope:

1. Establish the date, time, and place of birth.

2. Calculate the appropriate sidereal time.

We operate for convenience on a 24-hour day, but the real day length, the period of rotation of the earth relative to the universe, is four minutes shorter. Sidereal time is obtained from standard tables based on Greenwich in England, and corrections must be made for the time zone, longitude, and latitude of the birthplace.

3. Find the "rising sign."

The planets all move around the sun in the same plane, so we see them passing overhead always through the same belt of sky that extends all the way around earth. Situated along this line, which is called the ecliptic, are twelve main groups of stars, with the famous zodiac names. Some of these constellations are bigger and brighter than the others, but all are given the same value by dividing the belt up into twelve equal portions of 30°. The rising, or ascendant, sign is the constellation zone that is coming up over the eastern horizon at the moment of birth. This is not necessarily the same as the "sun sign." When someone says, "I'm Aries," he means that he was born between March 21 and April 20, when the sun rises at the same time as that constellation. If a person is born at sunrise, his rising sign and sun sign will be the same.

4. Find the "mid-heaven sign."

This is the constellation zone that is directly overhead at the time of birth. Like the rising sign, it can be found from standard tables.

5. Plot the positions of sun, moon, and planets on a birth chart.

This map includes all the planets, even those below the horizon at the moment of birth. All details are taken from a book called an "ephemeris"—meaning that which changes—which is published every year.

So far the technique is perfectly respectable; no scientist could take exception to the logic involved and no astronomer can find fault with the tables used in calculation. The division of the ecliptic into twelve zones is in some ways an arbitrary one, but it is convenient and, as long as all the zones are the same size, there can be no objection to their being compared with one another. The animal or character that is supposed to inhabit each of the twelve zones is more an aid to memory than a real star pattern or a cosmic force. In fact, since the ancient Babylonians set up their celestial Rorschach test and gave names to the splashes of stars, our axis has shifted slightly and the zones of the zodiac are no longer exactly in line with the constellations after which they were named. But this does not matter at all; the zones are precisely defined in the tables used to calculate a horoscope, and their symbolism is unimportant.

The basic tool of astrology is therefore a valid one and beyond dispute. Arguments arise only over the use of the tool, the way in which the horoscope is interpreted; but it is surprising how far science and astrology are in agreement. Astrologers begin their interpretation of the birth data by saying that things on earth are influenced by events outside. Scientists must agree. Astrology says that persons, events, and ideas are all influenced at their time of origin by the prevailing cosmic conditions. Science, which spends a large amount of its time measuring the continual changes in the cosmic scene, must concede that this is possible. Astrology claims that we are most influenced by the celestial bodies nearest to us, the ones in our solar system, and that the two most important are the sun and the moon. Once again science, now that it knows about photoperiodism and the action of solar and lunar rhythms, can only agree. Astrology goes on to claim that the relative positions of the planets is important to us, and science, with Nelson's work on the influence of planets on radio reception in hand, must grudgingly admit that this, too, is a possibility. Then astrology goes out onto more shaky ground with the claim that each of the planets influences life in a different way. But, since Gauquelin's work on the connection between planets and professions, even this idea now begins to have a certain scientific respectability.

The real division between the establishments of science and astrology comes, not when astrologers point to changes in the cosmos but when they claim to know exactly what these changes mean. Both scientists and astrologers describe celestial events and plot the discernible changes these produce in the environment, but the astrologers go further than this and have erected an intricate, and what seems to be completely arbitrary, framework to help them interpret what they see. Most practicing astrologers now no longer even bother to look any more, but rely entirely on the traditional framework to make their interpretations for them. As this is the present stumbling block between the disciplines, it is worth examining the nature of the tradition more closely.

Astrology is an equation in which the positions of all the large bodies in our solar system are variables. The positions of the moving bodies around a fixed spot at a given time are predictable, and they combine to produce a unique set of conditions that can influence anything taking place at that spot. Astrology claims that each of the bodies has a special effect on us (Mercury controls the intellect), but that this effect is modified by the stars behind it at the time. Each of the twelve star patterns in the zodiac also has its own special influence (Virgo is said to have critical, analytic attributes), so Mercury appearing in the zone of Virgo at someone's birth is thought to make that person not only intelligent, but able to apply this intellect shrewdly and well. On the horoscope, or map of the heavens for that time, the planet is shown inside the 30° arc that is thought to encompass Virgo's sphere of influence.

Also on the horoscope chart is a second subdivision into twelve sections that is not based on any known astronomical observation. These are called the "houses," and each of them, like the star zones, occupies 30° of the circle of the heavens. The first house starts on the eastern horizon and projects below it, and the rest follow on in sequence until the twelfth house, which lies just above the eastern horizon. So the rising sign is always in the twelfth house, but the zodiac zones and the houses never coincide exactly unless a baby is born just as one zone gives way to the next one. Like the planets and the stars, the houses also have traditional attributes. The tenth house, for instance, is said to relate to ambition and public standing. So if our subject with Mercury in Virgo also has these two in his tenth house, an astrologer would predict that the shrewd application of his intellect would probably make this person very famous.

So astrology claims that long experience has shown that planets have a predictable influence on character that is modified by secondary, though equally predictable, effects of stars in conjunction with the planet at that moment, and that the combined effects of these forces on a person are determined by the position of the planet/star combination in space at the moment of the child's birth. There are ten large bodies in our solar system, twelve groups of stars, and twelve areas they can all occupy, but astrologers believe that the most important associations are those actually on the eastern horizon at the time of birth (the rising signs) and those that will be there when the sun comes up (the sun signs). This tallies with Gauquelin's finding that it was the planet rising at birth that was linked with the profession. So, if a cosmic force exerts a special influence just as the earth turns toward it, it seems reasonable that this would be reinforced by the sun coming into view at the same time as well. Once again there is little in the mechanics of these suggested effects that would offend a broad-minded scientist, but it is with the specific attributes of the astrological tradition that difficulties arise. There is more of both to come.

Astrology goes on to claim that a person's character (as determined by a planet) and its manifestation (as influenced by a star group) are even further modified by the relationships of the different planets to each other. When a planet stands at a certain angle to another, they are said to be "in aspect." If the two can be seen together at the same point in the sky, they are in "conjunction" and said to exert a powerful influence on events. If one is on the eastern and the other on the western horizon, they are 180 degrees apart and in "opposition," which is said to be a negative, or bad, relationship. If one is on the horizon and the other is directly overhead, they are 90 degrees apart, in "square," and this, too, is bad. But if the angle between them is 120 degrees, they are in "trine," which is positive and good. These are the main aspects, but angles of 30, 45, 60, 135, and 150 degrees are also significant. In practice, a variation of up to 9 degrees from these set aspect angles is regarded as permissible.

When interpreting an aspect, the astrologer uses the traditional value of the angle between them to assess the combination of their traditional attributes. Uranus, for instance, is said to be connected with "sudden change" and Pluto with "elimination." Once every 115 years they come into conjunction; it happened in 1963, and astrology says that anyone born under this aspect is destined to become a world leader with enormous powers for either good or evil. It is fascinating at this point to look back at Nelson's work on radio reception. (229) He found that disturbance occurred when two or more planets were in conjunction or in 90- or 180-degree aspect to the sun. These are precisely the aspects that astrology claims are strong ones and can be "disharmonious" or "bad." Nelson also found that predictably good, disturbance-free conditions occurred when planets lined up in 60- or 120-degree angles to the sun. And these are the aspects that astrological tradition finds to be "good."

These factors and measurements are highly complex, but they form only a part of the vast latticework of intricate relationships used by astrologers. There are hundreds of thousands of recorded guides to interpretation, which cover millions of possible combinations of cosmic events. Even the most ardent devotees of astrology admit that their study lacks a clear philosophic basis, that the laws and principles governing it are still unco-ordinated, and that the records are scattered and contain many errors. But the sum total of what can be examined is an impressive body of opinion which is full of rich, interrelated symmetries that seem to form an elegant and internally consistent system.

Our next step must be to examine the evidence of astrology in action.

It is impossible to investigate the traditions themselves; most of them are supremely illogical and seem to have no basis in any kind of dialectic system, and their origins are obscured in myth and ancient lore and are not available for scrutiny. But we can test the effects of the traditions and their accuracy in interpretation. The proof of the astrological pudding lies in the ability of astrologers to stand up to the consumers' test. The most rigorous and scientific test to date was one made in 1959 by an American psychologist, Vernon Clark.

Clark's first test was to examine the astrologer's claim to be able to predict future talents and capabilities directly from a birth chart. (75) He collected horoscopes from ten people who had been working for some time in a clearly defined profession. These included a musician, a librarian, a veterinarian, an art critic, a prostitute, a bookkeeper, a herpetologist, an art teacher, a puppeteer, and a pediatrician. Half were men and half women, all were born in the United States, and all were between forty-five and sixty years old. These horoscopes were given to twenty astrologers, together with a separate list of the professions, and they were asked to match them up. The same information was given to another group of twenty people—psychologists and social workers—who knew nothing about astrology. The results were conclusive. The control group returned only a chance score, but seventeen out of the twenty astrologers performed far better, with results that were a hundred to one against chance. This shows that people's characters do seem to be influenced by cosmic patterns and that an astrologer can distinguish the nature of the influence just by looking at the horoscope, which is a traditional, ritualized picture of the cosmic pattern.

Clark then went on to test the astrologers' ability not only to distinguish between patterns but to predict the effect of a pattern. He gave the same astrologers ten pairs of horoscopes; attached to each pair was a list of dates showing important events such as marriage, children, new jobs, and death that had taken place in the life of the person who belonged to one of the two charts. The astrologers had to decide which horoscope predicted such events. The test was made more difficult by the fact that the two charts in each pair belonged to people of the same sex who lived in the same area and were born in the same year. Three of the astrologers got all ten right, and the rest again scored better than a hundred to one against chance. This shows that an astrologer can tell, from the birth data alone, whether an accident or a marriage belongs to a particular horoscope. Which means that he could, in theory, have predicted these events before they happened.

Still not satisfied, Clark arranged a third test. He thought the astrologers might have had too many clues to work with, and so he gave them a further ten pairs of birth data with no case history, no dates of important events, no personal information of any kind except that one member of each pair was a victim of cerebral palsy. Once again the astrologers were able to pick the right one far more often than could be attributed to chance. Clark concluded that "astrologers, working with material which can be derived from birth data alone, can successfully distinguish between individuals." In fact these tests, in which the astrologer works "blind," without seeing his subject, are like a physician diagnosing a disease without seeing his patient. To me, as a scientist, they provide impressive evidence that the astrological tradition is not just a meaningless jumble of superstitions, but a real instrument that can be used to extract more information from a simple map of the heavens than any other tool at our disposal.

These results, taken together with those of Nelson and Gauquelin, imply very strongly that cosmic events affect conditions on earth, that different events affect conditions in different ways, and that the nature of these effects can be determined and perhaps even predicted.

One field of prediction in which astrologers are very often consulted is, "Will it be a boy or a girl?" They enjoy some success in their forecasts, which is hardly surprising in view of the limited number of possibilities, but news filters out of Czechoslovakia about a new technique that promises much more than a 50 per cent chance of a right answer.

Eugen Jonas is the Czech psychiatrist whose interest in lunar rhythms led to the discovery of a successful natural method of birth control. In following up this work, he has hit on a new lunar correlation that makes it possible to predict the sex of a child with great accuracy. (168) The method is based on the moon's position in the sky at the time of conception. In classical astrology, each of the zodiac zones has a polarity, or sex—Aries is male, Taurus female, and so on. Jonas has discovered that intercourse leading to conception at a time when the moon was in a "male" star zone produced a male

child. At a clinic in Bratislava, he made the necessary calculation for eight thousand women who wanted to have boys,
and 95 per cent of them were successful. When tested by a
committee of gynecologists, who gave him only the time of
intercourse, he was able to tell the sex of the child with 98 per
cent accuracy.

Work now in progress on artificial insemination shows that
it is possible to separate male and female sperm by passing a
weak electric current through a sample of semen. (217) We
know that the moon produces regular changes in the earth's
magnetic field, and we know that life is sensitive to these
changes. It is a simple and logical step from these premises to
the assumption that a similar kind of sorting could take place
in semen in a living organism. The effect of environmental
fields on the sperm would be enhanced by the fact that semen
is made and stored outside the body of most mammals. Jonas'
discovery tells us two important things about this process. One,
that it seems to be governed by a regular, two-hourly cosmic
rhythm, one of the shortest yet discovered; and two, that
this rhythm is exactly as predicted in traditional astrology.

We are left with a picture of astrology far removed from
that given by stargazing newspaper columns, where facile
guidance is offered on the basis only of the sun sign. In many
people's minds the zodiac and astrology are synonymous, but
Virgo and her friends are only part of a very much larger
and more sophisticated complex. In fact the complex is so co-
hesive that it is difficult to understand how it could have come
about. The accepted background for astrology is that it owes
most to the Babylonians (or Chaldeans), who, being nomadic
in a climate that allowed an unobstructed view of the sky,
readily accepted the idea that divine energy is manifest in the
movement of the heavenly bodies. The textbook history goes
on to recount how this concept gradually became enlarged as
omens and portents were included, until the planets became

associated with every aspect of life. Then this ritual was handed on to and refined by the Greeks and the Romans and the Arabs, until it reached its full flowering in medieval times. John West and Jan Toonder reject this account and suggest, in a meticulous historical and critical survey called *The Case for Astrology*, that it owes much more to the Egyptians, who in their turn brought together the pieces of "an ancient doctrine that at one time fused art, religion, philosophy and science into one internally consistent whole." (339)

It is possible that the roots of astrology go back as far as the last ice age—a bone more than thirty thousand years old was discovered recently to be marked in a way that suggests lunar periodicity. But an awareness of the planetary paths and periods can be traced only as far back as the building of the first pyramid, about 2870 B.C. Five thousand years is only two hundred generations, and it is difficult to believe that this is time enough to compile a system whose most simple contention could only be checked a generation later. Some of the more unusual events take place so seldom—Uranus and Neptune have been in conjunction only twenty-nine times in recorded history—that this type of trial-and-error development is inconceivable. The picture of astrology growing slowly over the years, as bits and pieces of evidence were discovered and added from time to time, is an equally unlikely one. Trying to decide which cosmic pattern produces a particular effect is like trying to discover which particular gene of the thousands on a chromosome controls the color of an individual's eyes. The American Federation of Astrologers has thirteen hundred members, and the American Society of Geneticists has double this number, so it is fair to compare their efforts in an attempt to give some idea of the scope of the problem. The major tool in genetic research is the fruit fly; one fruit-fly generation lasts two weeks; two hundred generations would last eight years; work on the fly began in 1909, but it took more than fifty years for a full picture of even one chromosome to be completed. Even if we accept the problems as being roughly comparable, that represents a span of four-teen hundred human generations, or thirty-five thousand years of intensive research to build up the astrological picture. In fact, the scheme of traditional astrology is so much more com-plex that we are driven to the conclusion that it must have originated in some other way.

It seems obvious that astrology is not the result of some sud-den insight of the "*Eureka!*" kind; it never sprang fully formed from anyone's mind. So if it did not arise in either of these ways, there is only one other possibility: that it evolved, like a living organism, out of the very stuff of which it is made.

In the bush country around Darwin, in northern Australia, there lives a termite that constructs a weirdly shaped nest. Many termites cement fine grains of sand together with saliva and pack it into huge, rock-hard mounds, but this species builds slabs ten feet square and only a few inches thick that are scattered across the outback like enormous tombstones. The fact that every single one of them has its long axis ori-ented exactly along a north-south line gives the insect its name *Omitermes meridionalis,* the compass termite. Each termitarium is like an iceberg, with most of its structure be-neath the surface, and the part above the ground is honey-combed with ventilation shafts that form the air-conditioning plant for the entire fortress. Thousands of workers rush up and down the airshafts, opening and closing them like valves as they labor to keep the temperature in the deeper, brood chambers constant all day long. In the cool of the early morn-ings they need to take up as much heat as possible, and so the broad side of the mound faces directly into the rising sun. At noon they are more concerned with losing heat, so the mound exposes only its knife-edge to the sun, now directly overhead. Built into every single one of the termite laborers is an awareness of the sun's movements that leads it to construct its little bit of the mound so that the whole thing relates to the cosmos in a way that expresses the needs of the society. The termitarium is literally shaped by cosmic forces.

I believe that astrology arose in this way: that an awareness of cosmic forces predisposed man to certain ideas and patterns, and that, despite the fact that each contributing astrologer could see only his little bit of the structure, the final synthesis took on a natural and relevant form.

I know that this sounds mystic, but there are good scientific grounds for my belief. As chemistry was discovering that all life was built up of the same few basic substances, physics was investigating the substances themselves and discovering that fundamental particles of matter all behave in the same way. They all have a wave motion. We know that information, whether it is a sound signal or an electromagnetic impulse such as light, travels in waves; now the new field of quantum mechanics shows us that there are matter waves as well and that an organism receiving information is itself vibrant with wave patterns. If two waves of different frequencies are superimposed, there will be points along their path where the two touch, where they both peak together and interfere with each other. This interference is called a beat, and a number of beats in a regular sequence produces a rhythm. Everything in the cosmos dances to these rhythms.

John Addey, an English philosopher, has discovered such rhythms in human birth times. He tried to find out whether it was true that those born under the sun sign of Capricorn were longer lived than others, by collecting the data for 970 ninety-year-olds from Who's Who. (2) There were no more Capricorns than any other sign, of course, so he went on to see whether it was true that Pisceans were short-lived by collecting data on young polio victims. (3) Once again there was no connection, but when Addey looked at the data from both tests more carefully, he found a wave pattern running through the year. This was a regular pattern, which had 120 peaks in the year—it was vibrating in the 120th harmonic. A horoscope is built around the ecliptic circle of 360 degrees, so if the wave pattern is applied to this, it peaks once every 3 degrees. Addey went back to his test data and found that a child born every third degree was 37 per cent more likely to contract polio than a child born at other times.

Addey went on to apply wave analysis to other sets of data (339) and found that the birth times of 2,593 clergymen corresponded to the 7th harmonic and that 7,302 doctors fitted into the 5th harmonic. (4) This is probably the most important of all recent discoveries that give the old astrology and the new science a place to meet on common ground. It demonstrates quite clearly that astrological data are amenable to a statistical approach and that, treated in this way, they yield results that are in direct accordance with our knowledge of the basic laws of matter. The cosmos is a chaotic frenzy of wave patterns, some of which have been orchestrated on earth into an organized life system. The harmony between the two can be understood only with the aid of a score, and of all the possibilities open to us at this moment, astrology (for all its weird origins and sometimes weirder devotees) seems to offer the best interpretation.

I come to this conclusion from two directions: On one journey I travel as a scientist, picking my path with care and logic, guided by the map of established knowledge, and arrive satisfied that astrology, if not proved, has at least not been disproved. There is good evidence, which is soundly based and amenable to both examination and repetition, to suggest that there is enough truth in astrology to warrant that it be taken seriously and pursued further. On the other path I travel as an individual with a training in science but with a willingness to stop and consider almost anything out of the ordinary. I come upon astrology this way and live with it long enough to satisfy myself that there is something in it. To be sure, there are inconsistencies and vague, ambivalent statements—astrology is particularly weak and open to criticism in the field of prediction—but still I am left with a feeling of rightness. A feeling that, even if the goals are sometimes questionable and the reasoning often weak, astrology has hit upon a form that makes basic sense.

I do not believe that emanations from the planet Mars make a man "decisive, freedom-loving, and a pioneer." This is simplistic nonsense. But I do believe that there are complex patterns of cosmic forces that could predispose an individual to develop along these lines. The astrologers may be right in asserting that these conditions prevail when Mars is coming over the horizon, but even if that is true, the planet is merely a symptom of the over-all complexity. It is like the second hand on a watch, which provides a visible indication of the precise time but depends entirely on all the hidden springs and wheels that actually set the pace. I also disagree with the notion that birth is the critical moment. It seems far more reasonable to assume that cosmic forces are acting on everything all the time and that the moment of birth bears the same relation to the rest of life as the momentary position of Mars does to the rest of the cosmos. We know that the time of birth is related to lunar cycles, to solar rhythms, and to an inherited tendency to respond to these patterns in a certain way. It seems likely that birth, the early stages of fetal development, fertilization, and even intercourse are related in the same way, forming a continuum in which no one moment is intrinsically more important than another.

There are some mystical things about astrology, but there is nothing supernatural about the way it works. Man is affected by his environment according to clearly defined physical forces, and his life, like all others', becomes organized by natural and universal laws. To believe otherwise is tantamount to assuming that the Encyclopaedia Britannica was thrown together by an explosion in a printing works.

Chapter Three:

The Physics of Life

WE CHOOSE TO LIVE. We have to choose, because a hundred million impulses pour down on our nervous system every second and, if we were to accept them all, we would soon be overwhelmed and die in confusion. So the input is monitored and carefully controlled; of all the millions of incoming signals, only a small number reach the brain and a still smaller number get passed on to those areas where they can give rise to conscious awareness.

A tape recording always seems to pick up more background noise than there is in a real-life situation, but sounds such as passing traffic and the ticking of a clock are there all the time—our brain just ignores them. All life is selective in this way. From the background of continuous clamor, what Milton called "the dismal universal hiss," an organism makes its choice. The chosen pieces are not necessarily the most dramatic stimuli—the loudest sounds or the brightest lights; very often they are subtle changes in the environment made

conspicuous only because of their incongruity. While director
of a zoo I was once obliged to keep a pair of bat-eared foxes
in my house. These are tiny, delicate desert animals with
huge, leaf-shaped ears that quiver and scan like radar antennas, constantly seeking out new sounds. Heavy vehicles
thundered down a thoroughfare past the house, often loud
enough to drown out conversation with their clamor and
vibration, but even in the midst of this confusion the foxes
were able to hear sounds as soft as the furtive rustle of cello-
phane two rooms away and would appear like magic on the
arm of my chair to find out what I was unwrapping.

Living organisms select, from the barrage of electromagnetic
waves in their environment, only those frequencies likely to
contain the best information. Earth's atmosphere reflects or
absorbs large parts of the spectrum coming in from space:
infrared and ultraviolet radiation are partly eliminated, but
visible light, with a wavelength intermediate between these
two, passes almost unimpaired. So it is no accident that life
should be very sensitive to this potentially valuable source of
intelligence. Human vision responds to wavelengths from 380
to 760 millimicrons, which is exactly the range of frequencies
least affected by the protective blanket of the atmosphere.
We get a selective picture of the cosmos through a number of
narrow windows of this kind in our sensory system.

It used to be said that there were only five such windows:
those of sight, sound, smell, taste, and touch. But our ideas of
the architecture of life are being continually revised as we
discover new senses in ourselves and new combinations of the
old ones in other species. Bats "see" with their ears, building
up accurate pictures of their environment by sending out high-
frequency sounds and listening to the patterns of returning
echoes. Rattlesnakes "see" with their skin, following the
movements of prey in complete darkness with heat-sensitive
cells in two shallow dimples between their eyes. Flies "taste"

with their feet, trampling their food first to find out whether it is worth eating. The whole body is a sense organ, and most apparently supernatural abilities turn out on close examination to be variables of this kind, developed by a particular species to meet its own special needs.

In the red, muddy rivers of central Africa live a family of fish called mormyrids. They include some of the most peculiar-looking fish in the world, elongated and stiff-backed, with tiny eyes and drooping, elephant-trunk snouts. Some of them grub in the thick mud for worms, most of them operate only at night, and all of them have an extraordinary ability to respond to stimuli invisible to man. If a comb is drawn through hair, it becomes electrified with the power of less than one millionth of a volt, and yet, if such a comb is held near the glass on the outside of an aquarium containing a mormyrid, the fish reacts violently to the minute electrical field produced in the water.

Professor Lissmann of Cambridge has kept one species of mormyrid, *Gymnarchus niloticus,* for almost twenty years and made a detailed study of its strange world. (200) In spite of its degenerate eyes, which can only just tell the difference between light and dark, this fish maneuvers with precision in and out of obstacles, darting after other small fish, on which it feeds. Lissmann has discovered that it "sees" with electricity, which it generates in an electric organ made of a battery of muscles in its long, pointed tail. By dipping a pair of electrodes into the water, he found that the fish was sending out a constant stream of small electrical discharges at the rate of about three hundred per second. During each discharge, the tip of the tail becomes momentarily negative with respect to the head and *Gymnarchus* acts like a bar magnet, producing a field with lines of force that radiate out from it in a spindle shape. In open water the field is symmetrical, but an object nearby distorts the field and the fish feels this is an alteration of the electrical potential on its skin. The sensory cells are small pores on the head which are filled with a jelly-like substance that reacts to the field and sends information on to a special electrical sense area in the head which is so large that it covers the rest of the brain like a spongy hat.

Lissmann trained *Gymnarchus* to come to food hidden behind one of two similar ceramic pots at one end of its aquarium. The fish cannot see or smell the contents of the pots, but the walls are porous, and when soaked in water, present no obstacle to an electrical field. By using its electric location sense, *Gymnarchus* was able to tell the difference between tap water and distilled water, or between a glass rod one millimeter thick and another two millimeters thick, and always went for food to the pot that was the best conductor. If two or more fish are operating in the same area, they avoid confusion by adopting a slightly different frequency, which gives each individual its own distinctive electrical voice. When electrodes are connected to a loudspeaker and dipped into the water near the riverbank where the fish rest up during the day, one can hear a bewildering confusion of rattles, hums, and whistles as they conduct their electronic conversations.

Gymnarchus can tell the difference between living and non-living objects, even when the living one is completely stationary. It does not use shape as a clue, because it can distinguish a live fish from a dead one of the same species, so presumably it responds to an electrical signal of some kind. (199) Lissmann had found that many species of fish that are supposedly non-electric, do in fact put out strong discharges, and he suggests that they are in the process of developing an electric system of location, or may already use it to supplement their normal senses. Every time a muscle contracts, it changes its potential, so it is possible that a living organism, in which there is always some muscular activity going on, produces a field strong enough to be recognized by a specialist such as *Gymnarchus*. All the highly electrical organisms known, live in water, which is a good conductor. Air is a poor conductor, and a much greater source of power would be necessary for effective navigation. No species seems to have found the effort of developing such a system worthwhile, but it seems that all life forms can produce and perhaps recognize a weak electrical field.

LIFE FIELDS

Harold Burr, of Yale, demonstrated life fields with one of the most simple and elegant biological experiments ever made. He started with the principle of the dynamo, which is a machine that produces electricity from some purely mechanical source such as falling water or a passing wind. In its most simple form, the dynamo consists of an armature, usually a loop of copper wire, which is rotated inside a magnetic field so that it makes and breaks the field in rapid alternation. This produces an electric current. In Burr's experiment, the dynamo consisted of a live salamander floating in a dish of salt water. He assumed that the salamander, which is a small amphibian that looks a little like a lizard, was producing a field and that he would be able to interrupt this field and generate a current. So he chose salt water, which conducts electricity almost as well as copper wire, as his armature and rotated the dish around and around the floating salamander. It did break the field, and electrodes immersed in the water soon began to pick up a current. When this was fed into a galvanometer to measure the charge, the needle was deflected to the left and then to the right in the regular negative and positive pattern of a perfect alternating current. If the dish was rotated without the floating amphibian, no current was produced.

Having proved that even a small, fairly slow-moving animal

produces its own electric field, Burr went on to develop an instrument sensitive enough to measure the potential of the field. (57) He adapted a standard vacuum-tube voltmeter by giving it a very high resistance in order to prevent it from affecting the voltage by taking any current from the animal being measured. This meter he equipped with a scale and two perfectly matched silver-chloride electrodes. These are never put into actual contact with the specimen being measured, but are separated from it by a bridge of special paste or a salt solution of the same ionic concentration as the organism itself.

Burr's first test with the instrument was on a number of student volunteers. (60) The electrodes were fed into two small dishes of salt solution and the subjects placed their index fingers in the dishes, then reversed them to give an average reading. This was done at the same time every day for over a year, and Burr found that each person showed a small daily fluctuation, but that all the female students produced one huge increase in voltage, lasting about twenty-four hours, once each month. These changes seemed to take place near the middle of the menstrual cycle, and Burr thought they might coincide with ovulation. To test this idea, he turned to work on rabbits. The female rabbit has no regular menstrual cycle or breeding season, but true to her fertile reputation, can breed at any time. Like many small mammals, she is a "shock ovulator." All that is necessary is that the male should be rough enough during mating to stimulate the cervix strongly (some species even have an explosive dart in the penis for doing this), and ovulation occurs about nine hours later. Burr stimulated a female rabbit artificially, waited eight hours, anesthetized it, opened it, and placed his electrodes on the ovary. While the voltage pattern was being continuously recorded, he watched the ovary through a microscope. To his enormous delight, there was a dramatic change in the voltage at the exact moment that he saw the follicle rupture and release an egg. (56)

Ovulation causes a marked change in the body's electrical field. This finding was confirmed on a human subject who was about to undergo an operation but agreed to postpone it until Burr's voltmeter indicated that ovulation was taking place. (58) When her ovaries were uncovered in the operating theater, one contained a follicle that had just ruptured. This discovery of an electrical method of detecting ovulation, which is so simple that the subject just has to dangle her fingers in bowls of water, has been put forward as a system of birth control for those who cannot bring themselves to trust Eugen Jonas' lunar timetables. Both systems are far safer than the purely mathematical rhythm method, which, as many women have discovered to their dismay, makes no allowance for what can be a big variation in the time of ovulation. Burr's method has now also been used to ensure conception and for timing artificial insemination, but it does not end there.

Having discovered that a life field exists and that changes in the field are not random but connected with basic biological events, Burr wondered if the field would also be influenced by disruptions produced by disease. He took his equipment to an obstetrician, and together they tested over a thousand women in New York's Bellevue Hospital. (59) In 102 cases, they found abnormal gradients between the abdomen and the cervix, and in subsequent surgery for other complaints, ninety-five of these women proved to have malignant cancer of either the cervix or the uterus. So the life field changes even before the symptoms of the disease become manifest, and once the changes are understood, it seems likely to become a valuable early warning system and diagnostic aid. Burr goes even further than this: He claims that the gradient of the electrical response is directly connected to the rate of healing and that he can use his voltmeter as a sort of super X ray. (55) Internal scars do not show up well on normal equipment, but Burr has been able to determine the condition of surgical wounds just by following the changes in the external life field.

This field is one concerned with direct-current potentials and has nothing to do with brain waves or the impulses recorded by an electrocardiograph. Every time the heart beats or the brain is stimulated, it produces a measurable electric charge, but the life field seems to be the sum-total effect of these and all the other small electric charges that occur as a result of chemical events that continually take place in the body. The life field can be measured even with the electrodes held a little way from the skin, which indicates that it is a true field effect and not merely a surface electrical potential. The field persists as long as life lasts, undergoing regular small changes in healthy subjects and more dramatic aberrations in a diseased subject. Meas-ured over a long period, the rise and fall of voltage can be plotted in steady cycles that indicate the time when an individual is at his best and the times when his vitality is diminished and his efficiency is likely to suffer. In a healthy person, the cycles are so regular that they could be used to predict "high" and "low" times weeks in advance and warn someone in a hazardous occupation such as motor racing of days when he should take extra care or even stay at home in bed. In this respect, we are getting very close again to astrology, which specializes in predicting times that will be "auspicious" or "unfavorable" for undertaking particular proj-ects, so it is not surprising to discover that changes in the life field follow a cosmic rhythm.

It is obviously impossible to keep a man tied to a voltmeter for months on end, but there is a magnificent old maple tree in New Haven, Connecticut, that has been wired up for thirty years of continuous recording. (52) Analysis of this record shows irregular patterns produced by electrical disturbance from nearby thunderstorms and local fluctuations in earth's magnetic field, but it also shows that the tree responds to a 24-hour solar rhythm, a 25-hour lunar rhythm, and a longer lunar cycle that reaches its peak as the full moon passes directly overhead. Only one long-term study of this kind has been made on man. Leonard Ravitz made continuous recordings for several months that showed that the life field reaches a maximum positive value at full moon and a maximum negative value two weeks later, at new moon. (267) We know that the passage of the sun, moon, and planets all produce variations in magnetic conditions that radically alter the earth's field. And now we know that living things have their own fields, which are in turn influenced by changing patterns in the earth. The chain is complete. Here is a natural and measurable mechanism that can account for the connection between man and the cosmos. The supernatural makes way for Supernature.

The idea of having an electrical field we cannot see or hear or taste is in itself rather mysterious, so it is worth explaining that a field does not exist in its own right. It is simply an area in which certain things happen. If an electrical charge is brought into an electrical field, forces will act on it. Every atom carries an electrical charge and is therefore acted on by the field of an organism. Even a simple, single-celled animal such as *Euglena* has its own field and builds atoms and molecules into its structure, modifying its field by incorporating their charges. So a complex organism has a composite field which is a sum of all its component parts. This field can be measured as a whole to get the "flavor" of the entire structure, or separate measurements can be made of organs and perhaps even of individual cells within the organism. Each component has its own function and develops its own potential as a result of that function. Burr has been examining these differences and has come up with an exciting discovery.

He introduced microelectrodes into a newly laid frog egg and found that, even before the egg began to divide and develop into a tadpole, he could measure voltage differences in those parts of the egg that were due to become the nervous system. (50) The egg material that would eventually serve the function of communication was already displaying the voltage characteristic of that part of the organism. This implies that the life field has an organizing ability, that it is a kind of template, which lays down the form and function of the organism being developed. Edward Russell has seized on this one example of anticipation and elaborated it into a thesis just published as *Design for Destiny*. He sees the field as an integrating mechanism that not only designs the organism but lives on after it dies, as the soul. (285)

It would be splendid to find scientific proof of the soul, as advertised on the jacket of Russell's book, but I regret that this is not it. Burr took measurements from the frog egg that enabled him to predict where its future nerve cord would be formed, but at no point does he claim that the life field of the egg was identical to that of the adult frog. It would have to be the same if it existed before the frog as a blueprint, lived with it as intelligence, and survived it as a soul. All the available evidence points in the opposite direction. Burr showed that a life field deviated from the normal as an early warning signal of disease, but certainly never claimed that the change in the field produced the disease. His work demonstrates instead that the life field is very much a product of life, providing an accurate electronic mirror image in which certain details are detectable before they become apparent to our other senses. Life produces the life field, and when life dies, the field dies with it. *Gymnarchus* cannot distinguish a dead fish from a wax model.

During its life, any change in an organism is reflected by a change in its field. Burr proved this with another neat experiment. When two pure strains of corn are crossed, they produce a cob that contains a mixture of pure-breeding and hybrid seeds. These look identical, and internally they differ only in the arrangement of one small gene, which cannot be seen even with an electron microscope. But Burr showed that they had different electric potentials, and he was able to sort the seeds successfully into pure and hybrid plants just by using his voltmeter. (51) This is reminiscent of the astrologers successfully predicting later life patterns on the basis only of the horoscope, and it is worth pursuing the analogy. The measurement of electrical potential is like the identification of a rising sign: both are indicative of a pattern of events, but neither is a determining factor in itself. The life field is a vital discovery, but it is not the secret of life or of survival after death. It is more of a means to an end, a key to the understanding of Supernature.

One result of the new research into life and electricity is a theory that could explain how life is influenced by events outside our solar system. Together with light from the stars, we also receive an equivalent amount of energy in the form of very-short-wavelength cosmic rays. Most of these are absorbed in the atmosphere, where their energy is used partly to turn carbon dioxide into the radioactive isotope car- with a way of dating many fossils. The rest of the energy bon 14, which gets into all living things and provides us from this cosmic bombardment goes into ionizing the air, breaking up the gases into atoms that carry electrical charges. This charged air gathers at about sixty miles above the earth's surface in a layer called the ionosphere, which reflects the longer radio waves and makes it possible for us on the ground to send radio signals beyond the horizon by bouncing them off this invisible ceiling.

Part of the ionized air seeps down to lower layers of the atmosphere as ozone, which has a marked effect on life. In a concentration of only one part in four million parts of air, ozone kills many bacteria and is sometimes injected into the air conditioning of mines and underground railways for this purpose. (213) We can detect ozone in this concentration by its fresh, sort of seaside, smell, but we are also aware of ionized air in much lower concentrations and can even distinguish between positive and negative charges. (185) Air with a preponderance of positive ions has a depressing effect on man, while negative ions tend to be more stimulating. There is no way in which we could make distinctions of this kind without ourselves carrying an electrical charge that either attracts or repels particles around us. Ravitz showed that our fields are positively charged at full moon, so at this time we would attract negative ions to us and be more stimulated. (267) Which provides an elegant explanation for the fact that psychotic characters go into their manic phases at this time and that everyone bleeds more easily at full moon. The life field forms a perfect mechanism for linking us with cyclical events in our environment.

The moon produces tides in water, air, and earth, which alter the magnetic field, and this in turn affects the charge on our life fields. To accentuate this change and make us even more aware of the lunar rhythm as a basic timekeeper, cosmic rays produce ionized air, which reacts with our field and exaggerates our responses. We are sensitive to the moon, but this sensitivity is modified by events that originate many light-years away. Once again we find complex interrelationships that make earth and every living thing on it an integral part of the cosmos.

At the opposite end of the spectrum to the tiny cosmic rays are some very long waves, whose origins also seem to lie outside our solar system. The frequency of these waves is measured in tiny fractions of a cycle per second, their wave-length being millions of miles, and their energy is so weak as to be barely measureable, but we seem to be aware of them. A study made in Germany on fifty-three thousand people found that they took longer to respond to normal stimuli when waves of this length were passing by. (182) It is highly significant that the pattern of these very-low-frequency waves is almost indistinguishable from the patterns an electroencephalograph records in the human brain.

BRAIN WAVES

Electrophysiology began in the middle of the eighteenth century, soon after methods of generating electricity became available. At first the experiments were rather wild: it is reported that Louis XV in an idle moment "caused an electric shock from a battery of Leyden jars to be administered to 700 Carthusian monks joined hand to hand, with prodigious effect." (335) Later an awareness grew that not only was all living tissue sensitive to electric currents but the tissue itself generated small voltages, which changed dramatically when it was injured or became active. In 1875 an English physician found that the brain also produced such currents. The early experiments were done on the exposed brains of frogs and dogs, but as soon as more sensitive equipment was invented, investigations began in earnest on intact animals and men. In 1928 Hans Berger discovered that the current produced by the brain was not constant, but flowed in a rhythmic wave pattern, which he demonstrated on his "Elektrenkephalogram."

Today Berger's single wobbly line has been broken up into many components by instruments that can detect fluctuations as small as one ten-millionth of a volt. To give some idea of the minuteness of such a current, it would take about thirty

million of them to light a small flashlight bulb. Hidden
in the confusion of these very subtle stimuli are four basic
rhythmic patterns, which have been named alpha, beta, delta,
and theta. Delta rhythms are the slowest, running between
1 and 3 cycles a second, and are most prominent in deep
sleep. Theta rhythms are those with a frequency of 4 to 7
cycles a second, which seem to be connected with mood.
From 8 to 12 cycles are the alpha rhythms, which occur
most often in relaxed meditation and are disrupted by attention. And beta rhythms, between 13 and 22 cycles per
second, seem to be confined to the frontal area of the brain,
where complex mental processes take place.

Early research into these rhythms was confined to simple
experiments such as the effect of opening and closing the eyes,
doing mental arithmetic, and taking drugs, but the results were
very meager. To find out more about the scope and sensitivity
of the brain, Grey Walter and his associates decided in 1946
to try imposing new patterns of the existing brain rhythms
through the senses. They began by flashing a light at regular
intervals into the subject's eyes and found that this flicker
produced new, strange patterns on the graphs. At certain
frequencies the flicker also produced violent reactions in the
subject, who was suddenly seized by what seemed to be an
epileptic fit.

Walter turned immediately to the study of the normal,
resting brain waves of known epileptics and found that their
brain rhythms were grouped in certain frequencies. "It was
as if certain major chords constantly appeared against the
trills and arpeggios of the normal activity." This harmonic
grouping suggested to him that all that was necessary to get
the rhythms to synchronize in a tremendous explosion, was
an outside co-ordinator, a conductor who could bring the
separate chords together into a simultaneous grand convulsion. A flicker somewhere in the alpha-rhythm range, between

8 and 12 cycles a second, acted in just this way on epileptics, provoking them into a seizure at any time. This technique has now become a valuable clinical aid in the diagnosis of epilepsy, but it has also been discovered that a large number of otherwise normal people show a similar response under certain conditions.

Walter examined hundreds of people who had never had any kind of fit or attack and found that about one in every twenty responded to carefully adjusted flicker. They experienced "strange feelings" or faintness or swimming in the head; some became unconscious for a few moments or their limbs jerked in rhythm with the light. As soon as any such sensation was reported, the flicker was turned off to prevent a complete convulsion. In other subjects, the flicker had to be exactly matched with the brain rhythm to produce any effects. A feedback circuit, in which the flashing light was actually fired by the brain signals themselves, produced immediate epileptic seizures in more than half the people tested.

Driving down a tree-lined avenue with the sun flickering through the trunks at a certain rhythm can be very disturbing. There is a record of a cyclist who passed out on several occasions while traveling home down such an avenue. In his case the momentary unconsciousness stopped him from pedaling, so he slowed down to a speed at which the flicker no longer affected him and came around in time to save himself from falling. But a motorcar has more momentum, and the chances are that it would keep going at the critical speed and influence the driver long enough to make him lose control altogether. There is no way of knowing how many fatal crashes have occurred in this way.

In another case, a man found that every time he went to the cinema he would suddenly find that he was consumed by an overwhelming desire to strangle the person sitting next to him. On one occasion he even came to his senses to discover that he had his hands clutched around his neighbor's throat. When he was tested, it was found that he developed violent limb jerking when the flicker was set at twenty-four cycles per second, which is exactly the rhythm of film recorded at twenty-four frames a second.

The implications of this discovery are enormous. Every day we are exposed to flicker in some way and run the risk of illness or fatal fits. The flash rate of fluorescent lights at 100 to 120 per second is too high for convulsions, but who knows what effect it may be having on those exposed to it for many hours each day. The British Acoustical Society has become concerned about the low-frequency vibration produced by motor vehicles running at sustained speed. (318) These "infrasounds" are at the level of 10 to 20 cycles per second, which is below the limit of human hearing, but they can affect us in the same way as flickering lights. The Society warns that these sounds can produce symptoms of recklessness, euphoria; lower efficiency, and dizziness due to loss of balance. They believe that infrasounds are responsible for the way in which some drivers wander across the central strip of high-speed roads apparently quite oblivious to the danger of oncoming traffic, and that the vibrations may account for a large number of otherwise inexplicable accidents.

Professor Gavraud is an engineer who almost gave up his post at an institute in Marseilles because he always felt ill at work. He decided against leaving when he discovered that the recurrent attacks of nausea only worried him when he was in his office at the top of the building. Thinking that there must be something in the room that disturbed him, he tried to track it down with devices sensitive to various chemicals, and even with a Geiger counter, but he found nothing until one day, nonplused, he leaned back against the wall. The whole room was vibrating at a very low frequency. The source of this energy turned out to be an air-conditioning plant on the roof of a building across the way, and his office was the right shape and the right distance from the machine to resonate in sympathy with it. It was this rhythm, at seven cycles per second, that made him sick.

Fascinated by the phenomenon, Gavraud decided to build machines to produce infrasound so that he could investigate it further. In casting around for likely designs, he discovered that the whistle with a pea in it issued to all French gendarmes produced a whole range of low-frequency sounds. So he built a police whistle six feet long and powered it with compressed air. The technician who gave the giant whistle its first trial blast fell down dead on the spot. A post-mortem revealed that all his internal organs had been mashed into an amorphous jelly by the vibrations.

Gavraud went ahead with his work more carefully and did the next test out of doors, with all observers screened from the machine in a concrete bunker. When all was ready, they turned the air on slowly—and broke the windows of every building within half a mile of the test site. Later they learned to control the amplitude of the infrasound generator more effectively and designed a series of smaller machines for experimental work. One of the most interesting discoveries to date is that the waves of low frequency can be aimed and that two generators focused on a particular point even five miles away produce a resonance that can knock a building down as effectively as a major earthquake. These frequency-7 machines can be built very cheaply, and plans for them are available for three French francs from the Patent Office in Paris.

For many years now, seismic waves have been recorded in the same way as brain waves. Seismographs have been developed that are sensitive enough to pick up vibrations in the ground that we cannot consciously perceive. These records show when earthquakes are taking place even on the farthest side of the earth. During the Chilean earthquake of May 1960, for instance, the whole planet rang like a gong with long-wave oscillations that had periods of up to an hour. But it has now been discovered that an earthquake is also accompanied by, and preceded by, periods of low-frequency vibrations that fall into the range from seven to fourteen cycles per second. These start minutes before the first obvious shocks of the quake itself and provide an early-warning system to which many species seem to respond. The Japanese, who live right on a fracture system, have always kept goldfish for this reason. When the fish begin to swim about in a frantic way, the owners rush out of doors in time to escape being trapped by falling masonry. The fish have the advantage of living in a medium that conducts vibrations well, but even animals living in the air are able to pick up warning signals. Hours before an earthquake, rabbits and deer have been seen running in terror from the epicenter zones. Some people, particularly women and children, are also sensitive to these frequencies.

The fact that the frequencies coincide with those that make people disturbed and ill would account for the wild, unreasoning fear that goes with an earthquake. F. Kingdon-Ward lived through the great Assam shock of 1951 and described his feelings at the time. (175) "Suddenly, after the faintest tremor (felt by my wife but not by me) there came an appalling noise and the earth began to shudder violently . . . the outlines of the landscape, visible against the starry sky, blurred—every ridge and tree fuzzy—as though it were moving rapidly up and down . . . the first feeling of bewilderment—an incredulous astonishment that these solid-looking hills were in the grip of a force which shook them as a terrier shakes a rat—soon gave place to stark terror." This earthquake was a major one in which they were in great danger, but the feelings of terror seem to have no connection with the magnitude of the tremor. I remember running outside during a small earthquake in Crete in 1967 and, despite the fact that I was perfectly safe out of doors and was fascinated by what was going on, feeling an irrational fear so deep-seated that I was unable to sleep indoors for more than a week.

Vibrations of a frequency too low to hear could account for the feelings of depression and fear that seem to be attached to certain places. Many people feel intensely uncomfortable on the island of Santorini, in the southern Aegean, and few visitors stay more than a day or two. This island, which is now believed by some to be the site of old Atlantis, erupted violently in 1450 B.C. and suffered an earthquake in 1956. Since the recent disaster, a seismological station has been established there, which reports a constant undercurrent of very-low-frequency murmurs. Earth gives her warnings in a soft, low voice.

An unexpected discovery was made as a result of the Tashkent quake of 1966. For a year prior to the shock, scientists had been surprised to find that there were increasing concentrations of the inert gas argon in the city's water supply, which comes from deep artesian wells. On April 25 this had reached four times its normal level, and on the 26th the earthquake struck. The day following the disaster, the argon concentration was back to its normal level. The reason for the change is not known, but it forms yet another of those inconspicuous clues to which life may well be able to respond like magic.

The one thing that earth tremors, air tides, and cosmic rays all have in common is that they operate on very low energy and send out extremely subtle signals. The apparently supernatural ability of life to respond to stimuli such as the position of the unseen moon, the concentration of invisible ions, and the minute magnetic influence of a planet on the horizon can all be attributed to a single physical phenomenon—the principle of resonance.

RESONANCE

If a tuning fork designed to produce a frequency of 256 cycles a second (that is, middle C), is sounded anywhere near another fork with the same natural frequency, the second one will begin to vibrate gently in sympathy with the first, even without being touched. Energy has been transferred from one to the other. An insect without ears would not be able to hear the sound of the first fork, but if it were sitting on the second one, it would very soon become aware of the vibration—and thus of events taking place beyond its normal sphere. This is what Supernature is all about.

An event in the cosmos sets up the vibration of electromagnetic waves, which travel across space and create an equivalent vibration by resonance with some part of earth that has the same natural frequency. Life may respond to these stimuli directly, but more often it reacts by resonating in sympathy with part of its immediate environment. A flashing light on the same frequency as a brain rhythm produces resonance and alarming effects, even though the flicker may be too fast for us to see. A very weak electrical or magnetic field becomes noticeable because it resonates on the same frequency as the life field of the organism reacting to it. In this way, very subtle stimuli, too small to make any impression on the normal senses, are magnified and brought to our notice. The supernatural becomes part of natural history.

In most musical instruments, sound is produced by strings, stretched membranes, rods, or reeds, and an important part of all of them is a structure that increases the area of contact these vibrators have with the air. A guitar string has a sounding box and a clarinet reed has a pipe. The shape of the structure determines the way in which the air will resonate and the quality of the sound. Shape and function are very closely related, not only for the sender of the signal but also for the receiver. If the listener is to hear the sound properly, he cannot sit in a room of the wrong shape or wear a football helmet.

Ultimately, sensitivity to sound depends on vibrations being set up in the fluid of the inner ear, but the sound first has to be collected by the external ear. In man, the passage between the eardrum and the outside world is funnel-shaped, with the walls making an angle of about 30 degrees to the drum. This is exactly the angle best suited to magnification of sounds in the critical range. The most popular, and therefore presumably the most effective, old-fashioned ear trumpet is one that also has this angle of 30 degrees. This could be just coincidence, but I doubt it.

Sound, of course, is a vibration that can be conducted only through an elastic medium; it cannot travel through a vacuum. Electromagnetic waves do travel through free space, and we know far less about the factors governing their resonance. There is, however, one quite extraordinary piece of evidence which suggests that shape could be important in receiving even cosmic stimuli. It comes from those favorites of mystics throughout the ages—the pyramids of Egypt.

The pyramids on the west bank of the Nile were built by the pharaohs as royal tombs and date from about 3000 B.C. The most celebrated are those at Giza, built during the fourth dynasty, of which the largest is the one that housed the pharaoh Khufu, better known as Cheops. This is now called the Great Pyramid. Some years ago it was visited by a Frenchman named Bovis, who took refuge from the midday sun in the pharaoh's chamber, which is situated in the center of the pyramid, exactly one third of the way up from the base. He found it unusually humid there, but what really surprised him were the garbage cans that contained, among the usual tourist litter, the bodies of a cat and some small desert animals that had wandered into the pyramid and died there. Despite the humidity, none of them had decayed but just dried out like mummies. He began to wonder whether the pharaohs had really been so carefully embalmed by their subjects after all, or whether there was something about the pyramids themselves that preserved bodies in a mummified condition.

Bovis made an accurate scale model of the Cheops pyramid and placed it, like the original, with the base lines facing precisely north-south and east-west. Inside the model, one third of the way up, he put a dead cat. It became mummified, and he concluded that the pyramid promoted rapid dehydration. Reports of this discovery attracted the attention of Karel Drbal, a radio engineer in Prague, who repeated the experiment with several dead animals and concluded, "There is a relation between the shape of the space inside the pyramid and the physical, chemical, and biological processes going on inside that space. By using suitable forms and shapes, we should be able to make processes occur faster or delay them." (233)

Drbal remembered an old superstition which claimed that a razor left in the light of the moon became blunted. He tried putting one under his model pyramid, but nothing happened, so he went on shaving with it until it was blunt, and then put it back in the pyramid. It became sharp again. Getting a good razor blade is still difficult in many Eastern European countries, so Drbal tried to patent and market his discovery. The patent office in Prague refused to consider it until their chief scientist had tried building a model himself and found that it worked. So the Cheops Pyramid Razor Blade Sharpener was registered in 1959 under the Czechoslovakian Republic Patent No. 91304, and a factory soon began to turn out miniature cardboard pyramids. Today they make them in styrofoam.

The edge of a razor blade has a crystal structure. Crystals are almost alive, in that they grow by reproducing themselves. When a blade becomes blunted, some of the crystals on the edge, where they are only one layer thick, are rubbed off. Theoretically, there is no reason why they should not replace themselves in time. We know that sunlight has a field that points in all directions, but sunlight reflected from an object such as the moon is partly polarized, vibrating mostly in one direction. This could conceivably destroy the edge of a blade left under the moon, but it does not explain the reverse action of the pyramid. We can only guess that the Great Pyramid and its little imitations act as lenses that focus energy or as resonators that collect energy, which encourages crystal growth. The pyramid shape itself is very much like that of a crystal of magnetite, so perhaps it builds up a magnetic field. I do not know the answer, but I do know that it works. My record so far with Wilkinson Sword blades is four months of continuous daily use. I have a feeling that the manufacturers are not going to like this idea.

Try it yourself. Cut four pieces of heavy cardboard into isosceles triangles with the proportion base to sides of 15.7 to 14.94. Tape these together so that the pyramid stands exactly 10.0 of the same units high. Orient it precisely so that the base lines face magnetic north-south and east-west. Make a stand 3.33 units high and place it directly under the apex of the pyramid to hold your objects. The sharp edges of the blade should face east and west. Keep the whole thing away from electrical devices.

I have discovered that the speed of dehydration of organic materials depends very much on the substance involved and on the weather conditions. This much one would expect, but I tried keeping the same objects—eggs, rump steak, dead mice—in both pyramid and in an ordinary shoe box, and the ones in the pyramid preserved quite well while those in the box soon began to smell and had to be thrown out. I am forced to conclude that a cardboard replica of the Cheops pyramid is not just a random arrangement of pieces of paper, but does have special properties.

There is a fascinating postscript to this pyramid story. In 1968 a team of scientists from the United States and from Ein Shams University in Cairo began a million-dollar project to X-ray the pyramid of Chephren, successor to Cheops. They hoped to find new vaults hidden in the six million tons of stone by placing detectors in a chamber at its base and measuring the amount of cosmic-ray penetration, the theory being that more rays would come through hollow areas. The recorders ran twenty-four hours a day for more than a year until, in early 1969, the latest, IBM 1130, computer was delivered to the university for analysis of the tapes. Six months later the scientists had to admit defeat: the pyramid made no sense at all. Tapes recorded with the same equipment from the same point on successive days showed totally different cosmic-ray patterns. The leader of the project, Amr Gohed, in an interview afterward said, "This is scientifically impossible. Call it what you will—occultism, the curse of the pharaohs, sorcery, or magic, there is some force that defies the laws of science at work in the pyramid."

The idea of shape having an influence on the functions taking place within it is not a new one. A French firm once patented a special container for making yogurt, because that particular shape enhanced the action of the micro-organism involved in the process. The brewers of a Czechoslovakian beer tried to change from round to angular barrels but found that this resulted in a deterioration in the quality of their beer despite the fact that the method of processing remained unchanged. A German researcher has shown that mice with identical wounds heal more quickly if they are kept in spherical cages. Architects in Canada report a sudden improvement in schizophrenic patients living in trapezoidal hospital wards.

It is possible that all shapes have their own qualities and that the forms we see around us are the result of combinations of environmental frequencies. In the eighteenth century the German physicist Ernst Chladni discovered a way of making vibration patterns visible. He mounted a thin metal plate on a violin, scattered sand on the plate, and found that when a bow was drawn across the strings, the sand arranged itself into beautiful patterns. These arrangements, now known as Chladni's figures, develop because the sand ends up only on those parts of the plate where there is no vibration. They have been extensively used in physics to demonstrate wave function, but they also show very well that different frequencies produce patterns with different forms. By juggling around with powders of different densities and by playing notes with a wide range of frequencies, it is possible to induce a pattern to take on almost any form. It is interesting, and perhaps significant, that Chladni's figures most often adopt familiar organic forms. Concentric circles, such as the annual rings in a tree trunk; alternating lines, such as the stripes on a zebra's back; hexagonal grids, such as the cells in a honeycomb; radiating wheel spokes, such as the canals in a jellyfish; vanishing spirals, such as the turrets of shellfish— all these commonly occur. The study of this phenomenon, the effect of waves on matter, is called cymatics. (166)

The basic principle of cymatics is that environmental pressures are brought to bear in wave patterns and that matter responds to these pressures by taking a form that depends on the frequency of the waves. There are a limited number of frequencies involved, and nature tends to respond to these in predictable ways, by repeating a limited number of functional forms. The helical pattern of an updraft of heated air (a thermal) is mirrored in the growth of a creeper twined around a tree and in the arrangement of the atoms in a molecule of DNA. The manta ray flows through tropical waters with muscular waves that run in trains across its broad, flat back like wind-blown patterns on the surface of the sea. Mollusks without shells and flatworms that live in water move in exactly the same way. Given the same problem, nature will usually find the same solution. It could not do this with such widely divergent raw materials unless they were responding to identical pressures. There is even an example of convergent evolution at a molecular level in two enzymes, one from soil bacteria and the other from man, which have exactly the same pattern of amino acids at the "business ends." (184)

The recurrence of a small basic repertoire of shapes cannot be accidental. There are many variations on the chosen themes, but these are usually a compromise between the environmental pressures and individual needs. The embryonic material of most reptiles, for instance, is enclosed in one of the standard packages, a perfect sphere, because this is the shape that combines maximum volume with minimum surface area and use of materials. Crocodiles and turtles produce round eggs with thin elastic shells that have to be buried in moist soil to prevent their drying out. Birds, however, have gone an evolutionary stage further and become relatively independent of the ground and more concerned with parental care. They keep their eggs in the air, and to prevent desiccation, have developed a harder, less porous shell. But this raises a new problem. The brittle, non-elastic package is more likely to break under the pressure of gravity, so the eggs of nearly all birds are now spheres that have become rather pointed. They have been distorted in the one way that could give them the greatest possible mechanical strength without internal modifications of any kind. The basic shape was determined by environmental pressures and modified to meet specific needs.

In Switzerland during the past ten years Hans Jenny has been refining Chladni's figures and producing elegant proof that form is a function of frequency. One of his inventions is a "tonoscope," which converts sounds into visible three-dimensional patterns in inert material. (167) This can be used with the human voice as the sound source, and when someone speaks the sound for the letter O into the microphone, it produces a perfectly spherical pattern. The sphere is one of nature's basic forms, but it is startling to discover that the shape produced by the frequency of the O sound is exactly the shape we have chosen to represent it pictorially in our script. It raises specters of ancient beliefs that words and names had properties of their own. Today we still tend to regard personal names as something special, and find that children are often anxious to conceal theirs. Young children in particular always demand to know what the name of a thing is, never questioning that it has one, and regard this as a valuable acquisition. Is it possible that words have a power by virtue of their own special frequencies? Can magic words and sacred formulas and chants in fact exert an influence that differs from other sounds chosen at random? It seems so, and with Jenny's discovery of word patterns, I find myself looking with some discomfort and awe at St. John's assertion, "In the beginning was the Word."

As a biologist, I would have to paraphrase it as "In the beginning was the Sound of the Word," because there is an enormous national and individual variation in the speech sounds used to portray the same written word. (242) The International Phonetic Alphabet overcomes this difficulty by providing symbols to represent every shade of sound in most human languages. Analyzing this alphabet, one can see certain basic patterns. A speech sound is produced by allowing air to resonate in the throat, mouth, and nasal chambers, while subjecting it to some sort of modification by uvula, palate, tongue, teeth, or lips. There are two basic kinds of sound—vowels, which are produced without friction or stoppage, and consonants, which are characterized by friction, squeezing, or stoppage of the breath in some part of the passage. Vowel sounds are always accompanied by vibration of the vocal cords and have far more power than the largely unvoiced consonants. The power of vowels ranges from nine to forty-seven microwatts, while consonants seldom reach two microwatts, so the vowels carry further and are more easily received. Resonance in the fluid of man's ear makes the vowel sounds ah, aw, eh, ee, and oo, in that order, the easiest of all speech sounds to hear. (The vowels in Swahili, which is a lingua franca for over two hundred tribes in East Africa, are pronounced exactly like this.) Consonants, on the other hand, are often explosive, as when the air is released suddenly from behind an obstruction as in a "p" sound, or else they are fricative, as when air escapes gradually, as in the formation of an "s" sound. These produce little power, but they have much higher frequencies than the vowel sounds. When calling a cat, which is an animal designed to respond to the high-frequency sounds of its prey, people of all languages use combinations of these two short-wave consonants.

So the sounds of words do have different physical properties. If resonance can be produced between an air column in a sender's throat and another in a receiver's ear, then similar transfers of energy can take place between the throat and other parts of the environment. When Joshua's people "shouted with a great shout," the walls of Jericho fell down. The sudden loud cry of a samurai swordsman breaks the nerve of an adversary, and the trill of a soprano shatters glass. These are sustained effects, much like the burning heat of the midday sun, but we know that life responds to things as subtle as the moon filtered through twenty feet of water, so it is not unreasonable to assume that living matter is sensitive in different ways to the equally subtle frequency changes and patterns in human speech.

Linguists have not solved the problems of the origins of speech. There are many ideas, some with picturesque names, such as the "bow wow" theory, which holds that language arose in imitation of sounds that occur in nature, or the "yo he ho" theory, to the effect that it came from grunts of physical exertion. But there does not seem to have been any concerted attempt to look for biological origins among the basic sounds in the phonetic alphabet. Jenny's demonstration that the "oh" sound has a spherical shape is dramatic, but it should not come as a surprise. It feels right. We make a round mouth to produce the rounded sound, and when doing it, even our eyes round out. A face making the "oh" sound is also making the expression that most primates use to indicate an aggressive threat. Students of animal behavior assume that the face arose from various compromise body postures that occur in threat situations and that the expression is accompanied by a hard "oh"-sounding grunt to reinforce the effect. But it is also possible that the sound came first and produced the face, and, taking it one stage further, that the sound itself was adopted because it had the effect of disturbing an opponent. Its frequencies produced the right kind of resonance, perhaps including infrasounds, to mesh with an opponent's brain waves and put him to flight in panic. The Japanese have developed this use of sound to a fine art with the fighting cry, or kiai, of the samurai. It is said that a kiai in a minor key produces partial paralysis by a reaction that suddenly lowers the arterial blood pressure. A major key, if loud and sudden, certainly has the opposite effect.

Music provides another example of waves spaced in a meaningful manner. Donald Andrews has incorporated harmonic motion into a complex theory of the universe that he calls the "symphony of life." In this system atoms provide the musical notes, each one vibrating like a spherical bell. Molecules are chords composed of orderly patterns of these notes, and the music is played on instruments whose shape is provided by the organism itself. Andrews showed that even a violin lying still on a table is always humming gently to itself, and he believes this to be true of all matter. Certainly muscles under tension produce an audible sound. In one imaginative experiment, Andrews went around Baltimore Museum tapping bronze and marble statues with a hammer and recording the sounds on a high-speed tape in the hope of capturing the essential vibrations characteristic of their shapes. He did in fact find that identical shapes in the size ratio of two to one produced the same fundamental tone but an octave apart. This is exactly the effect one gets by halving the length of a violin string, and it suggests that three-dimensional objects could operate on the same basic musical principles.

The cosmos is full of "noise," irregular jumbles of wavelengths, but all its useful signals are regular patterns. Combinations of musical notes chosen at random jar on our nerves; we find them unpleasant. But tones with certain regular intervals between them are harmonious; we find them pleasing. A note played together with another one that has exactly double its frequency, that is, one octave higher, makes a very harmonious sound. Three notes go well together as a chord if their relative frequencies are in the proportion 4:5:6. These are purely mathematical relationships, but we know from experience that these are the ones to which man responds. Music is being played to other animals on farms and in zoos with similarly marked effects. Preferences differ from species to species, presumably because their structure and sensitivity, and therefore their resonant frequencies, differ. Research is now going on into the effect of music on plants. It has been discovered that geraniums grow faster and taller to the accompaniment of Bach's Brandenburg Concertos. If the dominant frequencies in these pieces of music are broadcast to the plants, they have some effect, but growth is more marked if the frequencies occur in the spatial relationship so carefully designed by the composer. Bacteria are affected in the same way, multiplying under the influence of certain frequencies and dying when subject to others. It is not a long step from this discovery to the old idea that frequent repetition of certain chants or songs could cure disease.

There are other spatial relationships that have an effect on us. Artists have known for centuries that certain proportions are more pleasing than others. If people are presented with a large number of four-sided shapes ranging from a square to a very long, thin rectangle, most of them will choose a shape whose length is a little more than one and one half times its height. (33) This shape, which the majority of people find to be the most pleasing, is called the Golden Mean; its exact dimensions have been established as a ratio of 1 to 1.618. There are enormous differences between the traditional arts of different peoples, but it seems that aesthetic tastes in all are governed by similar basic laws. (98) A study in London found cross-cultural color and design similarities in large-scale tests with British and Japanese students. Our response to proportions is presumably governed by the common distance between our eyes. A man who had been blind in one eye from birth and never known binocular vision, would probably find a square more pleasing. We know that people with only one eye have an unequal development of one half of the brain and that this is reflected in their brain waves. Having different rhythms, they respond to different frequencies.

Following discoveries about the nature of light, magnetism, and electricity in the nineteenth century, the theory of a "vibrating universe" became very popular in occult circles, but it was Pythagoras, in the fifth century B.C., who first developed the idea. The notion that all the universe is connected in a grand design has always been fundamental to magic, and the Pythagoreans used the mathematical relationship of musical intervals to express this pattern numerically. They were the first professional numerologists. Devotees of number systems point to the seven colors in the rainbow, the seven days in the week, the seven seals of Christendom, the seven Devas of Hinduism, the seven Amsha-Spands of Persian faith, and so on, claiming occult properties for this and other special numbers. Goethe was obsessed with three, Swoboda swore by twenty-three, and Freud believed in periods of twenty-seven. It is difficult to see biological significance in any of these intervals, and tempting to dismiss the whole idea on the grounds that any number is as likely as any other, but it seems that this is not true.

An American mathematician noticed that the earlier pages in books of logariths kept in his university library were dirtier than later ones, indicating that science students, for some reason, had more occasion to calculate with numbers beginning with 1 than with any other number. (261) He made a collection of tables and calculated the relative frequency of each digit from 1 to 9. Theoretically they should occur equally often, but he found that 30 per cent of the numbers were 1, whereas 9 only occupied 5 per cent of the space. These are almost exactly the proportions given to these numbers on the scale of a slide rule, so the designers of that instrument clearly recognized that such a bias existed. This preponderance of the number 1 may have been caused by the fact that the tables were not really random, but bigger tables provide a similar bias. The ecologist Lamont Cole worked with a Rand Corporation publication that gives a million random digits. (262) He selected numbers at regular intervals to represent the level of metabolic activity of a unicorn at the end of each hour over a long period. There should have been no relationship between the numbers and no kind of cyclic pattern, but Cole is now credited with the shattering zoological discovery that unicorns are busiest at three o'clock in the morning. (77)

It is possible that these discrepancies may be due to some peculiarity in our way of counting, but it looks as though the bias follows a natural law. Nature seems to count exponentially. Not 1 2 3 4 5, but 1 2 4 8 16, the numbers growing by a logarithmic power each time. Population increases in this way, and, even at an individual level, things such as the strength of a stimulus and the level of response to it vary in an exponential way. This is, however, nothing more than an observation; it does not explain the anomolous way in which numbers behave.

The unexpected grouping of similar numbers is something like the unusual grouping of circumstances that we call coincidence. Everyone has had the experience of coming across a new word or name for the first time and then seeing it in a dozen different places in quick succession. Or of finding oneself in a small group of people, three of whom have the same birthdays. Often these coincidences come in clusters: some days are particularly lucky, while on others it is just one damn' thing after another. Several people have made it part of their life's work to collect information on coincidences of this kind. The biologist Kammerer was one, and it was he who gave the phenomenon the name of seriality. He defines a series as "a lawful occurrence of the same or similar things or events . . . which are not connected by the same active cause" and claims that coincidence is in reality the work of a natural principle. (171) Kammerer spent days just sitting in public places noting down the number of people passing, the way they dressed, what they carried, and so on. When he analyzed these records, he found that there were typical clusters of things that occurred together and then disappeared altogether. This kind of wave pattern in events is familiar to all stock-brokers and gamblers, and every insurance company runs its entire business of assessment on similar tables of probability.

These "coincidental" clusters are a real phenomenon. Kammerer explains them by his Law of Seriality, which says that working in opposition to the second law of thermodynamics is a force that tends toward symmetry and coherence by bringing like and like together. In a strange, illogical way, this idea is rather persuasive, but there is no good scientific evidence to support it and the theory is not very important to us here. It is enough to know that there is a discernible organization of events. Taken together with musical and artistic harmony, with the non-randomness of numbers, and with the periodicity of planetary movements, we begin to get a picture of an environment in which there are recognizable patterns. Superimposed on the cosmic chaos are rhythms and harmonies that control many aspects of life on earth by a communication of energy made possible by the shape of things here and their resonance in sympathy with cosmic themes.

BIOPHYSICS

We are all sensitive to the physical forces around us, and it seems that there are ways of enhancing this sensitivity. One has been in use for at least five thousand years. Bas-reliefs from early Egypt show figures in strange headgear carrying, at arm's length in front of them, a forked stick; and Emperor Kwang Su of China is depicted in a statue dated 2200 B.C. carrying an identical object. Both, it seems, were in search of water.

Many animals have an extraordinary sensitivity to water, and some, such as the elephant, succeed in finding it underground. In times of drought, elephants often perform vital community services by using their tusks and pile-driving feet to expose hidden water sources. It is possible that they can smell the water percolating through the soil or that they have come to have a fairly elementary knowledge of geology, always digging at the lowest point on the outside curve of a dry river bed, where water is most likely to collect. But there are instances in which neither of these solutions is tenable, and we are left with the possibility that some other sense is being used. Like the surface of the earth, two thirds of most animals is water. One of the preconditions for resonance is that there should be similar, or at least compatible, structures in sender and receiver, so if the energy is broadcast by a water source, it could probably find a response in the body of most mammals. Our brains are 80 per cent water, which makes them even more liquid than blood, so the resonance might take place there, but the response seems to be most manifest in the long muscles of our bodies.

The classical method of water divining, or dowsing, is to cut a forked twig from a shade tree such as willow, hazel, or peach and to hold it out in front of the body parallel to the ground. In this position the muscles of the arm are under some tension; it is claimed that as the dowser approaches water, this tension somehow extends into the twig and induces it to move. The patterns of movement depend very much on the individual. Some say that an upward thrust of the dowsing rod indicates the upstream side of a water flow and the pattern of gyration indicates depth, but others disagree completely. There is a tremendous variation in technique among dowsers. Instruments in use include metal rods, coat hangers, whalebone, copper wire, walking sticks, pitchforks, bakelite strips, surgical scissors, pendulums, and even, it is said, a German sausage. For each dowsing aid there are as many different ways of holding it and interpreting the way it moves. Just one thing takes all this extraordinary pantomime out of the area of sheer farce—the dowsers enjoy a very high rate of success.

Every major water and pipeline company in the United States has a dowser on its payroll. The Canadian Ministry of Agriculture employs a permanent dowser. UNESCO has engaged a Dutch dowser and geologist to pursue official investigations for them. Engineers from the U. S. First and Third Marine divisions in Vietnam have been trained to use dowsing rods to locate booby traps and sunken mortar shells. The Czechoslovakian Army has a permanent corps of dowsers in a special unit. The geology departments of Moscow State and Leningrad universities have launched a full-scale investigation into dowsing—not to find out if it works, but to discover how it works. There is obviously something in it.

Serious research into dowsing seems to have begun in France in 1910. It was largely instigated by the Vicomte Henri de France, who published *Le Sourcier Moderne* and was, in 1933, partly responsible also for the formation of the British Society of Dowsers. Research in both countries is summarized in two books, *The Divining Rod* (16) and *The Physics of the Divining Rod* (204), which are interesting but clearly show the limitations of small-scale private projects. The fact that these are conducted without proper supervision and are poorly reported allows most Western scientists to dismiss the subject altogether, but in Russia research into dowsing now enjoys state backing, and it is there that the biggest advances are being made.

These researches began when an official commission appointed well-known geologists and hydrologists to work in conjunction with dowsers from the Red Army. After thousands of tests the commission reported that forked twigs responded, both to underground sources of water and to electrical cables, with a force that was measured as high as 1,000 gram centimeters. They found that no matter how quickly a dowser walked, or how carefully he was screened with steel plates or lead armor, the rods still responded. The report also mentions that the twigs were successful for only two or three days, and that a broken one could not be repaired without a loss of sensitivity. In some of the tests, lead, zinc, and gold were detected at a depth of 240 feet, and the commission concluded that dowsing could be used with striking success to locate underground electrical cables, pipes, damaged points in cable networks, minerals, and water. They suggested that the old Russian name meaning "wizard rod" be abandoned, and so today research on dowsing carries on under the safe, new, demystified name of "The Biophysical Effects Method."

In 1966 a Leningrad mineralogist, Nikolai Sochevanov, directed an expedition to the Kirghiz region, near Russia's border with China. They started with a survey in an airplane equipped with a magnetometer of the kind used by mining companies for aerial prospecting. Inside the plane Sochevanov and several other "operators" stood with dowsing rods at the ready. Flying over the river Chu, they found that the vast amount of water in the center of the river had no effect, but that all of them could feel pressure on the rods near the shores, on either side. Tests in other parts of the world have shown similar results, and it seems to be true that water influences man most strongly not where a large mass is moving at great speed but where it is in friction with the soil, particularly where soil surface in contact with the water is large, as it is in ground saturated with water moving slowly through tiny capillaries. Flying over known mineral deposits, Sochevanov experienced marked reactions, and, in follow-up tests on the ground, his team located a seam of lead only three inches thick at a depth of almost five hundred feet.

With larger deposits near the surface, they found that the rods were being jerked right out of their hands, so

Sochevanov designed a new, steel instrument that could rotate freely. This is a U shape with roller-bearing handles about two feet apart at the ends and an 8-inch loop twisted into the center of the curve. He claims that the number of turns made by the rod gives an indication of the depth and size of the underground deposit and has engineered an automatic recording device that is attached to the instrument and graphs its behavior. In large-scale tests with hundreds of operators, profiles have been constructed of whole areas of land. One such survey was made on 21 October 1966 in an area near Alma-Ata where three million cubic meters of rock were to be destroyed by explosives in a development project. The team covered this site just before the explosion and returned immediately afterward to make a second survey. Their rods reported enormous changes in underground patterns, and for four hours following the explosion, the shape of the profile continued to change as they plotted it. Finally it settled down, and when seismographs indicated that the tremors had subsided, the dowsers found that the pattern had returned almost to its preblast configuration. The small differences between the "before" and the "after" patterns were later determined by excavation to be due to underground fractures produced by the explosion.

Sochevanov made field tests with dowsers operating inside moving vehicles, with their recording devices linked to the drive shaft. He found that the rods continued to respond, but that at greater speeds they made fewer revolutions. The fact that there was any response at all inside a metal vehicle seems to indicate that the energy involved is not electrical, and any attempt to strengthen incoming signals by attaching long wire aerials to the dowsers' wrists has so far only diminished the response. Powerful magnets strapped on operators' backs had no effect, but leather gloves killed the response altogether. Groups of dowsers linked together had no cumulative effect, but when a seasoned dowser touched the hand of a non-operator, the rod came to life in the novice's hands.

Experiments in all countries suggest that, whatever the dowsing force may be, it cannot work on the rod alone. A living being has to act as a "middleman." The Dutch geologist Solco Tromp has shown that dowsers are unusually sensitive to the earth's magnetic field, and respond to changes in the field that can be verified with magnetometers. (323) He has also discovered that a good dowser can detect an artificial field only one two-hundredth the strength of the earth field and that he can use his rod to chart its extent in an experimental room. Dowsers tested in the Laboratoire de Physique in Paris were able to tell whether an electric current was switched on or off simply by walking past a coil at a distance of three feet with their dowsing rods held at the ready. (279) At the University of Halle it has been discovered that dowsers show an increase in blood pressure and pulse rate in some fields. (233) The Soviet scientists divide all people into four basic groups according to the way the dowsing rod "sees" them. The rod is attracted to the first group which includes all women (who have a 40 per cent higher success rate in dowsing than men). Group two consists of men who repulse the rod completely, while those in the last two groups repel the rod from shoulders and waist respectively. Polarity maps of the human body, prepared with an electrocardiograph by Tromp, support this grouping.

Dowsing fields, areas in which dowsers get strong responses, have been confirmed with proton magnetometers sensitive enough to measure the magnetic field in an atom. Experiments with these naturally occurring fields have produced interesting results. Mice placed in a long enclosure half on and half off a dowsing zone refused to sleep inside the field. (323) Cucumbers, celery, onions, maize, privet hedges, and ash trees will hardly grow at all if planted in the ground above a dowsing zone. It is said that ants always build their nests directly in a zone and that bees swarm on branches above such a field. It has also been suggested that rheumatics experience muscular contractions and pain in the joints in a field produced by water, and that strong dowsing zones of any kind have a bad effect on human health. The dowsing literature is full of incidents involving "noxious rays" and "harmful radiation" that can be minimized by moving a chair or bed from the afflicted zone or by planting complex coils of copper wire inside the field to "neutralize" it. It is very difficult to judge these reports objectively and to know how big a part suggestion played in the alleged cures, but the fact remains that an electrocardiogram attached even to the body of a non-dowser registers a difference in potential when the person moves into a dowsing zone.

The literature also abounds with accounts of dowsers locating missing persons, criminals, and dead bodies by following the indications of a "sensitized" rod. This is usually a pendulum with a hollow bob containing something belonging to the person being sought, or one that has been "tuned" by holding it over a sample object to find out how long the thread needs to be to produce the right reaction. There have been many celebrated and well-publicized successes with this technique, the most impressive being those in which the dowser locates his prey by working not in the field but over a large-scale map of unfamiliar territory. As far as it is possible to judge, from records that are seldom scientific, of events that by their very nature are unrepeatable, the method works. Knowing something of the influence of shape on frequency, it is possible to speculate that the two-dimensional shapes on maps or photographs might have some properties similar to real objects, but the mind boggles at the idea.

This technique, of using a pendulum to acquire information not only about an object's location but also of its character, has become known as "radiesthesia"—meaning sensitivity to radiations. It is used, among other things, for sex detection. The Japanese have always been expert in the difficult art of determining the sex of day-old chicks, but now they are able to do it even before the eggs hatch, with the aid of nothing more than a bead on the end of a piece of silk thread. Eggs pass by the expert on a conveyor belt with their long axes north-south. The bead is held over the line and swings along the same axis if the egg is sterile, gyrates in a clockwise circle for a cock chick, and anti-clockwise for a hen. The factories claim a success rate of 99 per cent for this system. There are practitioners in England who apparently can sex humans in the same way when provided only with a drop of blood or saliva on a piece of blotting paper. (20) They have been used several times to assist police forensic laboratories in murder investigations.

It is very easy to say, as dowsers do, "All matter gives off a ray, and the human body, acting in much the same way as the receiver of a wireless set, picks it up." (322) But glib statements like this tell absolutely nothing about the process or the biology involved. The sum total of hard knowledge about dowsing seems to amount to this: Water, by the action of friction between itself and the soil, creates a field that could have electromagnetic properties. Rubber and leather insulate this field, but metals seem to have no effect. Metals themselves, perhaps by their position in the earth's magnetic field, also exert a field effect. The fields created or modified by inorganic objects are appreciable to some animals and people. An unconscious sensitivity to these fields can be made manifest by using an object such as a rod or a pendulum as a visible indicator of field strength and direction.

Man has used dowsing techniques for such a long time that we may find animals that can do the same thing. Antelope and wild pigs have curved horns and tusks, which are similar in shape to the traditional forked twig, and both these species are very successful in finding hidden water sources. Could it be that their built-in dowsing rods help in some way? The best human dowsers can work with their bare hands, so it is possible that even animals without antennas can navigate in this way. As far as I know, no student of bird migration has ever considered this possibility. If the willow twig works in man's hands, how does it function when attached to the tree? The roots of trees are positively geotropic—they grow directly toward the source of gravity—but they also seek out sources of water. Perhaps they do this by dowsing?

The discovery that animals are sensitive to the dowsing field and react strongly to it will not surprise anyone who has ever watched a wild mammal settling down to sleep. The choice of a resting place naturally has to be made very carefully with regard to warmth and shelter and safety from predators, but often an animal will choose a place that seems to be far less appealing on these grounds than another only a short distance away. Domestic dogs and cats show the same behavior, and their owners know full well that it is no good making this decision on the pet's behalf—they have to wait until the animal chooses its own place and then put the sleeping basket there. There are some places on which an animal will not lie on any account. That humans have similar abilities has been shown by Carlos Castaneda in a recent book on Yaqui beliefs that is the most vivid and exciting piece of ethnography I have ever read. (67) The sorcerer Don Juan has told Castaneda that there is one spot on the porch of his house that is unique, where he can feel happy and strong, and that he must find it for himself. Castaneda tries for hours, sitting everywhere in turn and even rolling around on the floor, but nothing happens until he focuses his eyes on a spot directly in front of him, and the whole world out of the corners of his eyes turns greenish yellow. Then, ". . . suddenly, at a point near the middle of the floor, I became aware of another change in hue. At a place to my right, still in the periphery of my field of vision, the greenish yellow became intensely purple. I concentrated my attention on it. The purple faded into a pale, but still brilliant, color which remained steady for the time I kept my attention on it." He decided to lie down on this spot, but "I felt an unusual apprehension. It was more like a physical sensation of something pushing on my stomach. I jumped up and retreated in one movement. The hair on my neck pricked up. My legs had arched slightly, my trunk was bent forward, and my arms stuck out in front of me rigidly with my fingers contracted like a claw. I took notice of my strange posture and my fright increased. I walked back involuntarily and . . . slumped to the floor." He had found his spot.

In 1963 a 12-year-old South African named Pieter van Jaarsveld became world famous as "the boy with X-ray eyes" for his ability to detect water hidden deep underground. He used no sort of dowsing rod but claimed to be able to see water "shimmering like green moonlight" through the surface of the soil. Pieter was very surprised to learn that other people could not see it equally well. I think that soon, as we begin to realize that nature and the classic five senses are only a small part of the real magic of Supernature, more of us might begin to join him in seeing things as they really are.

PART TWO

MATTER

"What does a fish know about the water in which he swims all his life?"

ALBERT EINSTEIN, in *The World As I See It*, 1935.

THE GREEK PHILOSOPHERS sliced matter up into thinner and thinner sections until Democritus put a stop to the discrimination by declaring that there was a limit beyond which particles became indivisible or a-tomic. More than two thousand years later John Dalton showed that all matter in the universe was composed of basic building blocks, or atoms.

Both of them were right, but we now know that one further division is possible and that atoms can be split into even more fundamental particles. At first it seemed as though these operated on a planetary principle, with electrons traveling in orbit around a central nucleus. More recently it has become apparent that electrons are more like clouds of electricity vibrating with wave patterns. None of this can be seen, but there is clear evidence that at the center of the fog is a collection of nuclear bits and pieces that contain nearly all the mass of the atom and nearly all of its energy. If the atom were to be inflated until it filled an Olympic stadium, this nucleus would be the size of a pea lying alone in the center of the track. There is proportionally as much empty space inside the atom as there is in the universe.

All matter is like this. Take a man and squeeze the empty spaces out of him, like the holes in a sponge, and you are left with a little pile of solid substance no larger than a flyspeck. We are the hollow men and our insubstantial bodies are strung together with electromagnetic and nuclear forces that do no more than create the illusion of matter. In this respect there is little to separate the living from the non-living; both are composed of the same sparse fundamental particles interacting with each other in the same elementary ways.

The only real difference is that the atoms of life are organized. They have become arranged into self-replicating patterns that defy cosmic chaos by constantly repairing and replacing themselves. Feeding on order, they learn to recognize and respond to it; the more organized they are, the more responsive they become. Life must be in close touch with matter, and at the highest levels this means that it not only takes energy and information from its surroundings but returns them as well.

In this second section I want to look at the ways in which life can influence its environment.

Chapter Four:

Mind Over Matter

ECOLOGY IS LARGELY CONCERNED with the intricate system of interactions between life and its environment. The vast herds of zebra and wildebeest in Serengeti respond to environmental signals that initiate their annual migration, and in trekking in their millions from the plains of Olduvai up into the woodland of the Mara, they cut a swath through the country that leaves a mark for years to come. Beavers respond to the signs of approaching winter by building a dam to protect their lodge, and in doing so they flood an area of land and change its character completely. Man responds to environmental challenges in a direct and often brutal way—clearing areas for agriculture, losing land to the sea by neglect and erosion, and reclaiming it with his monstrous machines.

These are direct physical connections between living and non-living matter, but there are other links, which are far less obvious. Each year the transpiration of plants puts five thousand cubic miles of water into the air, from which it falls on the earth as rain. The respiration of man, and other kinds of combustion he finds necessary to sustain himself, are using up more oxygen than the environment can provide and creating a carbon dioxide build-up that could initiate a new ice age, with all its dramatic effects on matter. At even the most simple individual level, there is evidence of indirect action of this kind. A musk ox that returns each evening to sleep in the same spot melts the snow with its body heat and exposes a patch of earth that lingers on into the summer as a livid scar in the carpet of green that everywhere else enjoyed the full protection of a winter snow blanket.

Beyond these oblique effects of life on matter, there are other connections that are even more tenuous. They depend not on direct muscular action, nor even on indirect breathing and heating, but on the effects of the fields of force that surround all living things. I believe that these apparently supernatural forces are capable of physical description and understanding, but the whole thing is so new and yet so bedeviled by old superstitions, that we have to tread softly and come up on the subject unawares.

A living organism depends on outside information. This arrives in three forms—electromagnetic waves, such as light; mechanical pressures, such as sound; and chemical stimuli, such as those giving rise to taste and smell. If the organism is an animal, all three kinds of signal are converted by sense receptors on the outside of the body into impulses of electrical energy that carry messages in to the central nervous system. The fact that all news traveling along the nerves is conveyed by the same kind of vehicle can be shown by diverting the traffic. If a nerve fiber from the tongue is connected to one leading from the ear to the brain, a drop of vinegar in the mouth is "tasted" as a loud and startling explosion. This is how hallucinations occur, by drug- or stress-induced short circuits in the sensory system that allow music, for instance, to reach the brain as patterns of light. So what we usually refer to as the quality of a sensation depends entirely on which part of the brain is being stimulated at that time.

A nerve fiber is a very long, thin cell that not only generates an electrical charge when stimulated but passes it along to the next cell by a series of chemical changes that flow down its length like a smoke ring traveling along at two hundred miles an hour. Every time this happens it is exactly the same. Both the amount of current and the speed of travel are always the same, and no further action can take place until the whole event is over. A strong signal from the environment cannot generate a larger electrical charge in the nerve; it simply does so more often. So the intensity of the sensation as appreciated by the brain depends only on the frequency of the impulses coming in.

As an impulse passes along a nerve fiber, it uses a small amount of oxygen and gets rid of a small quantity of carbon dioxide. There is a slight local rise in temperature and a pulsation in the fiber that can be seen with a strong microscope, but the most noticeable effect is a change in the electric field. With suitable apparatus and electrodes on the skin, one can follow an impulse started by a prick on the finger all the way up the arm and record its arrival in the cortex on the opposite side of the brain. This communication shows up as a change in electrical potential, and the apparatus, by recording the passage of a single charge, can even be used to find out if a particular nerve is working properly or not. If one such impulse creates a measurable electric field that can be detected outside the body of a complex organism, it is clear that millions of similar events taking place all the time must produce a considerable surrounding field.

Pavel Gulyaiev of Leningrad University has developed a very sensitive high-resistance electrode that is even more

effective in measuring field intensity than Harold Burr's equipment. (294) There is still some secrecy surrounding his instrument, but it seems to be similar to magnetic-field detectors in use in space research. Gulyaiev's equipment can
detect an electric field as much as a foot from the exposed
sciatic nerve in the leg of a frog, and has also been successful
in charting a human field some distance from the body. (129)

This field lasts only a fraction of a second, as each impulse
passes along the fiber, but if the stimulus is prolonged, then a
constant stream of impulses create a standing field that persists for a while. If the stimulus is strong enough, it can
affect a muscle directly and produce a reflex action. For
instance if you tread on a thorn it takes only one twentieth
of a second for the nerve impulses to get to the spinal cord
and back to the muscles that pull the foot away. Most
stimuli, however, need to be sorted by the brain, and this
takes four times as long. In the giraffe it takes as much as
one third of a second for impulses to travel seventeen feet
from a foot all the way up to the brain. Then the brain has
to consider the stimulus, register it as painful, and send out
the message to take appropriate avoiding action. Until such
action is taken, and while it is under way, the brain continues
to broadcast to the muscles involved and sets up an electrical
field far stronger than that provoked by the initial stimulus.
Gulyaiev and others have shown that this brain-induced field
has the highest intensity and can be detected at the greatest
distances from the body.

PSYCHOKINESIS

In 1967 a Kiev film company produced a costly professional
film about a middle-aged Leningrad housewife. (271) She is
shown sitting at a table in a physiology laboratory after being
medically examined and X-rayed to ensure that nothing is

hidden on or in her body. She puts out her hands, with the fingers spread, about six inches above a compass in the center of the table and tenses her muscles. She stares intently at the compass, lines etched deeply into her face showing the strain of a body under acute tension. Minutes pass and sweat breaks out on her brow as she continues the struggle, and then, slowly, the compass needle quivers and moves to point in a new direction. She starts to move her hands in a circular motion and the needle turns with them, until it is rotating like the second hand on a watch. The field produced by the body can, under certain conditions, it seems, be stronger even than the field of earth itself.

There are many instances on record of matter apparently being directly controlled in this way. Most deal with grand-father clocks that "stopped short, never to go again, when the old man died," or with pictures that fell from the wall at the precise moment of some distant calamity. By their nature, events of this order are unrepeatable and yield nothing to further analysis. They are lumped together under the name of telekinesis—the ability to move things from afar—and effectively ignored by all except hard-core parapsychologists, but once in a while someone is discovered who seems to be able to move things from afar on demand.

The most impressive of all early laboratory tests on this phenomenon was arranged in London by Harry Price, who made a name for himself in the thirties as a highly skeptical investigator of ghosts. (309) His subject in this test was a young girl, and the task he set her was to depress a tele-graph key that closed a circuit and lit a small red light bulb, without touching any of the apparatus. He made the test difficult by blowing a mixture of soap and glycerine into a large bubble and placing this carefully over the whole apparatus. The bubble was then imprisoned under a glass cover, which was enclosed in a wire-net cage that stood in the center of a latticework fence of wood. Despite all these barriers, witnesses report that the girl was able to make the light bulb flash on and off several times and that, at the conclusion of the test, the soap bubble was found to be intact. This is a neat demonstration and seems to have been honestly reported, but like most older experiments on the occult, it has loopholes which modern scientists pounce on and hold up to ridicule. The report fails to say whether the key was seen to move, which could be important, because we now know that it is possible to induce current from a distance.

The whole pattern of investigation changed in 1934 when a lecturer in the psychology department at Duke University, in North Carolina, was approached by a young gambler who claimed that he could control the fall of dice by will power. The lecturer was J. B. Rhine, already involved in a long-term statistical study of telepathy, but what the gambler showed him right there on the office floor was enough to start him off on an entirely new track.

Rhine and his friends bought some ordinary plastic dice and began throwing them. They actively tried to will two dice to fall so that the total of their sides added up to more than seven. There are thirty-six possible combinations of two dice, and fifteen of these are greater than seven, so they expected to hit their target 2,810 times out of 6,744 throws. They actually scored 3,110, which was so far from chance coincidence that it could occur only once in well over a billion times. Rhine concluded that it was possible that the mind could influence the fall of the dice, and so he set out to investigate what he called "psychokinesis"—physical motion produced by the mind.

Tests of this kind had been made before, but what Rhine brought to investigation of the occult was a scientific method based on statistical analysis of large numbers of tests. The value of his system is shown clearly in this first test. Here the average rate of scoring should have been fifteen out of thirty-six, but it turned out to be 16.5. Such a small deviation can easily be ignored in one test, but when it occurs over hundreds of tests it takes on an entirely different meaning, whose significance can be assessed only by sophisticated statistical analysis. This is not just mathematical juggling, but a method of defining what can reasonably be ascribed to coincidence and what must be taking place for some other reason. In most scientific research, a result is said to be significant if it would have occurred by chance along no more than five out of a hundred times, which is odds of nineteen to one, but Rhine deliberately took extra precautions by ignoring anything that could have occurred by chance more than one out of a hundred times.

After twenty-five years of testing, Rhine concludes that "the mind does have a force that can affect physical matter directly." (275) He feels that the weight of evidence in favor of psychokinesis (PK) is so great that "merely to repeat PK tests with the single objective of finding more evidence of the PK effect itself should be an unthinkable waste of time."

These are some of the findings.

Rhine's tests, when assessed by his own statistical methods, show an over-all significance at a high level of chance. These methods have been criticized, perhaps rightly, but analyses by independent statisticians have revealed other trends hidden in the figures that are even more important. (254) The success of every person being tested shows fluctuations during the course of an experiment; nearly all subjects scored well at the beginning and again near the end of every series. This suggests that decline in the middle of the test is due not merely to fatigue but to a loss of interest. "Position effects" of this kind were most marked in tests where the subject was doing his own recording and could follow the trend of the score. (256) It was almost as though the person throwing the dice was influencing the pattern of their fall—which is exactly what the tests were designed to find out. A bias that consistently produces better results in one part of the test than another is far more likely to be due to personal influence than some defect in the experiment. The extent of this bias was nicely demonstrated by an English mathematician who was able to produce exactly the same deviation from chance values by getting subjects to throw, at random, dice loaded with lead at one corner. (180)

Other tests produced further evidence of mental influence. In one series it was shown that subjects succeeded better with targets, such as double six, that appealed to them. (268) And in another series, higher scores were always obtained when the subject was allowed to throw dice of the size he liked best. (151) Strong interest in the outcome of the test was obviously important. If the subject was consciously trying for a particular combination, but knew that the experimenter was interested in another number, then this one also came up more often than expected. (274) The importance of psychological factors in the testing was clearly demonstrated in a very long series, of two hundred thousand throws, made by a man-and-woman team. After analyzing their results, which showed a marked and changing pattern determined by their relationship to each other, a statistician decided that the scores could not be ascribed to chance or to "biased dice, wishful thinking, recording errors or any other reasonable counter hypothesis." (255) He concluded, "PK is left as the only adequate cause of these effects."

Through all tests it is obvious that the mood of the subject played an all-important part. The best results of all dice tests were produced by an experiment in the form of a competition between four successful gamblers convinced of their good luck and four divinity students equally convinced of the power of prayer. (114) It seems to be vital for the operator to be excited by the experiment and keen to see if he can succeed in making the dice do as he wants them to do. In no tests yet made have investigators repeating someone else's work ever managed to do quite as well as the original subjects. Rhine remarks that "those struggling to make their own trails and to develop their own methods in uncharted territory have again and again shown themselves more likely to get evidence of PK." (275)

This trend for researchers to get the results they badly want has naturally led to criticisms of the work on the grounds of experimenter bias and a lack of objectivity. Scientific investigation should ideally be neutral, but it seldom is, and in the life sciences the hazards are particularly great. For example, among the mass of information on the way in which white rats negotiate mazes, there is one very revealing item. It deals with an experiment on a number of rats that were specially chosen, on the basis of past performances in mazes, for their similar abilities. Their cages were marked at random with labels reading "CLEVER" and "STUPID," and each rat was tested by several research workers in a new series of maze experiments. The "clever" rats produced the best scores, but only when wearing their badges of merit. If the labels were changed around, their performances suffered accordingly. (282)

In order to avoid criticisms of this kind of bias, Rhine eliminated all contact with the dice by designing an electric machine to do the throwing for him while he stood nearby and exercised his will. (273) The results were even better. A physicist from Pittsburgh was still worried about bias during the recording stage, and so, to eliminate "record error, the loss or selection of data, selection of the experiment, retroactive choice of the target and optional stopping," he built a machine to do everything. The device shook and threw the dice and then photographed and filed the result without ever letting the subject see how well or badly he was doing. (223) All the experimenter had to do was press a button to start each throw going while he wished for a particular outcome. After 170 thousand throws he found he had results with odds of more than a hundred to one against chance. But if he completed the machine and added an automatic starter, so that there was no human involvement at all, the results were strictly according to chance.

Taken together, these experiments suggest that, for dice at least, there is evidence of a force of mental origin that can influence the movement of physical objects.

If the PK effect depends on the action of a subtle force, it would seem that these tests provide a very insensitive instrument for measuring it. Following the publication of Rhine's first results, several different techniques were developed elsewhere. In Germany, a seventeen-year-old schoolboy produced incredibly high scores with coins. He tossed a coin ten thousand times and was able to predict its fall correctly with results that had odds of a billion to one against chance. And in a test with a roulette wheel he scored seventy-five direct hits in five hundred spins, which has odds of millions to one against it. (25)

In other laboratories work went ahead on the assumption that not everyone can produce exceptional scores of this sort but that all people have some PK ability, which can probably be detected only by very sensitive tests. John Beloff, a psychologist at Queens University, in Belfast, reasoned that microscopic particles should be more easily influenced than macroscopic ones and hit on the idea of using what he calls "nature's own dice." (21) In the nucleus of every atom there are two basic types of fundamental particles—neutrons and protons. There are 275 different combinations of these particles that form stable alliances and make up most of earth's matter, but there are about fifty other naturally occurring chemical elements, with an unstable nucleus that sends particles shooting off as radioactivity. Beloff suggested that as these particles come off at random they would provide a perfect test of PK ability, which could be directed at either stopping them or increasing their rate of emission.

Two French scientists took up Beloff's suggestion and chose uranium nitrate as their radioactive source and a Geiger counter as the means of measuring the rate at which particles were given off. (70) Their subjects were two schoolboys, who were naturally fascinated by the experiment, and their task was either to accelerate or slow down the blips on the counter. They succeeded with scores of a billion to one against chance.

Helmut Schmidt, at the University of Durham, in North Carolina, used the same principle in designing a sort of electronic coin flipper. His radiation source powered a binary generator, which produced one of just two kinds of reaction at random once a second. He arranged nine light bulbs in a circle on a display board and connected them so that only one could be lighted at a time. A "heads" reaction made the light jump in a clockwise direction around the ring, while a "tails" reaction made it go the other way. His subjects concentrated on making it move consistently in either direction instead of flashing backward and forward at random. In thirty-two thousand trials they managed to do this with odds of ten million to one against chance. (295)

The outcome of these two studies suggests that Beloff was right—that PK action works most effectively at a subatomic level. This is a vital discovery, because we now know that the so-called particles in the atoms are not solid at all, but apparently consist of wavelike areas of electromagnetic action. There is only one kind of force that can influence an electric field—and that is another field. The psychokinetic force begins to look like an electric-field phenomenon.

A mechanical engineer in South Carolina has produced evidence in support of this theory. He built a clock driven by an electric current that had to pass through a bath of salt solution. (80) In the presence of electricity, salt breaks down into charged ions of sodium and chlorine, which move toward opposite electrodes and carry a current through the solution. The speed with which the ions form determines the flow of the current and therefore the rate of movement of the hands on the clock. He thought that PK could act on the ions and either speed up or slow down the clock—and it worked, with odds of a thousand to one against chance. Which seems to show that PK can bring a purely electrical force to bear on particles of atomic as well as subatomic sizes. The only drawback to the whole electrical theory is that there are examples of what seem to be PK forces acting on electrically inert substances, such as plastic and wood.

Haakon Forwald, a Swedish engineer, set out to describe PK in terms of the energy it exerts. He built a ramp sloping down onto a table and at the top installed a device for releasing a number of cubes simultaneously. The cubes rolled down the incline and out onto a table, where they could land on one or the other side of a center line. Forwald tried to make them go in one direction, and by measuring their displacement from the center line was able to calculate how much force was involved. With beechwood cubes weighing two grams each he found that the average force involved in moving the cube from a control position was about three hundred dynes. (104) A dyne is "that force which, when acting on a mass of one gram, will accelerate it by one centimeter in each second." This is a very precise physical measurement, and there is great satisfaction in being able to give a hard numerical value to the energy involved in at least one PK action. It helps to make the whole phenomenon seem more normal and legitimate, but it does not explain how it works.

Forwald also worked with zinc, bakelite, copper, cadmium, silver, lead, and aluminum cubes. He found that different materials reacted in different ways but that the distance they were deflected was not related to their weight. He suggested that, as his mind seemed to be trying equally hard to move all the cubes, any differences must be in the cubes and that they might themselves be liberating energy. (105) He explains that perhaps "the mind action is of a relaying kind that is able to start an energetic process within the atom but does not convey energy to it." Forwald tested the cubes for traces of any secondary radiation that would be produced by this sort of reaction, but found none.

The idea of a mental force acting only as a trigger makes sense when applied to all these PK experiments in which normal people try to influence objects that are already moving. Most of the results are not at all dramatic and gain significance only when viewed statistically. So it is possible that a small number of the falling dice or spinning coins drop into a state of equilibrium, where they could quite easily go either way, and it is on these that a very tiny force, perhaps no more than the pressure of a light beam, acts to produce the desired result. But this theory cannot even begin to account for some of the extraordinary things that are being done by people with special PK talents.

WILL POWER

Of all these special people, none is more talented or consistent than Nelya Mikhailova. She was born just ten years after the Russian Revolution, and at the age of fourteen was fighting in the front lines of the Red Army. She was injured by artillery fire near the end of the war and spent a long time recovering in the hospital. It was during this period that she began to develop her strange abilities. "I was very angry and upset one day," she recalls. "I was walking toward a cupboard when suddenly a pitcher moved to the edge of the shelf, fell, and smashed to bits." (233) After that, all kinds of changes began to take place around her. Objects moved of their own volition, doors opened and closed, lights went on and off. But, unlike most people plagued by poltergeist activities, Nelya realized that she was somehow responsible and that she could control the energy. She could summon and focus it at will.

One of the first to study her talents was Edward Naumov, a biologist from Moscow State University. In a test in his laboratory, he scattered a box of matches on a table and she circled her hands over them, shaking with the strain, until the whole group of matches moved like a log run across to the edge of the table and fell off one by one to the floor. To rule out drafts of air, threads, or wire, Naumov put another batch of matches under a plexiglass cover, but Nelya still made them shuttle from side to side. (233) Five cigarettes were then placed under the jar, and Nelya showed that she could be selective, picking out only one of them and making it move. Afterward the cigarettes were shredded to make sure that nothing was hidden inside.

Two famous Soviet writers have examined her, admittedly in uncontrolled conditions, but their accounts give some idea of the scope of her talents. Lev Kolodny visited her apartment for an interview and was startled to see the top of his pen being pursued across the table by a glass tumbler. "Both objects moved to the edge of the table as if they were in harness. The tablecloth wasn't moving—the other glasses besides mine were still sitting there. Could she be somehow blowing on them to make them move? There was no draft of air and Mikhailova wasn't breathing heavily. Why didn't a jar in their path also move? I ran my hands through the space between Mikhailova and the table. No threads or wires. If she was using magnets, they wouldn't work on glass." (181)

Vadim Marin, who was dining out with Nelya, reports, "A piece of bread lay on the table some distance from her. Mikhailova, concentrating, looked at it attentively. A minute passed, then another . . . and the piece of bread began to move. It moved by jerks. Toward the edge of the table, it moved more smoothly and rapidly. Mikhailova bent her head down, opened her mouth, and, just as in the fairytale, the bread itself (excuse me but I have no other words for it) jumped into her mouth!" (233)

In both these accounts the possibilities of fraud and hypnotism exist, but at least one series of experiments have been conducted under controlled conditions, where there was no chance of dissembling. Genady Sergeyev, neurophysiologist at the Utomskii Institute, in Leningrad, set up the tests in a physiology laboratory. Mikhailova was strapped into an electroencephalograph and cardiograph harness and initial measurements were made of her resting physiology. Sergeyev discovered that she had a magnetic field surrounding her body that was only ten times less powerful than that of the earth itself. (271) At a later date this was confirmed by tests made at the Leningrad Institute of Meteorology. Sergeyev also found that she had an unusual brain-wave pattern, with fifty times more voltage being generated at the back of her head than the front.

The testing began with one of the most difficult and impressive PK demonstrations ever made. (233) A raw egg was broken into saline solution in an aquarium six feet from her, and, with cameras recording every second, Nelya struggled until she was able to separate the white of the egg from the yolk and move the two apart—an act that nobody could ever attribute to hidden strings or magnets.

While the demonstration was taking place, her EEG showed intense emotional excitement. There was great activity in the deeper levels of the reticular formation, which co-ordinates and filters information in the brain. The cardiogram showed an irregular action of the heart, with that confusion between the chambers that is characteristic of great alarm. The pulse soared to 240 beats a minute, four times its normal level, and high percentages of blood sugar were recorded together with other endocrinal disturbances all characteristic of a stress reaction. The test lasted thirty minutes, and during this time Nelya lost over two pounds in weight. At the end of the day she was very weak and temporarily blind. Her ability to taste was impaired, she had pains in her arms and legs, she felt dizzy, and she was unable to sleep for several days.

All this is startling enough, but at the same demonstration Sergeyev also introduced a new and vitally important instrument. At the moment, it is known only as the Sergeyev Detector, and in principle seems to be similar to one that has recently been used at the University of Saskatchewan. (320) Its basic components are capacitors and a preamplifier connected to a cardiograph, and it is tuned to respond to changes in the life field. Sergeyev had the instrument near Nelya during the laboratory test, and at the exact moments that she seemed to be moving objects with her PK force, he recorded big changes in the electrostatic and magnetic measurements of her field. (233) As she strained to bring her influence to bear, the electrostatic field began to pulse until it was undergoing a regular fluctuation at a rate of four cycles a second. This turbulence was precisely linked at that moment to the pulse rate of four beats a second and to a heavy theta brain-wave action at the same frequency.

The body rhythms seemed to be producing a beat that was picked up and amplified by the field around her and concentrated on the spot where her eyes were fixed. Sergeyev claims that these vibrations in the field act like magnetic waves. "The moment these magnetic vibrations or waves occur, they cause the object Mrs. Mikhailova focuses on, even if it is something non-magnetic, to act as if magnetized. It causes the object to be attracted to her or repelled from her."

Part of this attraction could be due to an unusually wide electrostatic field that is being aided by a pulsing magnetic field. It has been recently discovered that the fundamental particles in most atoms can develop a spin that produces spin waves and a fluctuating magnetic field of the very kind necessary to reduce friction between an object and the table on which it rests. This is pure conjecture at the moment; nobody has yet observed this sort of magnetic interaction on or near objects being moved by PK activity, but there is growing and astonishing evidence of the necessary force being generated by most living bodies. Leonard Ravitz has found that mental changes can produce measurable effects on instruments used for charting the life field. (265) With them he claims to be able to determine a person's state of mind and even the depth of hypnosis. Neurophysiologists in Canada are using a field detector to determine at a distance whether a patient's level of anxiety is high, medium, or low. It is no longer possible to doubt that a field of some kind surrounds the human body like a cocoon.

THE AURA

Reports that the field pulsates are going to bring great gladness to the hearts of spirit mediums everywhere, who have always insisted that their sensitivity was due to "vibrations." Many, including the famous New York clairvoyant Eileen Garrett, have reported seeing spirals of energy leaving a newly dead body. (113) And now Sergeyev claims that his detectors sprang into action near the body of a man whose heart and brain waves had stopped, and was therefore chemically dead, but who still seemed to be releasing electrical energy. The idea of an energy cloud, or "aura," surrounding the body goes back many centuries. Old pictures of holy men show them standing in a luminous surround long before Christians invented the halo. This haze with the mythical properties was first investigated by Walter Kilner of St. Thomas' Hospital in London, who found in 1911 that, by looking through colored-glass screens, he could see a radiant fringe about six inches wide around most bodies. (174) He claimed that this aura changed shape and color according to the well-being of the person wearing it, and he used it as an aid to medical diagnosis.

Our eyes are sensitive to light that lies between the wavelengths of 380 and 760 millimicrons. With very-high-intensity artificial sources we can extend this at either end of the spectrum into the areas of infrared and ultraviolet light. The fact that man's body sends out electromagnetic waves just too long for most people to see has been vividly demonstrated by the new "thermographic" technique, which translates heat radiation into wonderful color pictures. (308) Atoms generate infrared rays by their constant motion, and the warmer they are the more active they become. In thermographic portraits, cold hair and fingernails show up black or blue, cool ear lobes are green, the nose is a lukewarm yellow, and neck and cheeks glow with orange and red. The system is now being used to detect tumors, arthritis, and cancer, which show up as isolated hot areas. So the body does radiate on a wavelength just outside our normal vision, and this radiation changes according to the health of the transmitter.

Perhaps Kilner was right. The range of human sensitivity is quite wide; some people hear sounds that to others are supersonic, and some people see wavelengths that to others are invisible. Those who claim to be able to see an aura surrounding living things could be supersensitive at the infrared end of the spectrum. Waves of this length are beyond the capability of the cone-shaped cells in our retina, which appreciate visible colors, but they may be within the range of the rod-shaped cells that are more sensitive to low light intensities. Occult books that give instruction on "how to see the aura" usually recommend that it be looked for in dim light, with the eyes partly closed and the head turned so that light strikes the corner of the eye. These are precisely the conditions most suitable for bypassing the cones, in the center of the retina, and stimulating the much more sensitive rods, around the edges. Animals with good night vision have no cones and no ability to see color, but they can operate in almost pitch dark, and it seems that many have some sensitivity to infrared radiation put out by their prey. It has been shown that owls can detect a silent, stationary mouse at a distance but are unable to locate a piece of dead meat of the same size and shape. If all nocturnal animals are able to see some infrared and therefore detect the "aura," we now know why the two animals most often chosen by witches for their "familiars" were owls and cats.

All those who claim to have seen the aura describe it as surrounding the body in a smooth egg shape, wider at the head than the feet. It is interesting that this same shape crops up in reports dealing with aura-like phenomena described by other cultures. In the second beautiful book on his conversations with a Yaqui man of knowledge, Castaneda records a discussion about ordinary looking and really "seeing." (68) Don Juan says, "I like to sit in parks and bus depots and watch. Real people look like luminous eggs when you *see* them." He goes on to explain that sometimes in a crowd of egglike creatures he spots one who looks just like a person, and then he knows that there is something wrong and that, without the luminous glow, this is not a real person at all.

Following up Kilner's work, the Cambridge biologist Oscar Bagnall has tried to describe the aura in physical terms. He claims that it can most easily be seen after "sensitizing" the eyes by looking for some time through a solution of the coal-tar dye dicyanine or pinacyanol. To make this easier, he has designed goggles with hollow lenses that can be filled with the dye dissolved in triethanolamine. (12) Bagnall reports that the aura cannot be dispersed by a current of air but that it is attracted to a magnet held close to the skin and that, like the electrical field around a charged conductor, it extends farthest from a projection such as a finger or the tip of the nose. He describes the aura as being composed of a hazy outer layer and a brighter inner layer, in which there seem to be striations running out at right angles from the skin. Bagnall and other aura watchers say that every once in a while a much brighter ray "reaches out from the aura like a searchlight" and extends several feet from the body before vanishing again.

Compare that with this description: "Whole luminous labyrinths, flashing, twinkling, flaring. Some of the sparks were motionless, some wandered against a dark background. Over these fantastic galaxies of ghostly lights there were bright multicolored flares and dim clouds." This is no extract from an account of an LSD trip, but the report of a top Soviet academician to the Presidium on an investigation now taking place in Krasnodar, near the Black Sea. (233)

In 1939 the electrician Semyon Kirlian was called to a

university laboratory to repair an instrument used in electro-therapy. He noticed that when a patient received treatment with the machine, there was a tiny flash of light between the electrodes. He tried to take photographs with this light and discovered that it was possible to do this without a camera by inserting a plate directly between the high-frequency spark and his hand. On being developed, the photographic plate produced a glowing image of his outstretched fingers. Other living objects also made pictures studded with dots and flares, but with inert objects there was no image at all. Kirlian built his own machine to generate high-frequency electrical fields with an oscillation of two hundred thousand sparks per second between two electrodes. He also designed an optical viewer (now the subject of fourteen Soviet patents) to make it possible to watch the process directly without films or emulsion. (192) It was a view of his own finger under this instrument that provoked that pyrotechnic description from the academician.

Every living thing placed in the high-frequency discharge produces these patterns. A whole hand can look like the Milky Way, sparkling and twinkling against a glowing background of gold and blue. A freshly picked leaf shines with an internal light that streams out through its pores in beams that gradually flick out one by one as it dies. Leaves taken from plants of the same species show similar jeweled patterns, but if one of the plants is diseased, the pattern in its leaf is entirely different. Similarly the patterns produced by the same fingertip change with the mood and health of the man to whom it belongs. Kirlian says, "In living things, we see the signals of the inner state of the organism reflected in the brightness, dimness and color of the flares. The inner life activities of the human being are written in these 'light' hieroglyphs. We've created an apparatus to write the hieroglyphs, but to read them we're going to need help." (233)

For twenty-five years Kirlian and his wife battled to perfect their apparatus. A constant stream of visitors—physicists, physicians, biochemists, pathologists, electronics experts, and government ministers—came to see the results. All went away impressed, and the bibliography on the Kirlian process grew to massive proportions, but nothing happened until 1964, when suddenly the doors opened to them. They were set up in their own laboratory with all the latest equipment, and research projects began on Kirlian-designed machines in a dozen other centers. The results are now just starting to come in, and they promise to revolutionize many aspects of biology and parapsychology. The electric aura has arrived.

Basic to many branches of the occult is a belief in "astral," or "etheric," bodies, which are supposed to exist as spiritual doubles of our own physical bodies. People who have had a leg amputated say that they can still sense it and even complain of itches in absent toes. This can be explained by the persistence of old sensory patterns in the brain, but some psychics claim to be able to "see" phantom limbs still attached to the body. Now the Kirlian effect shows that they may be right. In Moscow a Kirlian machine has been used to take pictures of an intact leaf, then a third of the leaf is cut away and further pictures are taken. For a short while after part of the leaf has been removed, an image of that part persists as a "ghost," making up a complete sparkling outline of the whole original leaf.

This suggests that there is some sort of energy matrix in all living things and that it has a shape like that of the organism, but relatively independent of it. This is an incredible idea, but in Russia they are taking it seriously. At the Kirov State University, in Alma-Ata, a group of biophysicists and biochemists are trying to study this energy body with the aid of an electron microscope. (233) They claim that it is "some sort of elementary plasma-like constellation made of ionized particles. It is not a chaotic system, but a whole unified organism in itself." They call it the "Biological Plasma Body."

Plasma sounds like something out of a Victorian spiritualist meeting, but has a physical reality now. A plasma is a gas that has been so completely ionized that all the electrons have been stripped off the nuclei of its atoms. This occurs in a thermonuclear reaction when the temperature is raised to three hundred million degrees C and the gas particles accelerate to speeds great enough to produce fusion, but there is no evidence that anything like this can happen at body temperature. Which does not mean that it is impossible; it just means that this whole branch of physics is so new that nobody knows exactly what a plasma is or what it can really do. One interesting fact that *is* known about plasma is that the only thing that will contain its energy effectively is a magnetic field—and we know that the body has one of these.

One of those to make the pilgrimage to see the Kirlians in Krasnodar was Mikhail Gaikin, a surgeon from Leningrad. After looking at the cavalcade of lights in his own hands, he began to wonder about their origin. The strongest flares shone right out of the skin like searchlights, but their positions corresponded with no major nerve endings in the body, and the pattern of their distribution showed no correspondence with arteries or veins. Then he remembered his experiences on the Zabaikal front in 1945 and the lessons he had learned from a Chinese doctor in the art of acupuncture. Acting on his hunch, he sent the Kirlians a standard acupuncture chart of seven hundred important points on the skin—and they tallied exactly with charts that the Kirlians had begun to prepare of the fires visible under their high-frequency machine.

Acupuncture literally means "pricking with a needle." It is

a very old and much respected Chinese system of medicine, which puts the emphasis on prevention of disease rather than a treatment of the symptoms. In the old days, a patient paid a doctor to keep him from becoming ill; if he did fall sick, the doctor paid him. (189) The essence of acupuncture is the belief that all matter contains two activities, Yin and Yang, and that well-being depends upon a proper balance between them. These activities are manifest as subtle flows of energy circulating in the body, which at some points come near enough to the surface to be manipulated. The key control points have, in thousands of years of practice, been literally pinpointed, and at each point an excess of the appropriate energy can be released either by fingertip massage or by inserting a metal needle.

Perhaps the most critical test of acupuncture is its efficacy as an anesthetic. Western journalists were recently invited to see a series of major operations in Peking conducted entirely without any other kind of anesthetic. Neville Maxwell reported on the removal of a tubercular lung from a patient who had just one thin steel needle inserted into his right forearm, which apparently numbed the whole chest area and allowed the operation to proceed while the patient chatted with the operating theater staff and sipped tea. "The onlooker could exchange words with the patient and, short of nudging the surgeons, could stand as near as he liked. After the operation was completed, the wound was closed, the needle removed, and Mr. Han was given a helping hand to sit up. Then the patient's arm was massaged and he was helped into his pajama coat, again with no sign of even a wince." And then Mr. Han gave a press conference. (209)

Chinese practitioners spend years learning to locate the acupuncture points precisely, but impatient Western students have always found this difficult. Now Gaikin and the Kirlians have built an electronic device to mark the points to within one tenth of a millimeter. The Russians proudly demonstrated this machine, now called the "tobiscope," at Expo 67, in Montreal, alongside the Vostok spaceship. With this instrument, medical laboratories all over the world are now using needles, electricity, and sound waves to stimulate the key points and produce dramatic cures. This development provides hard, practical proof of the effectiveness of acupuncture and the reality of the "plasma" with which it seems to be connected. (331)

If a biological plasma body exists, I would expect it to be produced by the organism. Once it exists, it is possible that it could exercise some sort of organizational function over the body that made it. There is one study that showed that a muscle that was surgically removed from a mouse and cut up into small pieces would regenerate completely if this mince was packed back into the wound. (289) But perhaps the best example is provided by the sponge. There are some colonies of unicellular animals that get together in large social groups, but sponges are more complex than this and are classified as single organisms. The cells in their bodies are loosely organized but occur in several forms, which fulfill different functions. There are collar cells, which live in cavities and wave whips to create the currents of water that flow through the animal's pores to bring it food and oxygen; there are sex cells, which produce eggs and sperm; and there are cells that build supporting skeletons of such superb geodesic construction that they serve as inspiration for aircraft designers. Some sponges grow to several feet in diameter, and yet, if you cut them up and squeeze the pieces through silk cloth to separate every cell from its neighbor, this gruel soon gets together and organizes itself—and the complete sponge reappears like a phoenix to go back into business again. A persistent plasma body would provide a perfect template for regeneration of this kind.

Whatever it may be called, "bioplasma" or "aura" or "life field," it is becoming difficult to avoid the conclusion that our sphere of influence does not end with the skin. Beyond the traditional confines of our bodies are forces we seem to produce and may be able to control. If you can accept this, then psychokinesis no longer seems strange. Nobody questions the fact that the mind controls and guides the muscles in our bodies, but to do this it has already demonstrated psychokinesis. An intangible thing like the mind, which has never been seen, jumps the gap between the unreal and the real, creating nervous energy, which directs muscular energy, which moves physical objects. From this situation to PK is only a short step; all we have to do is fill the gap at the other end. The Russians may well have done just that.

The relationship between mind and brain is still a complete mystery. Sir John Eccles, a great Australian neurophysiologist, described the brain as a system of "ten thousand million neurones . . . momentarily poised close to a just-threshold level of excitability. It is the kind of machine that a ghost could operate, if by 'ghost' we mean in the first place an 'agent' whose action has escaped detection even by the most delicate instruments." (92) This ghost in the machine of psychokinesis seems to have been layed by the sensitive instruments of Sergeyev and Kirlian. It could even be the same sort of ghost that the Germans call "poltergeist," the noisy spirit.

POLTERGEISTS

There is no shortage of good evidence for poltergeist activity, much of it provided by skeptical scientists, professional police officers, and hard-nosed reporters. The phenomenon is the same all over the world. Things fall off tables, light bulbs drop from their fixtures, liquids are upset, meaningless knocking occurs, stones fly through windows, and taps are left running. These apparently childish tricks often seem to be associated with an adolescent, usually a girl at the stage of puberty or a teen-ager in a stage of emotional adjustment. (142) In one well-known case, a twenty-year-old girl with delicate feelings was just getting involved in married life. The association of poltergeist activities with a person, rather than a place, is crucial. It suggests that unusual geophysical phenomena, such as a local aberration in gravity, play a less important part than forces of psychological origin. (292) There is an area at the head of the Songe Fjord in Norway and another in the volcanic crater of Kintamani on Bali, where pebbles are not as firmly anchored to the ground as they should be. But investigation, such as George Owen's meticulous study of the Sauchie poltergeist, show that when the central figure in one of these cases moves, the phenomena follow close behind. (237)

The psychoanalyst Nandor Fodor has described the poltergeist as a "bundle of projected repressions." (103) If this is true, the projection is completely unconscious. It could be psychokinetic energy just lashing out blindly, like the reflex movement that makes one knock a glass off the table when startled by a loud noise. But sometimes poltergeist activities show a measure of intelligence or purpose, as when writing appears on a wall or objects are aimed at a particular person. In these cases, the PK activity could be controlled by some deeper unconscious level, but even here the ghost is not a spirit so much as a manifestation of mind.

One of the features common to nearly all poltergeists is that people rarely see objects actually in motion, and, even in the few cases in which they do, I have not been able to find a single report made by anyone who saw an object *start* to move. This could be important. In laboratory tests with PK in ordinary people, effects often fail to appear when the subject is concentrating hard on them, and then suddenly appear when their attention is diverted. Poltergeist activities frequently stop as soon as an investigator arrives to examine them. Rhine describes some of his studies as "trying to develop film in daylight." (275) Just as darkness is an essential prerequisite for photographic development, so spontaneity seems to be important for PK by laboratory subject or poltergeist. The few special people who have learned to produce PK effects at will are obviously in a separate category. Rhine concludes that PK is "one ability which only operates under a narrow range of psychological conditions and is easily inhibited if these conditions are unfavorable." . . . In most persons it is inhibited all the time.

Perhaps the most useful clue to emerge so far from these investigations is Sergeyev's discovery that, during PK, the electrostatic field and the heart and the brain are all operating at four cycles a second. It has been known for a long time that the brains of very young children have slow wave patterns. Electrodes attached to the stomach of a woman in late pregnancy show that the unborn child is producing waves of fewer than three cycles a second—the same (delta) waves that adults develop when "sleeping like a baby." In the first three years of life delta rhythms are predominant, and only later do the pulses speed up to the alpha rhythms of meditation and the even faster rhythms of complex thought and calculation. At first it was believed that rhythms of four to seven cycles were just transitional between delta, which stop at three, and alpha, which begin at eight cycles a second. And it was assumed that these intermediate patterns were characteristic only of growing children, but later they were also found under certain conditions in adults and were given the name of theta waves.

Theta rhythms start in the thalamus, the area of the brain that seems to govern emotional display. They can be produced very easily in a young child by snatching a sweet or a toy away and holding it just out of reach. They can be produced almost as easily in adults by offending or frustrating them. In laboratory situations theta rhythms are often demonstrated by offering the subject a pleasant stimulus, such as having his forehead stroked by a beautiful girl, and then suddenly sending her away. As soon as the pleasant sensation stops, theta rhythms appear, flicker to a crescendo for a short while, and then disappear. Most adults are used to frequent disappointments, and it seems that they adjust to them by suppressing the theta quite quickly. In children the rhythms persist much longer and often lead to temper tantrums or purposeless destruction. It has been discovered that those adults who are subject to uncontrolled fits of violent aggression often have dominant theta rhythms in their brain waves. This is such a characteristic symptom that it has been used as a means of detecting this type of psychopath.

So it seems that, as young children, we all have a natural tendency to react emotionally to frustration by acts of aggression linked with theta waves in the brain. It seems, too, that animals react in the same way. Hebb tells of a chimpanzee that sat quietly for hours just watching a female in another cage, and then, as soon as she retired to her sleeping den, showed a sudden and violent display of rage accompanied by the chimp equivalent of our theta waves. (144) As children we flare up in the same way, but as we mature we learn to suppress the violent rhythms. The fact that this is a conscious and deliberate process has been demonstrated by Walter in laboratory tests where anger was artificially induced by exposing subjects to a light flickering at the theta rhythm, between four and seven cycles a second. (335) There is a wide variation in individual ability to exercise control, and it looks as though bad-tempered people are often just those who are not so good at holding theta down.

Textbook descriptions of behavior under theta rhythms

use the words "intolerance," "selfishness," "impatience," "suspicion," and "childishness." Which is a very good description of most poltergeists. It is tempting to draw parallels between the two and point out that poltergeist activities are most often associated with people who are going through difficult periods in their lives, when they would probably benefit a great deal by being allowed to produce a temper tantrum but have now grown too old for this to be socially acceptable. Perhaps the frustration builds up to a point where it can find release only through the unconscious, in pointless psychokinesis such as breaking windows and throwing things around. This is just guesswork; I have no proof to offer in favor of such a theory, but there are the records of Nelya Mikhailova's physiology to fall back on. While PK effects were being observed, she was operating almost exclusively on a strong, self-induced theta rhythm. Her blood-sugar and endocrine measurements show that she was in a state of controlled rage. These may be precisely the conditions necessary for PK to appear.

In communities of animals, high levels of aggression often appear and lead to fighting that is highly stylized so that emotions can be expressed without either protagonist being too badly injured. There are rules, but under certain conditions the rules break down and an animal finds aggression thwarted. This happens when two antelope are so evenly matched that neither will give way, or when two gulls meet on the edge of their respective territories, where neither has right of way. The rival tendencies to fight and to flee are brought into direct conflict with each other and a stalemate exists, but the level of emotion is so high that it has to find an outlet somewhere, and so a "displacement activity" occurs. The antelope may start scratching his hind leg as though he had suddenly become unbearably itchy, and the gull may start tugging at bits of grass as though he had an overwhelming need to build a nest immediately. In this way, pent-up aggression is expressed in action of an altogether different kind. Perhaps this is what happens in psychokinesis. Maybe the level of theta-induced anger is so high and so frustrated that it is displaced into another channel, and instead of the man kicking a chair over, which would be considered childish and reprehensible, his unconscious mind gets the force field to do it for him.

There are still a lot of maybes and perhapses in all this. We do not yet know the answers, but a pattern seems to be emerging. It is hard to find a logical place in biological evolution for psychokinesis below the human level. In all other species, aggression is easily expressed. Only in man is there conflict between aggression and social pressure. Only in man has the brain developed far enough to produce a mind that sets its own standards of behavior and consciously suppresses instinctive patterns that fail to meet this standard. Children have to be taught to do this, but at a time of life when the pressures on them are greatest, it is possible that they find an unconscious outlet. The few people who can produce psychokinetic effects at will, have presumably learned to do this by bringing this displacement activity under conscious control. Perhaps, as we learn more about ourselves, more of us will be able to do this equally well. At the moment it seems a little pointless to squander energy and lose two pounds in body weight every time we need to separate an egg. We can do things like this far more effectively with our hands, but these PK party tricks may be just kindergarten toys to a mind that can exert real control over matter.

Chapter Five:

Matter and Magic

IN THEORY, games such as roulette and dice depend only on chance, but if people believed this, gambling would soon die a natural death. Those who take part in horse racing, football, and poker clearly exercise a great deal of skill, and those who bet on the ability of their favorites also have to show some skill in assessment. But many of the most popular "games of chance" survive purely because the gambler believes that he can somehow control their outcome. He believes that by manipulating the objects involved, either directly or from a distance, he can exert an influence that will be to his benefit. He calls this influence luck, but it looks very much like psychokinesis.

Richard Taylor recently asked subjects in his laboratory to guess the sequence of colors in a shuffled pack of playing cards. After the first run, those with high scores were separated from the others, and in following tests the "lucky" ones continued to do much better than the "unlucky" group. Taylor cautiously concluded that "this data provides some empirical support for the popular notion of luck." (315) Similar evidence led the Director of the Netherlands Foundation for Industrial Psychology to say, "There are clear indications that some people have a certain flare for attracting good fortune." (326) These are valid comments, but both just miss the point that becomes clear as soon as one takes Taylor's test just one stage further. If a group of subjects are selected at random following the first run, regardless of their score, and told that they have done exceptionally well and are very lucky, this group continues to score significantly better than the others. Luck, it seems, is a state of mind.

All casinos know that certain individuals keep on winning slowly and consistently, and now the staff of a gambling magazine have produced a book that gives detailed instructions on how to join that fortunate few. They have examined the methods of laboratory investigation into psychokinesis and adapted them to the casino environment. Included in their advice is the importance of cultivating the proper attitude for winning, which they describe as "confident, relaxed, and almost playful." (283) We are still a long way from a situation where gambling houses are put right out of business by an invasion of parapsychologists, but there are signs that a few people are beginning to learn how to tip the odds in their favor.

For psychokinesis to be of any real use in gambling, it would have to be strong enough to move dice and balls. This is already a highly developed talent and it would seem to be more useful to start a survey of PK in action with examples at a molecular level. The objects most easily influenced are those already moving or in a state of disequilibrium; in our technology, few unstable systems are more common than silver nitrate in the emulsion of unexposed photographic film.

In the latter part of the nineteenth century, during an occult craze that had thousands tapping tables and pushing planchettes over ouija boards, another popular pastime was spirit photography, in which they tried to get pictures or "psychic images" to appear on photographic plates. Many claimed success, but not one of the results really stood up to close investigation, and interest waned. In Japan between 1910 and 1913, Tomokichi Fukurai made what seems to be the first scientific investigation of pictures produced by the mind. He succeeded in getting thought images transferred directly onto dry, wrapped photographic plates under apparently well-controlled conditions, but little attention was given to his results until the advent of the incredible Ted Serios.

THOUGHTOGRAPHY

Serios was born in 1918 in Kansas City, Missouri, the son of a Greek cafe owner. In 1963 he was an unemployed, often drunken, ex-hotel porter in Chicago when he met and impressed Jule Eisenbud, Professor of Psychiatry at the Medical School in Denver. Eisenbud put Serios through three years of intensive investigation and proved beyond reasonable doubt that he can produce recognizable images of distant objects just by staring into cameras. In front of scores of reputable witnesses, in a variety of carefully controlled situations, Serios has made hundreds of pictures of buildings, people, landscapes, rockets, buses, and racing cars. He has been stripped to the skin, medically examined, X-rayed, sewn into a restraint suit that allowed him to move nothing but his head, and tested with cameras and film provided by independent and critical observers. In spite of all precautions, and without touching any of the apparatus involved, he still succeeds in producing his "thoughtographs." (96) The full details of test situations, the testimony of witnesses, and the pictures themselves can all be found in Eisenbud's book, but it is worth looking at some of the results in relation to what we now know about psychokinesis.

Magnetic fields seem to have no effect on Serios. He has produced his pictures inside a field of twelve hundred gauss, which is thousands of times stronger than the earth's field, and inside a Faraday cage that reduced the natural field to one third its normal strength. He has also been tested inside the 5-inch-thick steel walls of a radiation counting chamber with a sensitive crystal pickup designed to detect electromagnetic radiation. It found nothing unusual when Serios was producing his pictures just eighteen inches away. He has been able to get pictures when the camera was pointed at him through half an inch of lead-impregnated glass in the window of a hospital chamber designed to exclude X radiation. Infrared and ultraviolet were also excluded when he worked through barriers of wood and plastic. These conditions virtually dispose of the possibility of any of the common kinds of electromagnetic radiation, from long, radio waves to short, gamma waves, being responsible for the pictures. It would be fascinating if Serios could be examined in Russia by the Sergeyev Detector to see if he produced the same reactions as Nelya Mikhailova, but the chances of co-operation at this level seem remote.

We know a little about the physiology of thought pictures. While working, Serios usually went into a state of "intense concentration, with eyes open, lips compressed, and a quite noticeable tension of his muscular system. His limbs would tend to shake somewhat, as if with a slight palsy, and the foot of his crossed leg would sometimes begin to jerk up and down a bit convulsively. His face would become suffused and blotchy, the veins standing out on his forehead, his eyes visibly bloodshot." During all tests he drank heavily and his heartbeat often ran very high. It is clear from this description that Serios builds up the same kind of rage as Mikhailova, but in his case it often broke out into abuse and attacks on the cameras that would not co-operate with him. There seem to be good grounds for the assumption that both operated on the same principle. The Russian demonstrations tell us little about the mental factors involved, but in the pictures of Ted Serios we have a vivid, ready-made analysis of his state of mind.

Eisenbud says that Serios sometimes seems to have control over the subject matter of his pictures, but that most of the time "Ted appeared to act like the passive observer of unidentified floating objects for which his mind was merely a reflecting screen." Sometimes there was conflict between images that he was consciously aiming at and other images that intruded despite his strongest efforts to keep them out, and Ted would act "like a slightly exasperated referee in a boxing match between two youngsters that can't quite keep to the rules." It seems clear that the pictures are expressions of his unconscious mind and their subject matter a reflection of his personality. When asked to produce a picture of the Arc de Triomphe, Serios would come up with a picture of a Triumph motorcar, in which he was far more interested. Cars and buildings are recurrent themes in his pictures. He has produced recognizable shots of Westminster Abbey, Munich's Frauenkirche, and the Denver Hilton Hotel. These show great detail, but the really interesting thing about them is that they also include detail that never existed and shadows that could not exist, taken from vantage points that would only be possible for a camera in a balloon. The source of the image seems to be something that Serios has seen in real life or in a photograph, but that has been hidden away in his unconscious and modified by memory and imagination.

Psychoanalysis of Serios indicates immaturity in many ways, and once again we find a link between psychokinesis and childlike behavior. A recent survey of children's imagination has revealed that a surprisingly large number of them have what is known as eidetic imagery. This is the ability to shut the eyes after looking briefly at a picture and still retain a vivid visual image of what has been seen. (130) The fact that the image is real and detailed has been clearly demonstrated in a most impressive way. A drawing of a man's face was broken down into a large number of meaningless squiggles and then split into two separate patterns that, on their own, meant nothing. The children were briefly shown one of the patterns and then allowed to look for a longer time at the other. Those with eidetic ability were able to summon up an image of the first pattern, mentally superimpose it on the second, and see the original face. In most of the children tested, images lasted about ten minutes, but others retained them for weeks. As the images faded, they transformed themselves like cinematic cartoons until they bore only a tenuous relationship to the original. This is exactly what happens to the pictures that Ted Serios produces. As children grow older and their minds become occupied with the paraphernalia of education, they seem to lose the eidetic ability, but in a few adults, such as Serios, who have little formal education and a simple view of life, the ability is retained.

This offers us a mechanism of mind capable of the precise visual recall necessary to produce accurate pictures, but it does not solve the problem of transmitting the pictures to film. We know that it helps to "become as little children," but we are still no closer to an understanding of the physics involved. Actually, as it is the emulsion on the film that is being affected, it is more of a chemistry problem. Perhaps the answer lies in other studies, of the influence of PK on chemical reactions.

Bernard Grad of McGill University has done pioneer work in this field. His subject was a faith healer who claimed to be able to cure disease by the biblical method of "laying on of hands." In a preliminary test involving three hundred mice with identical injuries, those held by the healer for fifteen minutes a day did in fact heal more quickly than those held by other people. (127) Grad tried to expose this ability to more critical analysis by narrowing down its effect in an ingenious experiment with barley seeds. The seeds were treated with salt and baked in an oven for long enough to injure but not kill them. Then twenty seeds were planted in each of twenty-four flower pots and watered each day. The water to be used was taken straight from a tap into two sealed glass bottles, and each day the healer held one of these in his hands for thirty minutes. An experimental procedure was designed so that no person knew which plants were being given the treated water, but after two weeks it was found that those given the benefit of the healer's hand on their water supply were not only more numerous but also taller and gave a higher yield. (124)

Grad tested the treated water and found no major changes, but a later analysis showed that there was a slight spreading between the hydrogen and oxygen atoms. (125) The change in what we know to be an unstable molecule was apparently triggered by the action of an individual human field. Following this clue, Grad tried to assess the personality involved in this healing response. He had water for a second barley-seed test treated by three different people. One was a psychiatrically normal man, one was a woman with a strong depressive neurosis, and the third was a man with psychotic delusional depression. The water treated by the normal man produced seeds that showed no difference from control ones, but the growth of all seedlings that received water handled by the depressed patients was greatly retarded. (126) The discovery of a negative as well as a positive response is important. It is conceivable, even in an experiment as carefully contrived as this one, that some factor could have been over-looked and that the positive result had nothing to do with the healer. But when a negative subject—a sick person—produces an appropriately negative response, then the original premise is greatly strengthened and the case for the healer looks good.

In this example, the man exercising his influence never saw the plants at all; he charged the water, and it did the rest for him. In an experiment in France, attempts were made to affect a living organism directly. (17) At the Institute of Agronomy in Bordeaux, two kinds of parasitic fungi—*Stereum purpureum* and *Rhizoclonia solani*—were seeded onto a growth medium in glass dishes, and for fifteen minutes a day the experimenters sat and stared at the dishes and tried to inhibit their growth by concentration. Special care was taken to ensure that the fungi were genetically pure, that the composition of the growth media was identical and that all dishes were kept at the same temperature and humidity. In thirty-three out of thirty-nine tests the fungi were inhibited, as compared with control dishes, to a degree that gave odds of many millions to one against chance. There can be little doubt that, for these two fungi at least, man can influence growth just by being nearby for a short while each day.

Gardeners have always contended that the exact time of planting is important, and our new knowledge of lunar rhythms has begun to make sense of their old superstitions about planting seeds only at the full moon. Now it seems that there might be something in the idea of the proverbial "green thumb." There are certainly some people who have an almost magical ability to make things grow, while others using exactly the same methods and spending just as much time in their gardens end up with nothing but withered leaves and aphids. The good gardeners may generate a field that has a beneficial effect on plant growth. And it is by no means impossible that a variant of this field could be equally beneficial to human beings. There are people who even in a crowd seem to radiate powerful goodwill or equally powerful evil. We are not a great deal nearer understanding this effect, but the experiments of Grad and those on the fungi make it impossible to deny that such effects could exist.

The inhibition of fungus, like the growth of barley seeds, could have been caused by a molecular change in the structure of water, but there is one experiment in which the induced change is behavioral and must be due to more complex chemical effects. Nigel Richmond tried exerting his will power over *Paramecium caudatum,* the little, free-swimming protozoan that rows itself along through the water of stagnant pools like a tiny blob of transparent jelly equipped with a thousand fluttering eyelashes. They are probably the most businesslike of all the single-celled animals, gliding purposefully around at speeds of almost one tenth of an inch per second. Richmond watched them through the eyepiece of a microscope that was divided by cross hairs into four equal segments. He located a paramecium that looked as though it was about to go somewhere, fixed it at the center of his sights, and tried to make it move into one of the four segments chosen at random. In three thousand such trials, he was successful with a score of ten million to one against chance. (277) *Paramecium* normally finds its way around by a trial-and-error system of swimming until it hits an obstruction or gets into an area that is too hot or too cold, too acid or too alkaline, then it backs out a little way and tries again. This avoiding reaction goes on until it gets away from an unfavorable area. So the animal, which knows only what it doesn't like, is a random system under normal circumstances and therefore a perfect surface on which PK can work by just tripping a balance minutely. It seems that man can do this with his mind.

These PK effects are being demonstrated by experimenters who have chosen to work in the fringe field of parapsychology. It is almost impossible to get finance for this kind of research; experiments are long and often very tedious, results are meager and difficult to publish, and scorn is plentiful and easy to find. It is safe to assume that anyone doing work in this area is an unusual person to begin with, so we cannot hold up Richmond, for instance, as proof that anyone can produce PK results. But even he came to the field without special training, so it is likely that with the right sort of approach, most people could do these things. If it is true that everyone has a latent PK ability, then a new question arises: Why? What do we get out of it? Gambling may be fun, but it is not a biological necessity. Pushing *Paramecium* around may be good for the ego, but it does not have real survival value. So why should evolution have given us this talent? The answer could be that there is a feedback and that the force field that carries our influence to the environment also brings information from it.

Hydra had nine heads, and whenever Hercules cut one off, two grew in its place. In the shallow water of unpolluted streams there is a naked little polyp that has the same ability and the same name. *Hydra pirardi* is just half an inch long with a body thin as thread that ends in five frayed tentacles. It has a marked preference for light and finds it in the same negative way as *Paramecium*. When a shadow, even that cast by its own body, reaches one of the tentacles, *Hydra* withdraws the arm abruptly and moves in the other direction. Its whole body is supersensitive to light, and yet it has no eyes or eyespots or light-sensitive cells of any kind. Light instead produces a chemical reaction in its body fluid—the viscosity of the protoplasm changes, fats saponify, and enzymes are inactivated. When light is removed, all these processes are reversed and the animal moves away and back into the light again. (38) This sensitivity is probably not confined to freshwater polyps.

EYELESS SIGHT

When the first white men arrived in Samoa, they found blind men that could see well enough to describe things in detail just by holding their hands over objects. In France just after the First World War, Jules Romain tested hundreds of blind people and found a few that could tell the difference between light and dark. He narrowed their photosensitivity down to areas on the nose or in the fingertips. In Italy the neurologist Cesare Lombroso discovered a blind girl who could "see" with the tip of her nose and the lobe of her left ear. When a bright light was shone unexpectedly on her ear, she winced. In 1956 a blind schoolboy in Scotland was taught to differentiate between colored lights and learned to pick out bright objects several feet away. In 1960 a medical board examined a girl in Virginia and found that, even with wads of bandage and tape over her eyes, she was able to distinguish different colors and read short sections of large print. (95) The phenomenon is obviously not new, but it has reached new peaks of sensitivity in a young woman from a mountain village in the Urals.

Rosa Kuleshova can see with her fingers. She is not blind, but growing up in a family of blind people she learned to read Braille to help them and then went on to teach herself to do other things with her hands. In 1962 her physician took her to Moscow, where she was examined by the Soviet Academy of Science and emerged a celebrity, certified as genuine. (161) The neurologist Shaefer made an intensive study with her and found that, securely blindfolded with only her arms stuck through a screen, she could differentiate among three primary colors. To test the possibility that the cards reflected heat differently, he heated some and cooled others, without affecting her response to them. He also found that she could read newsprint and sheet music under glass, so texture was giving her no clues. Tested by the psychologist Novomeisky, she was able to identify the color and shape of patches of light projected onto her palm or portrayed on an oscilloscope screen. In rigidly controlled tests, with a blindfold and a screen and a piece of card around her neck so wide that she could not see round it, Rosa read the small print in a newspaper with her elbow. And, in the most convincing demonstration of all, she repeated these things with someone standing behind her pressing hard on her eyeballs. (281) Nobody can cheat under this pressure; it is even difficult to see clearly for minutes after it is released.

Rosa really started something in Russia. Following her success, surveys were made and it was found that about one in six people could learn to recognize the difference between two colors after only an hour's training. Novomeisky soon had eighty students attending his classes in eyeless sight. They agreed that colors have textures that are more or less smooth to the touch. Yellow is very slippery, red is sticky, and violet has a braking effect on the fingers. (231) With the colored papers in insulated trays, they could feel these effects in the air above the cards. These students all had perfectly good eyes without their blindfolds, but at the Sverdlovsk Institute the same skills are being taught to the blind. Many sightless people say during these lessons that they were always aware of the difference in feel between the colors but that nobody ever told them what these meant. Some of the more advanced blind children at the Institute are reading colors through copper plate—they are "seeing" things invisible even to their teachers.

If light affects the chemistry of *Hydra* sufficiently to move it into a favorable environment, it does not seem unreasonable to assume that the body fluids of man could have some similar sensitivity. The fact that blind children are "seeing" with their ears and tongues and the tips of their toes, suggests that there are no special sensory cells at work but that the ability is scattered throughout the body and is one common to all cells. If this is true, it is possible that different frequencies and patterns of light affect the chemistry in different ways and that one can learn to appreciate this difference and distinguish among the sources of light. This explains why the Russians have found that the ability is best in bright light, and fades, exactly like normal sight, as darkness falls. But it does not explain why insulated trays help to broadcast the effect at a distance or why it fails when the objects, or the hands of the person, are electrically grounded. This may be where psychokinesis comes in.

Once again the ability is most strongly manifest in children and reaches a peak at the age of eleven. It could be that the human field plays a vital role in this kind of sensing, broadcasting in much the same way as the bat's sonar system, picking up echoes and translating them into meaningful patterns. When one of our primary senses fails, this branch of Supernature takes over to supplement the missing faculty, but even in normally sighted people it could be "feeling" the area in our immediate vicinity like the whiskers of a cat, giving us information that could be vital for survival.

If we do have a physiological response to light and this varies with the frequency of the light concerned, then this would explain some of the mystic values attached to colors. The apparent color of an object depends directly on the wavelength of the light it reflects, so it is possible that this physical difference could affect us in other ways. Manufacturers have discovered by trial and error that sugar sells badly in green wrappings, that blue foods are considered unpalatable, and that cosmetics should never be packaged in brown. These discoveries, given such commercial impetus, have grown into a whole discipline of color psychology that now finds application in everything from fashion to interior decoration. Some of our preferences are clearly psychological. Dark blue is the color of the night sky and therefore associated with passivity and quiescence, while yellow is a day color with associations of energy and incentive. For primitive man, activity during the day meant hunting and attacking, which he soon saw as red, the color of blood and rage and the heat that came with effort. So it was natural that green, the complementary color to red, should be associated with passive defense and self-preservation. Experiments have shown that colors, partly because of their psychological associations, also have a direct physiological effect. People exposed to bright red show an increase in respiration rate, heartbeat, and blood pressure; red is exciting. Similar exposure to pure blue has exactly the opposite effect; it is a calming color. Because of its exciting connotations, red was chosen as the signal for danger, but closer analysis shows that a vivid yellow can produce a more basic state of alertness and alarm, so fire engines and ambulances in some forward communities are now rushing around in bilious hues that stop the traffic dead.

Aesthetic, learned responses to color and more primitive, instinctive reactions have been combined into a very sensitive test of personality. The Lüscher Color Test was developed in Basel; it involves selection of personal preferences from a panel of twenty-five different hues. (301) Dark blue is said to represent "depth of feeling," bright yellow "spontaneity," orange-red "force of will," and so on. On the surface this sounds a little facile and suspiciously like the popular psychology of a newspaper horoscope, but the test concerns itself more with the order of preference and the detailed significance of color combinations. It is finding wide and enthusiastic reception in medicine, psychiatry, marriage guidance, and personnel selection.

A person's choice of color, in this test or for wallpaper in his bedroom, seems to be guided by the effect the color has on him, and can be used as an indication of his state of mind. A trained observer looks at the color and the person together and, by virtue of his special knowledge, can describe the connections between them. But we all have responses of the "My, that color suits you" kind. This could be because our own psychological reaction to that color agrees with our subjective assessment of that person's character, but the fact that there is usually widespread agreement about the combination suggests that something more basic is involved. I suggest that the principle of resonance is at work and that the wavelength of the color and the frequency of the person's field are in sympathy when we find their combined effect harmonious. This is a wildly mystical notion, fully in keeping with all the old superstitions about color, but it feels right to me when I look at the problem of color and camouflage.

The eggs of the lapwing plover are mottled, like the ground on which they rest; the wings of the carpet moth have a broken pattern, like the lichen-covered bark of its favorite trees; the body of the copperhead viper is a patchwork of hues exactly like the leaf litter in which it lives. All these wonderful effects serve the purpose of concealment and have been evolved over millions of years of natural selection, but they were not produced by the animals themselves. The colors and patterns cannot be seen by the animal wearing them; their effect is visible only at a distance, so an outside agency in the form of a predator has to come along like an art critic and pick out the least successful camouflage patterns, leaving the better ones alive to produce others of their kind.

This process works well over long periods of time, in which

adaptations occur over thousands of generations, but some species produce instant changes in their camouflage patterns. A chameleon very quickly takes on the pattern and the color best suited to any background on which it finds itself. Part of this ability depends on what it is able to see around it, but a completely blind chameleon still takes on the camouflage appropriate to its surroundings. It produces a pattern that, from a distance, harmonizes with the environment. This has long been a problem in biology, and I see no way of solving it now unless one assumes that there is a reciprocal interaction between the animal and its habitat. One has only to watch a chameleon in action to realize that it is not a matter of trial-and-error matching, of producing a black stripe on the tail because there is a corresponding black stripe just there on the background. What the reptile does is to assume a pattern that blends with the black stripe; it may not even be the same color, but it is always one that fits so well with the background that it is naturally congruous. The blind chameleon "suits" its surroundings; it does so in a flash, and from a distance the effect is perfect. It seems to me that this harmony can be explained only by assuming the existence of something like the life field, which picks up the frequency of the environment and translates this into an appropriate and resonant frequency of its own.

If such an ability exists, it could account for a phenomenon that is a cause of dissension even among occultists. Some claim that, just by holding an object, they can get information about its previous owners. Dealers in antiquities, whose livelihood depends on assessing objects correctly, will often just hold an Egyptian bronze cat or a piece of Mexican jade in their hands and say that it "feels right." They may be responding to any number of cues associated with the object, but can seldom point to any one as positive proof of authenticity, preferring to rely on a sense of "rightness" acquired by exposure to other objects with established pedigrees. This subliminal sensitivity is not uncommon, and although it is almost impossible to prove, it seems reasonable to assume that people leave some kind of mark on things around them. The alleged ability to read these traces has been called psychometry.

PSYCHOMETRY

A bloodhound can detect the traces of a particular person in a room long after he has left it, perhaps even after he has died elsewhere. The psychometrist claims to do the same, but not by smell. If a healer changes the structure of water just by holding it in his hand for half an hour, what effect does he have on a wristwatch he wears for half a lifetime? If a barley seed can tell the difference between ordinary and handled water, is it unreasonable to assume that a man can distinguish a brand-new object, untouched by human hand, from one that has been fondled for twenty years? I believe that there are differences and that they are discernible, but proving this is another matter. There have been casual tests made by presenting objects for psychometry in sealed containers, but no good, controlled investigation has yet been made. I predict that when one is, it will provide evidence of our ability to detect traces of human contact with things, but that there will be a limit to the amount of information we can get in this way. A fox can tell from traces on a tree not only that there is a male in the territory but who he is and what he last had to eat. Our territorial displays are now predominantly visual: the initials carved on the tree include a date and perhaps even an address, but there must have been a time when early man, with a comparatively poor sense of smell, could have made good use of a talent such as psychometry. (194) There are people today who claim to be able to tell the sex of the person who last used a particular Stone Age hand ax. This might once have been a very useful piece of information.

The nearest we can get to some sort of understanding of psychometry is an extraordinary series of experiments still going on in Czechoslovakia. They began with Robert Pavlita, design director of a textile plant near Prague. He invented a new weaving process that was so successful he could afford to retire and devote all his attention to his hobby of metallurgy. This continued until he discovered that an alloy of a particular shape had strange properties. If handled often, it seemed to accumulate energy and to attract even nonmagnetic objects. This sounds like electrostatic energy, which can be built up by friction in amber until it is strong enough to pick up paper, but static electricity does not work under water—and Pavlita's "generator" does.

He took it to the physics department at Hradec Králové University. There they sealed it on his instructions into a metal box alongside a small fan driven by an electric motor. Pavlita stood six feet away and did no more than stare hard at his generator. After a while the blade on the fan began to slow down, as though the current had been cut off; then it stopped altogether and began to rotate in the opposite direction. (233) For two years the department worked with him to try to unravel the mystery, but got nowhere. It has nothing to do with static electricity, air currents, temperature changes, or magnetism, but it works, and they now have a whole collection of generators in a variety of shapes that look like miniature metal sculptures by Brancusi. All of them have the same inexplicable ability to store energy from a particular person that can be released later to do a particular job, such as driving an electric motor.

At this point the government stepped in and appointed the physiologist Zdenek Rejdak to investigate the claims. He could find no indications of fraud and continued to work with Pavlita. Together they produced a generator shaped like a doughnut that killed flies placed inside the ring; then they went on to build a square one that accelerated the growth of bean seeds when placed in a pan of soil. And finally they turned out a small one that could be dropped into water polluted by factory effluent and would leave it crystal clear in a short while. An official chemical analysis of the water concluded that it could not have been purified with a chemical agent and added the splendid comment that the molecular structure of the water was slightly altered. Again this fact crops up, and we find reactions working first on the instability of the universal trigger substance—water.

So far the only theory put out about the generators is that their secret lies in the form, which is critical, and that only one configuration can produce a particular effect. These developments are very difficult to follow from a distance—as yet, no details of any of the generators have been published, but Pavlita has said that he got his original description and inspiration from an ancient manuscript, and we know that the libraries of Prague abound in untranslated and unexplored texts of the alchemists.

ALCHEMY

Alchemy flourished until 1661, when Robert Boyle published the *Sceptical Chymist* and demolished the old, Aristotelian idea of the four "elements"—fire, earth, air, and water. Eighty years later Black introduced quantitive chemistry, and soon after that Priestley discovered oxygen and Lavoisier analyzed air and water. This chemical revolution swept away the romance and adventure of the alchemist's quest and ushered in a new objectivity. The idea of converting one element into another was laughed out of the laboratory until in 1919

Lord Rutherford used alpha particles from a radioactive source to bombard nitrogen and turn it into oxygen. Today, with instruments such as the strong-focusing synchrotron, the transmutation of metals has become commonplace and the alchemists begin to look quite good.

There were two arms of alchemy, one outward and concerned with attempts to find the Philosopher's Stone, and the other hidden and more concerned with the development of a devotional system. The mundane transmutation of metals was merely symbolic of the transformation of man into something more perfect, through an exploration of nature's potential. The psychologist Jung realized this and regarded alchemy as the predecessor more of modern psychology than of modern chemistry. In his autobiography he makes it clear that he considers the roots of his psychology of the unconscious to have been firmly planted in the alchemical treatises that he spent ten years of his life studying. The elusive Stone was credited not only with the power of turning base metals into gold, but with the power also to prolong human life indefinitely. Colin Wilson describes this aspect of the search as "man's attempt to learn to make contact, at will, with the source of power, meaning and purpose in the depths of the mind, to overcome the dualities and ambiguities of everyday consciousness." (342)

The origins of alchemy lie in early agricultural communities, when technology had not yet been segregated from other aspects of daily life and the craftsmen who made metal farming implements and the dyes for weaving, carried out their trades to the accompaniment of religious and magical rites. The Egyptians, the Greeks, and the Arabs all contributed their skills and philosophies, and some great discoveries were made. In the Bagdad Museum are some stones found in a remote part of Iraq and classified as "ritual objects," but that have now been shown to be the cores of electric batteries invented two thousand years before Galvani. (240) Some pieces of bronze, dredged up off the shores of Greece at Antikythera and dated sixth century B.C., turn out to be components of an early computer for calculating astronomical positions. (333) So many of our proudest new achievements seem to have been anticipated by the alchemists and their contemporaries that one wonders what other lost skills we have yet to rediscover.

In the Mayan city of Chichén Itzá, in Yucatán, are hundreds of feet of reliefs, many carved almost in the round, by a people without metal tools. In the walls of the Incan city of Cuzco, in Peru, are vast blocks of stone of irregular shape that have been so perfectly cut that they jigsaw together without room to fit a knife blade between them. (290) Engineers and architects stand in awe of these achievements, which, with all our technical skills, we find hard to duplicate today. It may well have been done by a scientific development that has since been lost and smacks almost of psychokinesis. The Incas may have known how to soften stone. Colonel Fawcett, the British explorer who ultimately disappeared into the jungles of the Amazon, records in his diaries that on a walk along the river Perené, in Peru, a pair of large Mexican-type spurs were corroded to stumps in one day by the juice from a patch of low plants with red, fleshy leaves. A local rancher described them as "the stuff the Incas used for shaping stones." There are reports, too, of a small, kingfisher-like bird, probably the white-capped dipper *Cinclus leucocephalus,* which nests in spherical holes in the Bolivian Andes and bores these out of solid rock on the banks of mountain streams by rubbing a leaf on the stone until it is soft and can be pecked away. It seems that the Incas knew enough about chemistry to extract and distill this same substance. An excavation of a burial ground in central Peru turned up an earthenware jug containing a black viscous fluid that, when spilled on the ground, turned the rocks on which it fell into a soft, malleable putty.

This is the kind of discovery that most delighted the alchemists. In the course of working toward a higher consciousness, they learned almost by accident how to control matter and to liberate energy, so it is by no means impossible that in one of their texts are instructions for making generators like those of Robert Pavlita. Perhaps one of them was long and thin and looked like a magic wand.

One thing magic and science have in common is that both operate on the assumption that there is some scheme of order and regularity in the universe. Both attempt to discover this scheme by establishing relationships between things that are superficially different, and by analogical reasoning. The search for order is the only way life can survive in a cosmos tending toward maximum disorder. In man the search becomes more complex, because he looks not only for order but for meaning, so that he may be sure of being able to rediscover or even re-create that order. Superstition is one of the prices we pay for our habit of constantly scanning for patterns in everything. As Konrad Lorenz puts it, magic rituals have "a common root in behaviour mechanism whose species-preserving function is obvious; for a living being lacking insight into the relation between causes and effects it must be extremely useful to cling to a behaviour pattern which has once or many times proved to achieve its aim, and to have done so without danger." (203) In other words, if success follows a complex set of actions and you do not know which parts of the whole performance were the vital ones, it is best to repeat all of them exactly and slavishly every time, because "You never know what might happen if you don't."

So the Pedi, in South Africa, believe that infection can be cured by eating grain that has been chewed by a cross-eyed child and hung for three days in a gourd shaped like a snake that is suspended from a particular tree that grows near the water. And they are right, because under these conditions the grain grows a mold like *Penicillium*, with antibiotic properties, but the child's eyes and the gourd's shape and the species of the tree do not necessarily have anything to do with the cure. In just this way, alchemy stumbled on some great truths but produced theoretical structures in which the line of reasoning between cause and effect was cluttered up with all sorts of irrelevant mystical and magical red herrings. This has discouraged modern science from investigating the source material, which is a pity, because we can probably still learn a great deal from a discipline that flourished for over two thousand years and included devotees such as Roger Bacon, Thomas Aquinas, Ben Jonson, and even Isaac Newton.

The role of sympathetic magic and of superstition in psychokinetic phenomena is undoubtedly a large one, but I believe that, even without these props, we now have enough evidence to warrant the serious consideration of PK as a biological reality. There is a long way to go before we understand how it works, but we can already begin to think about its evolutionary implications. In man the ability seems to be manifest mainly in children, or essentially childlike personalities, and then most often as a casual, almost accidental effect. It is apparantly important to believe that the mind can influence matter, or at least not to disbelieve that it can. This suggests that its origins lie in some more primitive condition, which is preserved in the unconscious and later smothered by acquired cultural and intellectual pressures. But learning to produce PK effects on demand, by a conscious physical process, is probably a new development altogether.

We have no evidence as yet to suggest that any other species is capable of producing psychokinetic effects. We describe them as "mind over matter," but consciousness may not be a necessary precondition for PK. It is possible that many organisms at all levels of development are capable of generating the force fields that seem to be responsible for action at a distance. If this is true, then the ability could well turn out to be a major biological determinant, forging even closer bonds between life and its environment than even the most visionary ecologists dreamed possible.

I suspect that Supernature holds many such surprises in store.

PART THREE

MIND

"The answer is 'yes' or 'no,' depending on the interpretation."

ALBERT EINSTEIN, in *Scientific American*, April 1950.

MATTER IS A FORM of energy. Living matter is energy organized in such a way that it retains its unstable state. The brain is that part of living matter given over to the coordination of such organization. So far so good, but the next stage in evolution is impossible to describe in these simple, mechanistic terms. Life is an affair of chemistry and physics, but the mind is not amenable to this kind of analysis; it seems to be independent of energy.

Mind is something we experience, rather than something we observe. The physiologist watches an electric tide that sweeps across the living brain and rightly interprets this as one of the signs of mind, but his instruments cannot cope with the monster that produced these ripples on the surface. The ethologist studies patterns of behavior, and in these, too, he can see manifestations of mind; he can even produce behavioral changes that seem to depend on a change of mind; but none of this gets him very much closer to the problem. The mind is responsible for awareness, and probably the greatest contribution yet made by comparative ethology is the discovery that something like consciousness exists in other species and must have evolved a number of times in the course of evolution.

During the past five million years, evolution seems to have concentrated most of its creative energy in the process of human development. This intensity has produced a species substantially different from even his nearest living relatives, but I believe that even in the nebulous affairs of the mind this difference is largely one of degree. I have no intention of belittling the importance of the distinctions between man and other animals, but I cannot agree with those who would place man outside the order of nature. Lists of distinctive human characteristics usually include such things as his capacity for abstract thought, his ability to make and use symbols, and his engagement in apparently meaningless patterns such as play. But we now know that even birds can form abstract concepts—ravens can be taught to choose a food dish on the basis only of the number of spots with which it is marked. The dance language of the bees is a marvel of symbolism, indicating by movements such complex information as what to look for, in which direction, how far, and what lies in the way. And play not only occurs in animals but can take on almost aesthetic overtones—as in the absorption and skill shown by a chimpanzee with a paintbrush.

To me this continuity suggests that none of man's qualities is new. No component of our brain or behavior has been added by supernatural means to make us what we are. Not one of our abilities can be denied to some other animal somewhere, but what we have done is to arrange everything in an entirely new way. Man is a unique pattern, a new and powerful combination of old talents. For a long time, one or more of these abilities have been predominant and effectively masked the others, but we are now beginning to rediscover more of our extraordinary gifts.

In this section I want to look at some of the signs of mind and at the strange things we can do with it.

Chapter Six:
Signs of Mind

In 1957, following a series of nuclear weapons tests in the Pacific, concern began to grow about the dangers of radioactive fallout. The World Health Organization issued a warning in March that year about the genetic effects of radiation, and very soon afterward medical physiologists in several places reported with horror that the white-blood-cell count in a very large number of patients was undergoing a rapid and possibly damaging change. As it happened those effects were being produced by radiation from nuclear reaction—but not in the Pacific. The years 1957 and 1958 were ones of tremendous activity, but of a type beyond the controls of any test-ban treaty, because the explosions that irradiated earth were taking place in the sun. (300)

This discovery is now included in a growing body of knowledge that demonstrates the sensitivity of life to subtle stimuli, but time and again we still make the mistake of assuming that only the dramatic and obvious events around us can be of any importance. This kind of myopia has come to be known as the "Clever Hans" error in honor of a famous problem-solving horse who mystified scientists in nineteenth-century Europe. They believed that the animal was solving problems set out on a blackboard in front of it, while it was actually getting the information it needed for correct answers by watching the involuntary gestures made by the scientists themselves in expectation of these answers. A large part of animal communication is based on the interpretation of very slight manifestations of mood in others of its kind, and the horse simply responded to the gathering of very distinguished scientists as though they, too, were horses.

In physiological terms, the gulf that separates us from other animals is not a wide one, and despite the fact that we now have an elaborate vocal language and other sophisticated communication systems, our bodies continue to show external signs of our inner feelings. Instinctively we continue to respond to these signals. We can listen to a discussion on the radio and understand exactly what the speaker is trying to communicate, but where more spontaneous, emotional material is involved, we find the lack of vision a serious handicap. Anyone who has ever used a telephone knows how difficult it is to convey really complex feelings with the voice alone and how comparatively easy it is to tell lies to someone who cannot watch you while you do so. Deaf people, who miss the information provided by the voice, learn again to communicate by gesture alone, and now this old talent has been made a new psychoanalytic and research tool by students of body language, or kinesics. (100)

Laboratory and clinical studies of body language have shown that it often directly contradicts verbal communication and that the person who says "I am not afraid" will at the same time be sending out automatic signals that betray his fear. This outward manifestation of an inner feeling is by no means restricted to the long muscles; it shows up even in the eyes. (147) Eckhard Hess at the University of Chicago discovered that there was a direct relation between pupil size and mental activity. In a series of tests in which subjects' eyes were photographed as they watched changing pictures, he found that the pupils expanded when looking at something interesting or appealing, and contracted when exposed to anything distasteful or unappealing. And the fact that we automatically respond to these changes in another person was demonstrated by showing a group of male subjects two pictures of an attractive girl that were identical except that her pupils in one of the pictures had been retouched to make them larger. When questioned about these photographs, the subjects reported that they could see no difference between them, but their eyes showed that they responded very much more strongly to the girl with large pupils. They presumably found her more attractive because unconsciously they were reading her signal, which says "I am very interested in you."

It is not surprising that the response of the pupil should be connected directly with mental activity. Embryologically and anatomically the eye is an extension of the brain, and looking into it is almost like peering through a peephole into a part of the brain itself. The reflex action of the eye in response to light is determined by the parasympathetic nervous system, and the emotional response is brought about by the sympathetic system. So both branches of our autonomic nerve network are involved, and we can expect to find that other parts of the body supplied by these systems are also going to show signs of mind.

In emotional situations, pupil reactions are connected with an increase in the heart rate and blood pressure, more rapid respiration, and greater sweating. One of the first places in which sweat appears is on the palms of the hands, in what is known as a psychogalvanic response. This is an electrical storm in the skin that suddenly breaks when the owner of the palm becomes anxious. It is used extensively in the so-called lie-detector tests, which measure the electrical resistance of the skin. The results of the tests are not usually acceptable in a court of law, because they give no indication of truth or falsity, but they do provide a measurement of emotional stress. Often this state is apparent from a distance when a nervous man rubs wet palms together or wipes them down his thighs to dry them. It is also of course immediately apparent when shaking hands, and this offers an explanation for the origin of the custom, which makes more biological sense than the traditional one of indicating a lack of weapons.

The reason for sweating on the palms of the hands rather than on the elbows or behind the ears seems to be connected with another kind of signaling from a distance: communication by smell. Most mammals mark out their territories with the secretion from special scent glands. Some antelope have glands in their feet and leave distinctive tracks wherever they go; others have to trample in their dung and carry the smell of this around with them on their feet. Tree shrews first prepare a little puddle of urine, trip about in it, and then scamper around, leaving smelly footprints everywhere. Bush-babies and lemurs urinate directly onto their hands before the leap, so every handhold becomes an advertisement for the occupier as distinctive as the nameplates we put up on our office doors and gateposts.

In a primate the most obvious areas for spreading smell are the hairless palms and the soles of the feet. Most of the higher primates have developed a sense of sight at the expense of their sense of smell, but they still seem to use their noses a great deal. None of the great apes urinate on their hands, but all of them have well-developed sweat glands on the palms, and these seem to carry a smell that is distinctive for every individual. One does not have to be a chimpanzee to appreciate the differences. Part of the palm smell is produced by food—just try smelling your hands a few hours after eating asparagus and you will find that the distinctive smell comes right through the pores of your skin. But part of every smell is also sexual in origin. Internal physiology is regulated by hormones, and it is now known that similar chemicals are secreted externally for communication and the regulation of the physiology of others. These are pheromones; migratory locusts secrete them to accelerate the growth of their young, ants use them to lay trails to and from the nest, female moths use them to attract males from a great distance. In man, striking sexual differences have been found in the ability to smell certain substances. (343) A French biologist has reported that the odor of a synthetic lactone can be detected only by mature females and is perceived most clearly at the time of ovulation. Men and young girls cannot smell this substance at all—unless they first have a huge injection of the female hormone estrogen. It seems that a chemical very like this one is part of man's natural bouquet and is secreted through sweat glands, largely in the palms of the hands.

So the palm not only becomes moist in moments of emotional stress, but in doing so it also communicates intentions, sex, and individual identity.

PALMISTRY

Apart from a unique smell, each person also carries an exclusive pattern in his hands. The dermis of the skin has a distinctive assortment of loops, whorls, and arches in the fingertips and on the palm. This is unlike any design ever borne by any other person. There is no authenticated case of indistinguishable patterns, even in so-called identical twins, so the shapes have been used for identification purposes ever since the Chinese perfected a system of classification in A.D. 700.

Dermatoglyphics is the study of the ridge and furrow patterns on the palms and on the soles of the feet. These are the designs that have always been used in police work and as such have been the subject of serious statistical study in several countries for a long time. More recently the patterns have become of interest to geneticists, because they show hereditary characters and, forming during the third or fourth month of fetal development, persist unchanged throughout life. The distribution of the ridges is determined by the arrangement of sweat glands and nerve endings and is so firmly established that it is impossible to destroy or change the patterns permanently. They reappear as healing brings the natural skin to the surface again after severe burns and even after skin grafting.

There is little controversy surrounding the ridges, as these are not the marks used by gypsy fortunetellers. Jan Purkinje, a Czechoslovakian physician, was the first to describe the patterns, and his classification and interpretation are still followed. In London, a Society for the Study of Physiological Patterns in the Hand has begun to collect data in an attempt to establish connections between distinctive patterns and certain pathological conditions. So far the results look promising, but far more are needed for statistical significance.

Superimposed on the art-nouveau background of finely etched designs in the hand are the more obvious lines and creases. These are the stuff of the fairground palmist, and surprisingly, it is with these lines that we find some exciting biological correlations. Anatomists describe the creases in the palm as "lines of flexure," but there is no good functional reason for these lines to fall in one position rather than another. Every hand seems to have its own idiosyncrasies, and the palmists insist that these mean something.

Sir Francis Galton, a cousin of Charles Darwin, was one of the first reputable scientists to take the idea of palmar diagnosis seriously. He made a collection of palm prints and presented them to the University of London at the same time that he endowed a professorship there and founded the science of eugenics. The Galton Laboratory has carried on with these studies and in 1959 showed that Mongolism was due to a chromosomal abnormality that also produced a characteristic line, known as the "simian crease," across the top of the palm. (158) Since then, about thirty different congenital disorders have been connected with particular patterns in the palm, some of which are apparent even before the disease appears. In 1966, abnormal palm prints were linked for the first time with a virus infection. Three New York pediatricians palm-printed babies born to mothers who had caught German measles during early pregnancy and found that, even if the babies were not affected in any other way, all had a characteristic and unusual crease in their hands. (306)

In 1967 a team of Japanese doctors extended their system of baby identification to include patients of all ages admitted to an Osaka hospital. After collecting over two hundred thousand prints and their relevant case histories, they discovered that there were many correlations between the patterns and the diseases treated. They claim that not only is the position of a particular line important, but that its length, breadth, the degree to which it has been broken up into islands or triangles, and even its color have diagnostic significance. They are now able to tell just by looking at a palm print, whether a patient is suffering or has recently suffered from organic diseases such as thyroid deficiency, spinal deformation, and liver and kidney malfunctions. They also say that it is possible to predict with a high degree of accuracy, whether a particular patient is likely to contract infectious diseases such as tuberculosis and perhaps even cancer.

There are an enormous number of nerves ending in the hand in sensors of heat and cold, pressure and pain. So many of these make direct connections with the brain that if human proportions were determined only by the nerve supply, we would have hands the size of beach umbrellas. If the palmists are right in asserting that these nerves carry a two-way traffic and that all internal physical conditions are mirrored externally in our palms, then it makes very little sense for a general practitioner to ask to see a patient's tongue. Even going on the evidence already clearly established, he could learn a great deal more by saying, "Good morning. How are you? Please put out your hand."

Fortunetelling by lines in the hand bears the same relationship to the serious study of chirology as newspaper horoscopes do to true astrology. Chirologists are concerned with the whole picture presented by the hand. They study the basic skin pattern with a magnifying glass to find changes in the texture and rhythm; they look at all the flexure lines and at the smaller lines that cross them, paying particular attention to the ways in which these are broken or intersect; they feel the underlying muscles and tendons and take note of the mounds and ridges these produce; they study the thickness and form of the palm, the relative lengths of fingers and thumb, the flexibility and shape of the joints, and the color and texture of the nails and skin. Only after making all these observations will a serious chirologist attempt to draw the threads together and make some assessment of the subject's physical and psychological condition.

The basic physiology behind their assumptions seems to be sound. The brain, the nervous system, and the sense organs are all derived from the ectoderm of the embryo at the same time as the skin. Their common origin means that they maintain very close connections throughout life, and it is not at all unreasonable to assume that many internal events will show up externally through the skin. Jaundice, a liver disease, typically shows up during the early stages as a yellow discoloration of the skin. Rheumatoid arthritis, which attacks the joints of small bones, may also appear as dry, silvery scales on the skin. These are obvious, external changes, but a great number of other internal physical disorders could well produce more subtle effects that can be recognized only by careful study of sensitive areas of skin such as those of the hand. There is certainly a very close connection between most skin diseases and mental states. Dermatitis, urticaria, acne, warts, and allergic reactions are all skin conditions that are produced almost entirely by anxiety and other types of emotional stress. So, theoretically there is no reason why it should not be possible to make judgments about a person's prevailing mental condition, and therefore about his personality, from signs appearing in the skin.

Most of these conditions affect only the general pattern and texture of the skin. The connection between internal physical and mental states and the crease lines in the palm is more difficult to establish. The lines do not follow the patterns of skeleton, muscles, tendons, blood vessels, nerves, or lymph or sweat glands. Anatomists claim that the creases are entirely random and concerned only with allowing the flesh of the palm to fold when the hand forms a fist. The characteristic and basic division of the palm by two roughly horizontal lines (the ones the palmists call Head and Heart) and two roughly vertical lines (those of Fate and Life), are almost certainly produced by the resolution of the various physical forces set up in the hand by flexion and tension. There does, however, seem to be some other principle, which governs their exact shape and the continually changing appearance of the smaller creases. If physical forces alone were responsible, one would expect the lines to remain stable in the hand of a man whose way of life and work were relatively constant from day to day, but long-term studies show that there is a constant fluctuation in the palm patterns. There is one dramatic record of a house painter who fell from a great height and suffered such severe concussion that he remained unconscious for two weeks and had to be intravenously fed. After a week in this condition, all the creases in his hands vanished as though they had been wiped off with a sponge—and then, as he regained consciousness, the lines gradually reappeared. (158)

Death masks are often most unlike the living person. Throughout life, even in deep sleep, the many fine muscles of the face are in states of variable tension produced by constant stimulation from the brain. The total effect of these waves of activity is to produce a pattern of expression that gives each face its unique features. (344) It is likely that a similar supply goes out from the brain to all parts of the body and constantly reinforces form and function. The exact pattern of the palm print, like that of the heartbeat or the life field, seems to depend on the maintenance of these signals, because the lines in the hand begin to break down when the impulses cease, at the moment of death.

The signals from the brain also determine how the hand will be used. In this, the science of body language is paralleled by an older one, in which the gestures are much more subtle, each one, however, being recorded at the time of performance in a written code that can be examined and analyzed at leisure.

GRAPHOLOGY

Camillo Baldo in 1622 published the first known book on the subject, which bore the title *Treating of How a Written*

Message May Reveal the Nature of Qualities of the Writer.
He was followed by Goethe, the Brownings, Poe, Van Gogh,
Mendelssohn, and Freud. Today graphologists, like the serious chirologists, have quantified their science and lifted handwriting analysis out of its fairground atmosphere to make it a
useful tool now widely used in psychoanalysis and in educa-
tional and vocational guidance.

There is nothing instinctive in handwriting; nobody is born
with the ability to put pen to paper. It is strictly a learned
pattern of behavior that has to be acquired over years of
painstaking effort under the careful scrutiny of a teacher. So
all written records show cultural and environmental patterns
that depend purely on where and when a person learned to
transcribe the traditional symbols. But after years of practicing the skill it becomes mechanical, and the automatic actions
are influenced more by personal factors. In an adult, the pen
places one letter after another almost unconsciously, while the
mind moves around the sound of the word. Between the
thought and the final result there is ample room for the expression of character, and there can be very little doubt
that the shape of each line in every letter carries the mark of
the author.

There are many examples of animals that show individual
differences in learned patterns of behavior. Young squirrels
encountering a hard-shelled nut for the first time make in-
discriminate scraping patterns on it with their teeth until at
last the nut yields and breaks open. As they gain more experience, they learn how best to apply the minimum effort
for the maximum return by following the fibers in the shell
and not working against the grain. Techniques differ in that
some individuals gnaw a piece out of the apex of the nut,
some make furrows running up to meet at the apex, some
circle the apex and lift off the lid, and some slice the nut
neatly and completely in half. (337) Each squirrel leaves a

pattern so distinctive that an expert can go into a forest and tell, just by looking at the shells, how many animals were involved. If he happens to be a good game ranger, then he can file "toothprints" of all the squirrels living in the area and not only keep track of their development and whereabouts but even get an idea of each individual's state of health.

There is a definite connection between handwriting and health. Some analysts claim that they can detect specific sicknesses from the script. It is true that loss of co-ordination due to something like Parkinson's disease would certainly produce gross deformation in writing. The American Medical Association reports, "There are definite organic diseases that grapho-diagnostics can help to diagnose from their earliest beginnings." (158) They list anemia, blood poisoning, tumors, and various bone diseases among these, but add that old age can produce substantially the same signs. A few skilled geriatricians believe that it is possible to use handwriting as a sort of X ray to distinguish between actual mental unbalance and normal senility. The general disruption of handwriting patterns that occurs in both emotional and physical disorders is clearly recognizable and almost impossible to disguise.

Like the serious astrologer or chirologist, a good graphologist is concerned with details. Before making an assessment, he collects several samples of script produced at different times, preferably with different pens, and never works with material specifically written for analysis. He examines the slant and weight of the writing; looks at margins, spacing, rhythm, and legibility; watches punctuation and the way in which t is crossed and i and j are dotted; studies the shape of loops and the way in which strokes begin and end. With all these characters, repetition is considered to be important; the more often a trait is recorded in the script, the stronger it is thought to be. The relative frequency is also measured, so patterns that indicate contrasting traits can be reconciled. If only a limited amount of script is available for analysis, graphologists can get most information from the signature of the subject. This is something that is written so often and with such specific reference to self that it becomes a stylized representation of the writer as unique as a fingerprint. Hence its use for the purposes of identification.

In the assessment of all behavior patterns, it is necessary to decide how much is determined purely by functional requirements, and once this quantity has been subtracted, the rest can be used as an indication of cultural and personal preferences. An aboriginal tribesman puts on as much clothing as is necessary to protect him from the sun or the cold, and whatever is worn over and above this must be there for other reasons; but great care should be exercised in attributing value to the extra items. They may be worn for traditional and cultural reasons, for the sake of convention and modesty, or there may be religious or magical significance in the garments, or perhaps social values, such as status or position, may be involved. Only when all these possibilities have been exhausted can we pick out, say, a necklace of cowrie shells, and say that these express the individual's personality and that he must be an outgoing character with a fine appreciation of nature. Then we discover that cowries are the local form of currency and that he was just on his way out to buy a new harpoon. This kind of pitfall is common to the life sciences and applies directly to studies such as graphology.

In writing, the letters and words are symbols of language and ideas. They are functional signals that have been dressed up in patterns with a variety of traditional and cultural nuances. With experience it is impossible to strip away the well-rounded curves; long sloping up-and-down strokes; and the liberal ornamentation that are affirmations of national identity and indicate only that the writer learned to use his pen in France. It should also be possible to recognize the fact that heavy lines may be caused by nothing more than the poor quality of the paper in an undeveloped country or the current fashion for felt-tipped pens in a prosperous one. This kind of preliminary scrutiny is not always done with the necessary care, but beneath all the misleading surface details there seem to be a number of basic patterns in graphology that can be used as a valid scientific means of assessing individual character.

I believe we all respond to subtle signals in other people's script even without training, and that a letter from a loved one carries an unconsciously coded message in every line and flourish that is quite distinct from the sense of the words involved. Why else should we be upset by a typewritten letter from a close friend, unless the machine comes between us and destroys the chance of reading the lines themselves?

An American psychologist says, "How long you make your strokes, how wide your loops, where you put the dot over the i, isn't a matter of chance. It's governed by the laws of personality; . . . the movements you make while writing are like gestures—they express what you feel. Anything that moves you, disturbs you or excites you—either emotionally or physically—shows up in the marks you make with your pen." (158) So now General Motors, General Electric, US Steel, and the Firestone Tire and Rubber Company all employ full-time executives to do nothing but watch these marks—and they seem to be earning their salaries.

The hand and its behavior provide one of the most sensitive external measures of the workings of the brain, but there are other outward signs of mind.

PHYSIOGNOMY

Most amoebae multiply in the immortal manner—splitting down the middle to form two daughter cells and then doing it again and again as necessary. But there are some species that go in for communal reproduction, getting together in groups of up to half a million that form a special sexual organism. *Dictyostelium discoideum* is normally an independent single cell that flows around in the usual erratic amoeba way, but whenever food is in short supply and there are a number of other amoebae around, the cells get together at central collection points and build towers that grow until they topple over into a small, glittering mass. This blob takes on a bullet shape and becomes a slug with a distinct front and back end, shows a communal sensitivity to heat and light, and migrates as one purposeful being to the most favorable environment. There it stands on end, forms a long, thin stalk, and lifts a spherical mass of cells up into the air like a balloon on a string. The separate amoebae making up the structure take on different functions, some forming the supporting stalk and others becoming spores that will be wafted away to liberate new free-living amoebae somewhere else.

This joint effort in a single-celled organism is a remarkable development. John Bonner has discovered that it is made possible by the fact that all amoebae are not created equal. There are visible differences between those that are destined to become the stalk and those that will be spores: the stalk makers are slightly larger than the others and move more quickly. So even in a society as old as this slug it is possible to pick out individuals on the basis only of their appearance and to use this to describe their behavior patterns and to predict their destinies.

In more complex organisms there are even more clues to work with; whole branches of science, such as paleontology, are forced to draw inferences about diet, habitat, and behavior directly from what is known about the structure of species long since extinct. Collaboration between engineer George Whitfield and zoologist Cherrie Bramwell at the Uni-

versity of Reading has produced new deductive information
of this kind about *Pteranodon ingens,* the largest flying creature ever to exist. (340) Working from scattered pieces of
skeleton, like a team rebuilding a crashed airliner, they es-
timate its wingspan at twenty-three feet and total weight at
only thirty-five pounds—and from this information deduce
that it was poor at powered flight, but was a very efficient
glider with an extremely low rate of sink and a very low flying
and stalling speed. These clues, together with a study of the
teeth, suggest that this vulturine gliding reptile lived at sea,
soaring in the rising air where the wind blows over the waves
and diving to snatch fish off the surface. They also suggest
that it nested on cliffs facing the sea and the prevailing wind,
and returned to its home by soaring up the face and flopping
down gently on the top. Putting a fossil head into a wind
tunnel, they discovered that the long, thin, bony blade pro-
jecting from the back of *Pteranodon*'s head was an aerody-
namic fin that balanced the loads on the beak when the head
swung from side to side in its search for prey. And that this
development allowed the animal to economize on the weight
of neck muscles and made it even better suited to the light
winds and warm, shallow seas of the Cretaceous.

Similar feats of scientific detection play a large part in the
search for man's ancestors. Dubois, who discovered the famous fossil man of Java in 1891, had nothing but a few teeth
to start with, but using these together with the skullcap and
a piece of thighbone, he was able to predict that Java Man was
primitive, with a brain midway in size between man and
gorilla, and that he walked erect. Later and more complete
finds showed that this diagnosis was correct. (346)

If reasoning of this kind is capable of producing verifiable
results with fossil forms, there is no reason why it should not
apply equally well to living ones. We know that the physique
of many men is directly related to the climate in which they

live. The Dinka people of Africa are tall and thin, because this gives them the greatest possible surface area for their body weight and helps them lose heat most effectively, while the Eskimo are comparatively short and padded with fat to conserve heat. The faces of Mongol people from northeast Asia are flat, which reduces frostbite; have fat-lidded eyes, which are thus protected against glare and snowblindness; and are smooth-skinned, which reduces the risk of condensation on hair around the mouth. Equatorial people tend to be dark-skinned, with a pigment that protects deeper layers from the sun, while Nordic people are very fair and able to take maximum advantage of occasional sunlight to promote the formation of vitamin D in their skins. (15) This sort of climatic engineering makes it possible to look at a man's shape and deduce something about his, or his ancestors', habitat and way of life. To a certain extent, this knowledge will tell us a little about his character, but it may be possible to tell quite a lot about personality types by looking directly at physical appearance alone.

Aristotle and Plato considered the idea, but the first scientific work on physiognomy—"knowledge from the body"—was produced by Johann Lavater, a nineteenth-century Swiss mystic. Charles Darwin included similar ideas in his *The Expression of the Emotions in Man and Animals* and pointed out that special body structures were evolved to signal certain emotions and that it would be reasonable to deduce from the presence of these structures that the relevant emotion played a large part in that animal's life. In more recent and less scholarly works on physiognomy, writers have tended to make rather fanciful generalizations such as "an indented chin is a certain sign of a warm, loving disposition," which, if they have any meaning at all, can only be applied to small, localized groups of people. And yet, if one wades through the literature on physiognomy, there is a germ of truth that makes biological sense.

Taking man as a single species, it is possible to see certain basic patterns of shape and proportion. The height of a man is usually six times the length of his foot; the face from the top of the forehead to the point of the chin measures one tenth of the height; the hand from the wrist to the tip of the middle finger is usually the same as the face from the hair line to the chin; the distance from the hair to the eyebrows is the same as that from the eyebrows to the nostrils and from the nostrils to the chin; and the height is normally equal to the distance between the fingertips with arms extended sideways. It is interesting that these world-wide human "norms" are exactly the proportions considered most harmonious by the classic Greek sculptors. There is naturally a tremendous variation over the world, but national, racial, and cultural averages can be established, and if an individual varies significantly from these standards, there must be a good biological reason for the deviation. William Sheldon in 1940 worked out a system of somatotyping that recognizes three extremes of body shape: The endomorph is essentially rounded, with a round head, a bulbous stomach, a heavy build, and a lot of fat, but he is not necessarily a fat man and does not change to another category when he loses weight—he just becomes a thin endomorph. The mesomorph is the classic sculptors' model, with a large head, broad shoulders, a lot of muscle and bone, not much fat, and relatively narrow hips. And the ectomorph is all sharp corners and angles, with spindly limbs, narrow shoulders and hips, and little muscle, so that even when fattened up he does not become an endomorph. (306) Everyone has a little of all three in his makeup, and a random group of people, say those called up for jury duty or traveling in the same train, will show all possible combinations, but a group chosen for particular physical prowess will favor certain shapes. Olympic athletes are seldom endomorphic. There does not, however, seem to be any correlation between shape and intelligence—a group of university graduates show a completely random pattern of combinations.

PHRENOLOGY

Franz Gall, an anatomist working in Vienna at the end of the eighteenth century, made a special study of neurology and decided that the brain was responsible for producing the phenomena of mind. For this heresy he was expelled from Catholic Austria. He continued with his work in exile and decided that not only were emotions produced in the head, but that different ones arose in different parts of the brain. (226) This was an astute and revolutionary idea at a time when the orthodox view was that the brain, whatever it did, worked as a whole. Up to this point Gall was absolutely right, but then he went off at a tangent and began to ascribe functions to parts of the brain on the flimsiest evidence. He remembered that two of his school friends with good memories also happened to have bulging eyes, and concluded from this that the faculty of memory must be located in the frontal lobes of the brain, just behind the eyes. He chose sites in the cerebral hemispheres for the functions of language and calculation on similarly vague grounds and published all his theories in a book that, much later, gave rise to the craze of phrenology. European society discovered it with delight, and "bumps on the head" became a fashionable parlor pastime in London and Paris. Life-size, bald, china heads were produced as guides, suitably inscribed with a patchwork labeled "sublimity," "ideality," "benevolence," and that splendid Victorian substitute for sex—"philoprogenitiveness." The subject quickly fell into disrepute, and serious anatomists ignored it altogether, which was a pity, because it embodied a useful idea that was lost for 150 years.

The phrenologists made two basic mistakes. They assumed that, if a faculty was particularly well developed in someone, then that part of the brain in which it was thought to be located would also be large and well developed; and they thought that these bulges in the brain produced corresponding bumps and indentations on the surface of the skull. Today we know that the volume of the brain has little to do with its effectiveness (Byron had a very small brain) and that bumps on the head are produced by thickening on the outside of the skull. There is no similarity between the ripples on the inside of the brain case and the bulges outside. But the phrenologists were right about functions being localized in certain areas of the brain—there is a center of language and another that controls sexual activity. It was not until 1939, when experiments were done on monkeys with parts of their brains removed, that science really grasped the fact that character and personality were localized in specific areas. In one operation, alterations were made to only one side of the brain, so that, with the left eye open, the monkey was violent and aggressive, and looking only through its right eye, it became indifferent and docile. Which, incidentally, provides an anatomical basis for the old belief that witches have one "evil eye," whose powers differ markedly from the other one.

While there may not be bumps of aggression on the head, the brain areas responsible for initiating aggressive behavior do set up patterns of muscle action that usually follow the same paths. A baboon has a repertoire of three basic facial expressions that accompany attack, aggressive-threat, and scared-threat behavior. In all these expressions, the eyes are open wide, and, depending on the level of aggression, the eyebrows move from a lowered frown up into a raised position. Constant repetition of these patterns by an individual in an insecure hierarchical position leaves its mark on his face. Vertical and horizontal lines begin to appear permanently on the forehead and produce a visible, external sign of a prevailing emotional state. Physiognomy works to the extent that it is possible to look at such an animal or man and predict that he will probably be more than ordinarily aggressive.

In apes and man a state of pleasure is indicated by a relaxation of the eyes and, at a high level, by an automatic inflation of small pouches on the lower eyelid. This response cannot be faked; it appears only in genuine happiness, and if it takes place often, leaves the pouch in a permanent state of partial inflation. This character has only recently been recorded by physiologists and ethologists, but it is well described in all the works on physiognomy.

The connection between other internal states and external appearance is less obvious. Physiognomists traditionally equate the round-faced, endomorphic type with a personality involving good humor and adaptability; the mesomorphic face, with the strong bone and muscle structure, is said to indicate an energetic and forceful character; and the slender, pear-shaped, ectomorphic face is supposed to show imagination and sensitivity. Broadly speaking, most psychologists agree with this assessment as applied to the extreme examples of the three types, but it is a generalization of little real value. Another criterion often used is the position of the ear: the farther back on the head it lies, the greater the intellect is said to be. Embryonically its position is determined by that of the auditory nerve, which will sometimes be displaced if the cortical area of the brain is well developed—so there may be something in this belief. The unsubstantiated idea of a strong, hooked nose being the sign of a leader probably originated in Roman times, when people with such noses did lead, but it would be fruitless to look for a nose of this shape among the very capable Asian and African leaders of the present. Many other physiognomic characters, such as red hair, brown eyes, and thick lips are similarly associated with racial stereotypes and mean nothing. Birds of prey kill for a living, and so we associate hooked beaks with violent and aggressive behavior, and we contrast this with the stereotype of the soft-billed, gentle dove. Nothing could be further from the truth. The social life of most birds of prey is quiet and well ordered, whereas there are few things more bloody and destructive than the battle between rival male doves. We tend to make the same sort of mistake in our estimation of human character and behavior.

The small strengths of physiognomy lie partly in physiology and partly in behavior. There are medical conditions, such as hyperthyroidism, that result in an excess of the thyroid hormone and produce over-activity and excitability—and one of the classic symptoms of the disorder is bulging eyes. There are external characters that can be acquired by the constant repetition of a muscular act that is directly connected to a particular mental state. These correlations are probably statistically significant, in that a large number of people who have a certain appearance will also behave in a predictable way, but comparisons should be made with care.

There are several offshoots of physiognomy—one of the most fanciful being "moleosophy"—the interpretation of moles on the body, the theory being that the shape and color of the mole and its position are indications of character. These marks on the skin are often congenital and hereditary, often occurring in exactly the same place on a child as in one of its parents, so their position is not determined by chance, but there is nothing to support the idea that a mole on the ankle indicates "a fearful nature" or that one on the ear will bring "riches far beyond expectations."

So much of our character is determined by learning and experience that any system of interpretation that relies on permanent physical features is likely to be inaccurate. People change, and transient patterns are far more effective indications of mood, because the best signals are those that, like the flashing light, produce a sudden and dramatic change. Blushing is one of these. Basically it is a reddening of the skin produced by dilation of the blood vessels and is most common in young females, but it seems to occur in all humans no matter what their sex or color and can almost be considered as a biological character of our species. Records show that girls who blushed freely fetched the highest prices in old slave markets, so there seem to be both sexual and submissive factors involved in the signal. Desmond Morris suggests that it is a powerful invitation to intimacy. As such, it probably serves the same function as breeding plumage in many male birds, which appears only at certain times and, when it does, it indicates a willingness and intention to breed.

All in all, it seems that there are limits to what one can learn about an individual's mental state, from observation only of the external signs of mind. Sensitive equipment such as electroencephalographs and life-field detectors give a closer view of the outward parts of internal processes, but even these are measuring only the fringes of the phenomenon. In order to really appreciate the potentials of the brain, it is necessary to learn new techniques of self-control and contact with others. A few of these keys to Supernature have already been discovered.

Chapter Seven:

Transcendence

TAKE A TOAD. Hold it flat between the palms of your hands; turn it over on its back and keep it there for a moment. Now remove your upper hand carefully and the toad will lie quite still with its webbed feet in the air.

This "experimentum mirabile" was demonstrated in 1646 by a Jesuit priest as an example of man's dominion over the animal world, but in fact it illustrates a far more fundamental principle—the domination of the rest of the body by the brain. Many species react in the same way. A crayfish that is made to stand on its head with claws on the ground and tail up in the air, stays in that position of supplication until disturbed. A hare held tightly upside down adopts a similar sort of waxlike pliability, and its limbs can be arranged in any weird posture. The snake charmer's grip on the back of a cobra's neck reduces it to instant and sometimes rigid immobility, suggesting that Moses was perhaps a better biologist than we give him credit for. Many zoos use this principle of immobilization for keeping small mammals and birds quiet while they are being weighed. In all cases, constriction seems to play an important role in producing the response, which may account for the comparative stillness of babies tightly wrapped in swaddling clothes.

Sudden immobility can be induced by a high level of fear. The Swiss psychiatrist Greppin tells of a campaign to eliminate the sparrows in his hospital grounds that ended after ten weeks in mass paralytic hysteria, with the birds dropping like stones into the bushes and then freezing into rigid postures as soon as they saw a man with a gun. (128) This sounds remarkably like the catatonic state that fear can produce in man. The explorer David Livingstone was once attacked by a lion at Mabotsa, in southern Africa, and described his reaction to being grabbed by the shoulder and mauled. "The shock produced a stupor similar to that which seems to be felt by a mouse after the first shake of the cat. It caused a sort of dreaminess in which there was no sense of pain nor feeling of terror, though quite conscious of all that was happening. It was like what patients partially under the influence of chloroform describe, who see all the operation, but feel not the knife. The singular condition was not the result of any mental process. The shake annihilated fear and allowed no sense of horror in looking round at the beast." (201) When the lion let go for a moment, Livingstone recovered and managed to get away.

There can be little doubt that under certain circumstances immobility has high survival value. Many animals escape from predators in exactly this way. Some, like the bittern *Botaurus stellaris*, enhance the effect of their leaflike feather pattern by adopting an elongated pose and swaying in time with the reeds around them. When a predator gets too close they fly away, but others, such as the stick insect, rely so completely on their immobility that they can be dismembered before they will move. Some vertebrates use this same kind of self-induced catatonia in emergencies.

The Cameroon toad *Bufo superciliaris* and the hognosed snake *Heterodon platyrhinos* both sham dead, turning over and lying on their backs with their tongues hanging out when threatened. But the mechanism is not perfectly developed in them yet, because they make the hilarious mistake when put the right way up or moved in any way, of immediately turning upside down again. The most accomplished death feigner of all is certainly the American opossum *Didelphis virginiana*, which has a superb fixed-action pattern to call on. In normal sleep the opossum keeps its mouth and eyes closed and its feet out of sight, but when attacked it collapses with eyes open, lying on its side with the feet visible and claws grasping the ground. The fact that the animal is still wide awake has been demonstrated in tests that show that it responds to loud noises by twitching its ears and by retracting its lips when prodded. There is no difference in body temperature, oxygen consumption, or blood chemistry, and EEG records show brain waves that are identical to those of a normal, highly alert animal. (107) "Playing possum" appears as a complete behavior pattern in isolated young animals at an age of 120 days, which is when they would normally be weaned and begin to wander off on their own. (230) So this species has developed a stereotyped, instinctive way of coping with attack that just imitates the automatic paralysis that some other species have to rely on to avoid death. In all of them, immobility clearly works well, inhibiting further attack by a predator and perhaps giving them a chance to escape later comparatively unharmed.

Immobilization can also be induced by disorientation. (122) At the Freiburg zoo they have built a mechanical device to supplement the effects of constriction. An animal is strapped tightly to the inside of the lid of a box, with its feet just touching the floor, and then the lid is spun on a swivel to bring the captive quickly up and onto its back, where it lies without struggling. The great French naturalist Fabre reported that most birds could be immobilized simply by swinging them to and fro or by tucking the head under a wing. (305) The degree of control varies with the amount of disorientation. Falcons are not paralyzed but are certainly made more amenable by hooding, and blinkers serve the same function on a horse.

Some birds do not respond just to being held or disorientated, but require a different kind of stimulus. They can be treated like toads and placed flat on the ground with their necks stretched out in front, but to get them to "freeze" effectively it is usually necessary to draw a sand pattern of long, steady lines radiating out from the beak. When released in this position, they lie there with eyes focused on the lines until they gradually recover or a puff of wind rouses them and sends them flying away. This concentration on a rhythmic pattern seems to be the basis of "fascination" techniques used by some reptiles. Many zoologists scoff at the idea of snakes fixing their prey with some sort of visual display, but it happens. (145) The African tree snake *Theletornis kirtlandii* has a vivid red tongue with a black forked tip that protrudes several inches out of the snake's mouth and makes extraordinary rhythmic movements. These not only attract the interest of small birds, but seem to put them into a bemused state that makes them easy prey. Two species of *Langaha* snakes in Madagascar do the same thing with a nose leaf and a comb on top of their head, and in Ceylon the pit viper *Ancistrodon hypnale* uses the colored tip of its tail to fascinate passing prey. The truly fascinating thing about all these displays is that the organs used by the snakes all move in the same way, vibrating at a regular three beats per second. Little is known of the brain waves of birds and small mammals, but this could be the frequency that is their equivalent of the alpha waves that occur during relaxed meditation in our brains. Vibrations of six or seven cycles a second make us irritable, but ten we find soothing. These are examples of immobilization being produced across the species line, but there is at least one example of the technique being used by members of the same species on each other. In certain spiders there is such a huge difference in size between the sexes that the male runs the risk of being mistaken for prey and attacked and eaten by his mate, so he approaches her only under the cover of a reassuring semaphore display that involves a sustained rhythmic movement of his palpi.

Immobilization can therefore be induced by constriction, disorientation, fear, a fixed behavior pattern, or rhythmic stimulation. In man all these techniques have been used, but in 1843 the Scots physician James Braid showed that a trance state could also be induced by suggestion, and he called the process hypnosis, from the Greek for sleep. (37)

HYPNOSIS

The process of animal hypnosis has been called catatonia, catalepsy, thanatosis, akinesis, and action inhibition; in man it has been known as mesmerism, animal magnetism, somnambulism, reverie, and druidic sleep. In neither case is there any evidence that hypnosis has anything at all to do with normal sleep, but there is widespread disagreement about exactly what hypnosis is.

Léon Chertok, Director of the Paris Institute of Psychiatry, believes that it is a fourth organismic state, which can be added to waking, sleeping, and dreaming. (72) It certainly differs in several respects from each of these three states of being, but the difficulty is that although hypnosis is held to be a genuine condition, nobody has yet come up with a satisfactory definition of it. Ivan Pavlov, the celebrated Soviet psychologist, thought that it was a defense mechanism that is similar in many ways to sleep. (241) He induced it in dogs by delaying the presentation of food for a long time after the sounding of the signal that the animals had come to associate with food. The dogs' tense expectation often led to catatonic states so severe that they could not move even when food was finally presented. Anatol Milechnin, a Uruguayan physician, uses this and other evidence to support his theory that hypnosis is an emotional reaction that can be produced either by shock techniques, such as the sudden firing of a gun, or by tranquilizing stimuli, such as stroking or soft singing. (211) The British psychiatrist Stephen Black combines both these ideas into the notion that hypnosis could be a reflex conditioned in very early life. (26) He suggests that during development in the egg or the uterus an animal is physically restricted and must remain relatively immobile, and that forcible restriction in later life produces a return to this condition of inaction. It is certainly true that most animals, when put into a trance state or feigning death, do adopt a fetal posture. This theory could also explain why rhythmic stimuli produce hypnosis. The dominant sound and sensation throughout an embryo's life is the continuous rhythmic beat of its mother's heart, and after birth it is most easily tranquilized either by being held close to its mother's left breast, where it can hear the heart, or by a metronome or a cradle that moves at seventy-two cycles per minute—the same rate as the pulse. (218) The hypnotic effect of solid-beat music and the trancelike state of some dancers can be explained in the same way.

In this climate of uncertainty the best way to examine hypnosis is to look at what little is known about the physiology of the condition. Hypnosis-like states occur in people that are clearly awake. A person lost in thought may read page after page of a book without any comprehension and listen to a whole conversation without hearing any of it; or an injured boxer may complete a bout without any realization of having done so. This narrowing of attention is very characteristic of the hypnotic state. Sleeping and dreaming can both be differentiated from waking by the differences of the patterns that show up on an EEG, but the brain waves of a hypnotized person are identical with the waking state. (81) A subject wired to an EEG machine shows, when resting with eyes closed, exactly the same pattern of waves as when hypnotized a moment later by means of a code word. (93) There seems to be no change either in cortical potential, pulse rate, skin resistance, or palmar electric potentials. (187) There is a slight rise in body temperature brought about by vasodilation during the trance state, and there seem to be small changes in the voltage of the life field. (265) But both these measurements are very subtle, and changes of this kind can also be recorded as a response to purely emotional reactions, so we are left with no known physiological indication of hypnosis.

The only way one can tell if someone is hypnotized is if he either responds to test suggestions or actually says afterward that he entered a hypnotic state. This is obviously very unsatisfactory and leads to the suspicion that a large part of the hypnotic phenomenon is self-determined, like the behavior adopted by a frightened opossum. Seymour Fisher, in an ingenious experiment, suggested to deeply hypnotized subjects that every time they heard the word "psychology" they would scratch their right ear. (101) After waking them, he tested the suggestion by using the word, and all of them dutifully scratched their ear. At this point one of his associates came into the room and they carried on a prearranged, apparently informal discussion about everyday topics in which the word "psychology" came up several times, but the subjects failed to respond to it. After some minutes of conversation, the associate left and Fisher turned back to his class, and when he next used the key word, all of them again produced the appropriate response. It seems that some hypnotic suggestions work only because the subjects do what they think is expected of them. When, by implication, the experiment was abandoned during the casual conversation, the suggestion was ignored as well.

Similar results are recorded for an experiment on pain in which all subjects were given exactly the same stimulus but showed a marked difference in their response. (195) Those who were being paid most to take part in the research also suffered the greatest amount of pain, apparently because they felt that they ought to suffer more. There is some reason to believe that hypnosis is governed in this way by psychological controls, but whatever causes the hypnotic state, there is absolutely no doubt about its effects.

One of the characteristics of pain is that it produces an increase in blood pressure. At Stanford University they compared the responses of hypnotized subjects, who had been told that they would feel no pain, with non-hypnotized subjects, who were asked to pretend that they were feeling no pain. (149) Observers could not tell the difference between the two groups by watching their reactions, but the blood pressure of all those feeling pain soared while that of the hypnotized subjects remained steady. Hypnotism seems to be a real painkiller and is now being used as the sole anesthetic in childbirth, dental work, and some major surgery. A chemical anesthetic works by blocking painful nerve impulses before they reach the brain, but hypnosis apparently acts by getting the brain to ignore the impulses. (314) In several surgical reports of hypnoanesthesia, the patients showed no overt signs of pain, but their pulse rate and blood pressure fluctuated considerably during the operations.

They were feeling something. It looks as though the mind, under the influence of suggestion, is exerting considerable control over the body. Part of the explanation may be that many of the reactions to pain are produced by anxiety, and if there is no worry regarding the source of the pain, we can tolerate surprisingly large amounts of discomfort. Injuries that would ordinarily be painful, often escape notice altogether during important occasions, when our attention is fixed elsewhere. Afterward we notice the bruise and wonder where it came from.

There seems to be almost no limit to the things that we can make our body do if we put our mind to it. Stephen Black gave subjects under hypnosis a direct suggestion that they would not be able to hear a tone with the particular frequency of 575 cycles per second, and in subsequent testing they showed no physiological startle reactions to the tone when it was suddenly played very loudly. They were also unable to feel the vibration of a tuning fork of the same frequency when it was placed against their ankle bones. (28) Several attempts have been made to induce color blindness or even total blindness by suggestion, and in one subject it was found that the brain no longer reacted normally to a bright light. (202) This is a sort of negative hallucination—not seeing something that was there—but positive hallucination of bright colors has also occurred complete with afterimages in the appropriate complementary colors. (97)

Of all skin diseases, warts seem to be most closely associated with psychological factors. Wart "charmers" ply their trade, apparently successfully, in most countries of the world, so it is not surprising to find that hypnosis works equally well. In one well-controlled study, fourteen patients with long-standing warts all over their bodies were given suggestions that those on only one side of the body would disappear. (305) In five weeks they did. Allergies seem to be similarly responsive to suggestion. An elegant test in Japan involved blindfolded subjects, all of whom were known to be allergic to a certain tree. (159) When the leaves of chestnut were placed on their left arms and they were told that these were from the allergy tree, all developed the usual dermatitis; but when the real leaves were placed on their right arms and said to be harmless, no reaction took place. All allergic reaction is produced by a foreign substance, such as pollen, that enters the body and combines with a protein to form a specific antibody that sometimes produces distressing side effects or allergic reactions. It is a relatively straightforward biochemical reaction that apparently has nothing to do with the brain, but there is now a wealth of evidence to show beyond doubt that the whole process is governed by mental factors. The classic test for tuberculosis, a bacterial infection, is the Mantoux skin test, which produces red allergic weal on the skin if the patient has TB antibodies in his blood, but it has been shown that a hypnotic suggestion not to react can produce a negative response to the test even in someone riddled with TB. (27) This nicely demonstrates the dominance of emotion over the wasting disease, which has long associations with depression and unrequited lovers "alone and palely loitering."

Other physiological mechanisms are also amenable to suggestion. (26) In deep hypnosis even the tendon reflex that makes a leg jump when tapped on the knee can be eliminated. (13) The heart can be speeded up or slowed down and the amount of blood circulating in any one limb can be increased. (298) Nearsighted people can be made to change the shape of their eyeballs and improve their distance vision for short periods. (173) And perhaps most impressive of all, the contractions of the stomach due to great hunger can be eliminated altogether by nothing more than the suggestion of eating a large meal. (196)

Many of these studies have been strongly criticized, most effectively by Theodore Barber, who hates the whole idea of hypnosis. (14) In some instances the criticism is justified —the effects listed might not have been produced by hypnosis; but the arguments are rather pointless and tend to conceal something very important. Whether produced by what is called "hypnosis" or by what others prefer to see as simple "suggestion," the fact remains that all these bodily functions, which are normally operated by the autonomic nervous system, over which we have no conscious control, are amenable to outside influence. Whatever the process may be, it has enormous biological significance and gives us our first direct contact with the elusive unconscious.

AUTOSUGGESTION

The whole problem of consciousness is full of pitfalls, many of them purely semantic, and it is a long way from satisfactory solution, but for our purposes it is enough to say that man has something the amoeba does not have. We have an individuality that seems to be based on our experience. The brain of a newborn child is in effect a blank sheet, which quickly becomes covered by records of experiences that have been useful to him. At first the child depends completely on others, and his most urgent need is therefore to get these others to do what he wants. Right from the very beginning, he starts to build up a system of communication based on information he slowly collects. This is stored in what amounts to a theoretical model of the world as he sees it. Our brains continue to build this structure throughout life, modifying and adding to it as necessary, but always comparing the input of daily events with the record of past experience of events of the same kind. At the highest levels, the brain calls on stored information to make judgments about things even in the absence of the normal stimuli—it can "think" for itself.

This ability is roughly what is meant by consciousness. We know that we have it, and we can recognize it in many other mammals and birds that seem to respond to us or to each other in the same way. We have reason to doubt its existence in reptiles, amphibians, and fish, and arguments go on continually about the possibility of consciousness, perhaps a sort of collective version, in the social insects. Few people think that worms or jellyfish have it, and it would be hard to find anyone who believed in conscious sponges or seaweed. It is very difficult to know where to draw the line and quite unnecessary to even try; all we need do is recognize the fact that the possibility of consciousness gets more and more remote as we look back along the line of evolutionary development. It is a comparatively new thing and best developed in the more advanced organisms.

Those processes we recognize as conscious are governed almost entirely by the central nervous system—the brain and the spinal cord—and these, too, are relatively new developments. So the remainder of the nerve network, the autonomic system supplying the gut, blood vessels, and glands, must be more primitive. This system governs the processes we call unconscious; its origins seem to lie a very long way back in organic history. Going all the way back to a time before the development of any kind of nervous system, early protoplasm must have been faced with one major problem—that of keeping itself intact in the struggle against disruption from outside. To do this it would at least have to be able to distinguish "self" from "non-self"; it would have to be able to recognize foreign matter and reject it if necessary. Immune and allergic reactions do exactly this by recognizing the shapes of intruding substances, and the fact that these reactions respond to unconscious suggestion could mean that the unconscious is a process common to all life no matter how simple it may be.

This could go a long way to explaining patterns of behavior and response that now seem supernatural.

The discovery of the double-helix shape of the DNA molecule highlighted the importance of form at a molecular level. We now know that an enzyme depends almost entirely on its form, and the ability of an organism to recognize an antigen is based solely on the shape of the foreign body. (5) Even the sense of smell is a product of shape: round molecules smell like camphor, disks smell like flowers, and wedges smell like peppermint. So the ability to distinguish between apparently similar smells can be explained quite simply by the fact that they probably have quite distinct shapes, and telling these apart is something even a blood cell can do. This makes responses of animals such as the parasitic wasps look a lot less uncanny.

The large American species *Megarhyssa lunator* runs up and down tree trunks until it locates the larva of the horntail moth hidden three inches below the bark. It does this partly with "ear" cells in each of its feet that are sensitive to vibration and can listen to the sound of the larva chewing, but the larva keeps dead still as soon as it hears movement on the bark. (143) And yet the wasps manage not only to locate the larva precisely, but to tell by the smell through three inches of tree whether it is the right species of larva and whether any other wasp has already laid her eggs on it. This highly sophisticated response to a subtle stimulus is made possible by reliance on an old and basically simple ability to recognize shape.

The ability of salmon to return across thousands of miles of ocean to the same rivers and streams in which they hatched, has now been shown to be due to sensitivity to the smell of that body of water as distinct from all others. (139) Eels are able to recognize a thimbleful of rose scent diluted in a lake covering fourteen thousand square miles. (317) Male moths can detect the presence of a female of their species as much as thirty miles away by the presence of only one molecule of her specific scent in the air. (186) This kind of sensitivity is completely foreign to us, who have such a poor sense of smell, but we can get some idea of the implications from a new mechanical nose invented by Andrew Dravniek of Chicago. This is capable of detecting the traces of smell left behind in a room by a burglar some hours previously and of matching these up with samples from suspects. As people who are related by blood have similar smells, it can also be used to assist blood-group analysis in proving paternity, and because the invasion of pathological organisms produces changes in the chemical balance of the body, it can detect disease long before the symptoms become apparent. (90) The machine performs these functions by the purely mechanical process of comparing chemical properties that depend on physical shapes. The man working the machine has to make decisions based on the information it gives him; he is the conscious mind controlling the unconscious mechanism. In this case the human is supplemented by a machine, but it is a reasonable model of the sort of relationship we enjoy with our own unconscious. We are only now just beginning to realize how much direct influence one has on the other.

At the Harvard Medical School, David Shapiro has just completed an experiment in which he trained a number of students to alter their own blood pressure. (304) They were wired up to a sensitive gauge, and every time the pressure showed a momentary fall, the men were rewarded by being shown an enlargement of a nude pinup from the center pages of *Playboy* magazine. They had no idea what the experiment was about, but the fact that their conscious attention was attracted at the same time as an unconscious process was going on, forged a link beween them and made it possible for the men to control the usually random fluctuations of blood pressure at will. In another, similar experiment, business executives with dangerously high blood pressure were taught the same useful skill. (71)

It has long been known that individuals with vivid visual imagination have few alpha rhythms in their brain waves, whereas non-visualists, who prefer to verbalize things, have persistent alpha activity. These characteristic rhythms are apparently partly hereditary, but they depend also on environmental factors and experience. Identical twins start life with identical EEG records, but these differ later to show even slight variations in character that would normally be noticeable only by close friends. In most people alpha rhythms appear best when the eyes are closed and the person is relaxed and thinking about nothing in particular. If they persist strongly when the eyes are open, this is usually a sign of mental illness of the sort that produces isolation from reality. Such complete dissociation can be harmful, but alpha is so relaxing that it performs a valuable biological function and it would be useful if we were able to summon it up at will. An inexpensive machine is being marketed to do just this. This "alphaphone" is a simple instrument that monitors the brain waves and, by lighting a bulb or ringing a bell, lets a user know exactly when he is producing the alpha rhythms. This simple reinforcement acts in the same way as nudes on blood pressure, and after a few hours of use anyone can learn to exert conscious control over alpha and produce it on demand—a sort of instant version of the meditation techniques that normally take years of practice and self-denial to learn.

At Boston City Hospital the physiology of true meditation is being investigated with a number of adepts skilled in the transcendental techniques of Maharishi Mahesh Yogi. All show a sharp increase in alpha rhythm, a decrease in the breathing rate and oxygen consumption, a decrease in heart rate and blood pressure, and an increase in the electrical resistance of the skin. (22) There is also a dramatic drop in the level of lactate in the blood, which persists for some time after the end of meditation. High lactate levels are associated with stress, so the total effect of the self-induced changes is a sudden and significant release from tension. Those who practice these techniques report that they find them an effective and often preferable substitute for drug-induced experiences.

In Japan some fascinating work has been done on the patterns that occur during Zen contemplation. (172) The priests produce sensory deprivation by sitting in the "lotus position" for long periods of time with their eyes wide open and fixed on some object. At the beginning there is no alpha activity, but soon alpha rhythms appear and become very strong, diffusing all over the scalp. In the Zen masters, the waves may persist for half an hour or more without change. In normal people, alpha seldom lasts more than a minute or two. (6) Similar work on yoga meditation shows that there is prolonged alpha activity, but in one study made on a Bengali sect, the alpha broke down when the adepts entered the state of ecstasy they call "samadhi." (83)

The conscious control of involuntary functions is commonplace in yoga, Zen, and some African cults. Pulse rate, breathing, digestion, sexual function, metabolism, and kidney activity can all be influenced by and at will. Skilled practitioners, after years spent perfecting what amounts to a system of conditioned reflexes, can slow the heartbeat almost to the vanishing point, reduce the body temperature to what would normally be lethal levels, and reduce their respiration to no more than one breath every few minutes. In this state the whole organism is reduced to a condition similar to that of a hibernating animal and can be buried alive for days without ill effects. (335) The reflexes that normally make us shy away from intense pain can be diverted so that nails are driven through the limbs and spikes through the cheeks or tongue. And while this is being done, the sympathetic nervous system can be locally suppressed or stimulated so that bleeding is prevented or encouraged. The pupils, which normally respond to light and emotion, can similarly be controlled. There is nothing supernatural about any of these talents; many of them have been objectively studied and imitated in the laboratory. It takes time and practice to cultivate the right paths of control, but physiologists have succeeded in doing such unlikely things as making their hair stand on end or their pancreas secrete more than the normal amount of insulin.

Some of these skills are developed purely as a means of livelihood, but in many instances they are simply by-products of the process of self-realization. In parts of the world where life is difficult they may also serve some very practical function. The art of *lung-gom* in Tibet produces the ability to travel very rapidly across some of the inhospitable upland wastes of that country. The training consists of living in complete darkness and seclusion for thirty-nine months of deep-breathing exercises. Alexandra David-Neel tells of seeing a monk, from the monastery in Tsang renowned for training in swiftness, in full flight. "I could clearly see his perfectly calm impassive face and wide open eyes with their gaze fixed on some invisible far distant object situated somewhere high up in space. The man did not run. He seemed to lift himself from the ground, proceeding by leaps. It looked as if he had been endowed with the elasticity of a

ball and rebounded each time his feet touched the ground."
(84) It is said that one of these skilled walkers covered a
distance of over three hundred miles in about thirty hours—
between sunrise on one day and midday of the next. That is
an average of about ten miles an hour across all kinds of
country by day and by night. Marathon runners, by comparison, travel at an average of twelve miles an hour, but
only for just over two hours at a time on good roads.

Another useful Tibetan custom is *tumo*. This accomplish-
ment is aimed at combating cold, and in a country that is
almost entirely above ten thousand feet altitude, it is a
talent greatly respected. Initiates learn a complex set of
breathing and meditational exercises and retire to a remote
area to train. Each day they bathe in icy streams and sit
naked in the snow thinking of internal fires. When the training is complete, a test is made on a windy winter night by
wrapping the student in a sheet that has been dipped into
the river through a hole in the ice and has to be completely
dried just by body heat at least three times during the night.
After qualification, the adept never again wears anything
more than a single cotton garment in all seasons and at any
height. Several Everest expeditions have even reported seeing
completely naked hermits living well up among the permanent snows.

The insistence of both Tibetan and Indian cults of mind
and body on the importance of breathing is an interesting
one. Ancient yoga texts proclaim that "Life is in the breath"
and that the body absorbs "life force" or "prana" from the
air. (152) Deep breathing, of course, causes hyperventilation
and can produce hallucination and even unconsciousness, but
there is more to it than that. The biologists working at the
Kazakh State University on the Kirlian process have discovered that the flares in the skin glow more brightly when
the lungs of the subject are filled with pure oxygen—and the

effect is even more impressive with ionized air. (233) So it looks as though surplus electrons from oxygen may actually provide fuel for the energy in the life field.

If it is possible to exert conscious control over unconscious processes, then the reverse is also bound to occur. It shows up in fact in all the psychosomatic disorders that surround us. At least half of all the ills of mankind can be diagnosed as originating in the mind. Witch doctors always treat all diseases by magic as well as by herbal cures, and their success rate with skin complaints, blood-pressure difficulties, peptic ulcer, incipient coronary thrombosis, and hysterical blindness is as high as, if not higher than, that of specially trained and magnificently equipped Harley Street surgeons. Even "accidental" injuries such as broken limbs can often be attributed to psychological causes. Recent research shows that the statements "It happened by accident" and "It happened by chance" are not synonymous, and that some people at certain times really are accident prone. (212) Personality traits, psychological conditions, and even physiological patterns can be identified in individuals who are nothing more than "accidents looking for a place to happen."

Taken to its limit, autosuggestion can even kill. Every year thousands of people die simply because they believe that it is inevitable. Witchcraft may have powers that are truly supernatural, but it does not need them while people are capable of wishing themselves to death. It is not even necessary to consciously believe in forces of evil; the unconscious can manage very well on its own. There are vivid and graphic descriptions of otherwise rational people in New York and London wasting away when they have been told that someone is abusing a doll constructed in their image—and of these same people making rapid and complete recoveries when they knew, or even thought, that the doll had been destroyed. (302)

Witches and witch doctors often depend upon crowd re-actions to work their magic, because if a number of people are involved they reinforce each other's suggestibility by a process of social facilitation. All farmers know that a solitary pig never gets fat and that several pigs together each eat far more than they would alone. The same is true of many aspects of behavior. The emotional tension of a magic session or a political meeting or a revivalist gathering quickly com-municates itself to all present and allows a leader to put across ideas that individually and under normal circumstances few of the audience would accept. Much has been written about "mass hypnotism" and the ability of certain people to create widespread hysteria or common hallucinations. While it is entirely possible to hypnotize a small group of care-fully selected suggestible subjects simultaneously, only about one in twenty people fall into this category, and the odds against a crowd being composed entirely of such people are overwhelming. So there has never been an authenticated demonstration of the Indian rope trick in public. (69) But the fact remains that in the infectious frenzy that can be produced by facilitation in a large crowd, the barriers of reason and conscious free will are lowered and simple ideas spread rapidly and take root wherever they fall. Contagious activity of this kind is equally common in other species. The adoption of a ritual posture by one bird in a dense colony of gulls often spreads in ripples throughout the entire area. If one penguin on a beach raises its beak, stiffens up in an "ecstasy display," and gives the rallying call of its species, the whole seething mass all the way around the bay take up the cry.

The spacing of individual fish in a shoal is determined by the vortexes that each fish sets up in the water around him and that are appreciated by the lateral-line sense organs of his immediate neighbors. (39) Part of the communication of intentions is certainly carried out through these organs as well, but the cohesion within a school is too good for this to be the only explanation. It may be that all dynamic groups of this kind, including wheeling flocks of starlings and vast floods of lemmings, are in a state of mild hysteria that enables them to act almost as a single organism. In a sense, all instinctive social communication is similar to hypnosis in that it depends on an unconscious response being made to a special stimulus. When the system was being set up, the stimulus must have been repeated insistently, like the light flashes or the repeated instructions of the hypnotist, before the appropriate response became almost automatic. Familiarity with this kind of conditioning may well account for the predisposition of all animals to immobilization techniques and for man's susceptibility to hypnosis and suggestion.

In man the unconscious has become very much more than that part of the brain which looks after mundane domestic physiology. The greater part of all Western psychiatry is based on the existence of the "unconscious" of the Freudians or the "collective unconscious" of Jung. From being only a control mechanism intent on recognizing shape, it has become a real alternative to conscious thought processes, with its own special capabilities. There is evidence that much real creativity is based on the unconscious and that many writers, artists, and composers gain access to it by self-induced hypnosis. Goethe said that many of his best poems were written in a condition that bordered on somnambulism. Coleridge is supposed to have composed *Kubla Khan* in his sleep, and Mozart described his musical inspirations as rising like dreams, quite independent of his will. Newton even resorted to solving his most troublesome mathematical problems by sleeping on them.

DREAMS

Since all life depends in one way or another on the energy of the sun, the most insistent beat in the metabolism of every species is the circadian rhythm—the alternation of light and dark. At first, when the early life forms were directly dependent not only on the energy but also on the heat of the sun, activity must have been confined to the hours of light. This is certainly true of land-living animals, and even today most cold-blooded species become inactive during the cool of the night, when their body temperature falls almost as fast as the temperature of the air. Birds and mammals have developed a vital independence from this system by controlling their internal temperature, so that many of them can be active in the dark, but even these emancipated species still take a break during part of each 24-hour period.

Invertebrate animals, with the possible exception of octopus and squid, simply seem to become inactive: they just stop moving; but, for most warm-blooded animals, sleep is an active process. Niko Tinbergen points out that sleep is a true instinctive pattern, because it is preceded by appetitive, or preliminary, behavior such as looking for or traveling to a special place, and involves the assumption of a particular posture. (321) Some fish, such as the carp *Cyprinus carpio*, lie flat on the bottom of their pools after dark, and the giant golden sunfish *Mola mola* floats on its side like a huge disk on the surface of the sea. They seem to be sleeping and can even be captured if cautiously approached. Birds certainly sleep, most of them with their eyes closed and their head tucked underneath a wing. Those which sleep on perches cannot afford to relax completely, and those which sleep on water often make continuous paddling movements with one leg so as not to drift in to shore, within range of predators.

Aquatic mammals have to develop the same kind of reflex, floating up to the surface every now and then to breathe. Dolphins appear to sleep with first one eye open and then the other, changing every few hours. Cows and many other ruminants sleep with both eyes wide open and carry on chewing their cuds regardless. The peculiar arrangement of their digestive system relies on gravity, so they have to keep their heads up, too. Even those animals such as elephants and giraffes that are traditionally supposed never to sleep, do in fact do so, often even lying out flat on the ground to sleep.

So sleep is widespread among higher animals, many of which spend one third of their lives doing it, but despite its prevalence we still know very little about the process. In man we can describe it reasonably accurately as a condition in which the eyelids close, the pupils become very small, the secretion of digestive juice and urine and saliva all fall sharply, the flow of air into the lungs diminishes, the heart slows down, and the brain waves change with loss of consciousness. As we fall asleep, the alpha waves gradually disappear as the rhythm slows down to the long, quiet delta waves, at one to three cycles per second, that are characteristic of deep sleep. Brief bursts of faster waves, or "spindles," are usually mixed in with the slower ones.

All these patterns can be artificially induced by electrical stimulation of certain areas of the brain; in one study a shock in the upper part of the brain stem induced a cat to groom itself, curl up, and settle down to sleep. (148) But most evidence points to the fact that there are areas of "wakefulness" in the brain and that it is when these cease to be stimulated that we feel sleepy. The area primarily responsible for keeping us awake is the reticular formation, a sort of master control at the base of the brain for activating the entire central nervous system. Chemical anesthetics inhibit this area and produce sleep for as long as the effect of the drug lasts, but any mechanical interference with the reticular activating system abolishes wakefulness altogether and produces prolonged coma and death. Consciousness is lost during sleep, but it does not always return with waking. (108) Animals from which the whole cortex of the brain has been removed, still sleep and wake and move around, eating and excreting, but without the vital gray matter they can never learn or show any of the awareness of true consciousness. Sleepwalkers are not so much asleep as unconscious. They move around with their eyes open and perform quite complex acts before eventually returning to bed, but remember nothing of it in the morning. It is quite possible that the dreaded "zombies" of the Caribbean, who are said to have returned from the grave, are people with congenitally or accidentally damaged cortex areas, or people whose brains have been affected by drugs so that they seem to be walking dead—awake but still unconscious.

It is very difficult to keep a normal person awake for long periods, but many experiments have been done to study the effect of sleep deprivation. After several days without sleep, the grip is still as strong as ever, so muscle action has not been impaired; subjects can still perform complex arithmetical problems, so the conscious activities of the brain have not been affected; they can still respond immediately to a light flash by pressing a buzzer, so reaction time is apparently not prolonged. But the sleepless people cannot sustain long periods of concentration; they make numerous errors and have to keep on going back to correct them. (341) After longer periods without sleep, these small lapses into momentary unconsciousness grow until the subjects begin to see things that are not there: they begin to dream with their eyes wide open.

Proper dreaming occurs during sleep, but it is not just a

part of ordinary sleep. Orthodox sleep alternates several times during the night with periods of a very different, almost paradoxical, kind of sleep. It is during these times that dreams take place. In orthodox sleep the brain produces big, slow waves of delta rhythm, the eyes are still, and the heartbeat is regular, but some of the muscles, and particularly those of the throat, are still tense. In paradoxical sleep the brain produces more rapid waves, almost like those of wakefulness, the eyes move rapidly to and fro, and the heartbeat becomes irregular, but despite all this mental activity going on, the muscles of the body, including those of the throat, are more relaxed and the sleeper is much more difficult to awake. (235) The relaxation of the muscles amounts almost to paralysis, with even reflex twitches being eliminated, so the nightmares in which we struggle to escape but are unable to move are a true reflection of our physical condition.

When we first fall asleep, most of us start with the orthodox variety and only change to paradoxical sleep after about two hours. If an experimenter monitors a subject constantly and wakes him every time he starts to show rapid eye movements, then a state of deprivation builds up and the subject tends to start right away with paradoxical sleep as though determined to make good the deficit. It seems that both kinds of sleep are equally important, but for different reasons.

We tend to think of bodies as relatively permanent structures, but individual cells have a very short life and are continually being replaced, not just on the skin and in the gut lining, where they are rubbed away by friction, but even in the bones. Friends may look unchanged to you after long absences, but if several years have elapsed there will not be a single cell present that was there last time you met. Regeneration and replacement depend on the synthesis of new protein, and most of this seems to take place during sleep.

In orthodox sleep it seems that the body tissues are most affected; after strenuous athletic days, people spend more than the usual amount of time in orthodox sleep. Human growth hormones are manufactured during this time, and the rate of cell division increases soon after falling asleep. The tissues of the brain differ from those of the rest of the body in that they stop growing after a certain age and concentrate largely on repair and maintenance. Most of brain growth occurs during the two months just before birth and the month after it. In this time the cortex of gray matter is produced, and the baby not only sleeps twice as long each day as the normal adult, but it also spends proportionally twice as much time in paradoxical sleep. It seems that, while the body is repaired in orthodox sleep, the brain receives attention in the alternate periods, when more blood flows to the head and more heat is generated there.

As soon as it was discovered that the rapid eye movements of paradoxical sleep were a sign of dreaming, the idea grew that there might be some correspondence between these and body movements and the content of the dream. (234) Active dreams seem to involve more movement, but it is unlikely that the eyes are actually moving to look at dream pictures, because men who have been blind from birth show exactly the same behavior in their dreams. Recordings of heart and breathing rate, body temperature, pulse wave, and skin potential show that these vary directly with the emotional content of the dream, so it is nevertheless a very real experience.

Analysis of dream content shows that they do not necessarily form a continuing story that runs in episodes throughout the night, but they do tend to start off with a subject related to the experiences of the previous day before shifting to earlier periods of life. This has given rise to the theory that dreams help a person assimilate the events of the day by re-running some of them and comparing them with previous experience before filing the lot away in the memory banks. It fits in with the fact of dream debt building up, presumably because of the pressure of unsorted experience accumulating in the cortex. There is in fact strong electrical activity during paradoxical sleep in the very area just below the cortex that is thought to be the site of the memory.

The symbols in dreams seem to be the direct action of the unconscious, censoring and shaping images to suit its own purpose. Freud based his system of psychoanalysis largely on dreams. His interpretations were sometimes a little simplistic and are not followed rigidly today, but he seems to have been right in assuming that the unconscious was not amenable to direct investigation and could only be examined at second hand by inference. His emphasis on the sex drive is sometimes criticized as an exaggeration based on the minds of the frustrated young women of nineteenth-century Vienna, but it has been vindicated somewhat by Calvin Hall in a recent study. (234) Hall made lists of all the dream objects that psychoanalysts took to be symbolic of the male sex organ and came up with 102 symbols for penis, including stick, gun, pen, rod, dirk, etc. Then he went through Partridge's *Dictionary of Slang* and found that all of these, plus another ninety-eight the analysts had never thought of, have been in use as coarse English descriptions of the phallus for hundreds of years.

There is constant argument about whether animals dream. Many of them go through movements that look like patterns of hunting and feeding while they sleep, but these usually take place during orthodox sleep even in those animals that also have paradoxical periods. Cats, dogs, chimps, and horses all have alternating periods of both kinds of sleep, but it will probably never be possible to say for certain whether they actually dream in one or the other. It seems likely, though, that the two sleep patterns serve the same restorative functions for these species as they do in man.

In cats paradoxical sleep occurs throughout life, but in many apparently less intelligent animals it can be found only in very young individuals. Sheep and cows show signs of both states of sleep before weaning, when their brains are still growing, but later the paradoxical patterns disappear altogether. In species such as raccoons and monkeys, which are much more inventive and aware, there are strong indications of paradoxical, rapid-eye-movement sleep at all ages. There seems to be a direct correlation between this kind of sleep, which is closely associated with dreaming, and a high level of consciousness. A survey of the animal kingdom therefore shows a gradation of awareness. At the lowest levels organisms are either active or inactive, but in more advanced species and particularly among birds and mammals, the period of inactivity takes on special active functions of its own. In the most complex animals it is even divided into two different kinds of sleep, associated with separate physiological and psychological processes. And now, in man, it seems that there is an extra step, one that has given rise to a new kind of awareness.

This new development is highlighted by chemicals that produce changes in behavior. Drugs can be divided into several broad categories on the basis of the kind of change they make. The first group are those, such as the amphetamines, cocaine, and caffeine, which stimulate metabolism; in biological terms we must consider these as being similar in action to the reticular system of the brain, which produces wakefulness. The second group have the opposite effect; these are the barbiturates and tranquilizers, which act as sedatives and are biologically equivalent to the process producing sleepiness, but the interesting thing is that they result only in orthodox sleep. After a long period on sleeping pills, people show symptoms similar to those which occur in subjects that have been deprived of paradoxical sleep and the chance to dream. When taken off these drugs, all experience a tremendous rebound of paradoxical sleep, which looks as though it is trying to make up for lost time. Some dream sleep occurs under the influence of the opiates, heroin and morphine, which of course also produce delirium and euphoria and act as painkillers. Biologically their action is much like strong autosuggestion or hypnosis, which produces the same kind of dissociation and anesthesia. But beyond these three categories, which simulate the basic life states of waking, sleeping, and dreaming, is one more group of chemicals: the hallucinogens.

HALLUCINATION

Hallucinogenic drugs and practices reveal something that seems to be peculiar to man. They illuminate the fringes of an expanse of mind and experience so vast that it is difficult to comprehend. Sidney Cohen, Director of the Institute of Mental Health, in Maryland, describes the brain as "an under-powered self-scrutinizing symbol factory whose main job is body management. Its side line consists of reflecting on what it is, where it is going and what it all means. Its unique capacities for wonder and self-awareness are quite unnecessary for purposes of physical survival." (76) The glimpses we are beginning to get of the scope of the brain do indeed raise some unprecedented evolutionary questions. No biologist would say that the brain's extracurricular activities were unnecessary for survival: the brain is part of us and we are as much a part of the ecology as every other species. What we have done to our environment is as natural as thunder or lightning. Our brains have made us a major evolutionary force, and it is going to take a great deal of imagination and creativity on their part to think us out of present dilemmas. But I must agree with Cohen that the extent of man's potential is awe-inspiring; we seem to have acquired abilities so far beyond even our present dramatic needs that we look top-heavy. Nature seldom does thing without good reason, and yet she has gone to some trouble over the past ten million years—a very short time by her usual standards—to equip us with an enormous cerebral cortex of seemingly unlimited capacity. We have acquired this incredible organ at the expense of several others, and yet we use only a minute part of it. What was the hurry? Why have we raced along this line of development so fast? We could certainly have got by with much less. At the moment, we are like a small family of squatters who have taken over a vast palace but find no need to move beyond the comfortable, serviced apartment in one corner of the base-ment.

An almost subliminal awareness of the rest of the structure has always tantalized us. Brief glimpses into other rooms have led a few adventurous individuals to make more deter-mined efforts to explore, but traditional methods have been only partially successful. Some have tried rhythmic tech-niques, such as Christian chants or the swaying movements of Hindu prayer or the whirling dances of the dervishes, to in-duce a trance state that would get them across the barrier. Some have tried altering their body chemistry by deep breathing or fasting or going without sleep. Some have sought dissociation in physical pain by self-flagellation or mutilation or hanging from the ceiling. The Sioux Indians used heat and thirst in their sun ritual to produce a sort of crude delirium; the Egyptians tried social isolation in their temple rituals. The one thing all these methods have in common is that they cut down on the usual flow of information with which the envi-ronment threatens to swamp us; they either eliminate the sensory input or make it monotonous and meaningless. When this is done, some of the doors in the mind open up a little.

The technique of sensory deprivation has been refined in several recent investigations. At McGill University subjects were confined to a small soundproof room and wore goggles that admitted only diffuse light. At Princeton they were kept in a tiny, lightproof, soundproof, constant-temperature cubicle. And at Oklahoma and Utah they were immersed in a dark tank of water kept at blood temperature so that they received no light, sound, or touch sensations from their environment. The immediate response in all studies was to retreat from this monotony into sleep, but once this avenue of escape was closed and they could sleep no longer, the volunteers began to experience other difficulties. All subjects lost track of time and underestimated its passing: some slept for more than twenty-four hours and claimed that it was only an hour or two. Disorientation and lack of feedback from the environment made it difficult for them to think seriously and to make normal judgments. Dreams began to appear more frequently, sometimes with frightening intensity, and sooner or later the total unreality of the situation led most of the subjects to the experience of hallucinations. These were not just simple sensory "ghosts" such as flashes of light or the sound of bells, but fully fledged happenings, complex and entirely convincing. (329) What seems to take place is that in normal circumstances the vast amount of information we receive is monitored by the reticular formation, which sorts it out and passes along only what we need and can handle at any one time. Under conditions of sensory deprivation very little is coming in, so each small piece of information receives far more than the usual amount of attention and becomes enormously magnified. Our vision is restricted, so we blow up what we can perceive to fill the whole screen, like a film taken through a microscope. So part of the hallucination is simply an improved close-up view of reality, but there is more to it than that. Left without its normal barrage of stimuli, the brain embellishes and elaborates on reality, drawing on its store of unconscious paraphernalia to fill the time and space available. And yet not even this goes far enough, for there are some qualities to hallucination that seem to lie outside both the conscious and the unconscious capabilities of the brain.

Almost every subculture has at some time sought out a root, herb, or berry to further the process of dissociation. The Persians had a potion called soma, which, according to the Sanskrit chronicle, "made one like a God." Helen of Troy had nepenthe. In India and Egypt they have always had hashish or marijuana. In Europe and Asia there was the beautiful crimson-spotted mushroom *Amanita*, which killed flies but only drove Norsemen berserk. Mexico is favored with the morning glory, the peyote cactus, and several "divine mushrooms." All these plants contain chemicals that produce transcendent states, and most have been used as adjuncts to religious and magical ceremonies, but the most shattering and significant of all psychedelic substances does not occur naturally in the wild, and had to be extracted from ergot fungus, which grows on grain. This is lysergic acid diethylamide, or LSD.

LSD has been tested on a wide variety of animals, but it seems to have little effect on any of them except perhaps the spider, who builds a rather more fancy web. It seems to be specific in its action on the highest levels of thought, and even a minute amount, about one three-hundred-thousandth of an ounce, produces profound effects on man. Depending on how it is taken, these begin within about half an hour, reach a peak after an hour and a half, and end six or even twelve hours later. Most of the action on the brain seems to be confined to the reticular system and to the limbic system, which modulates emotional experiences. So it is working directly on those areas responsible for filtering and comparing sensory information and on those which determine an individual's feelings about this material. Speech, walking ability, and most physical activities are completely unaffected. Blood pressure and pulse are normal, reflexes are acute, and there are no unpleasant side effects. It seems that LSD acts only on the area of higher consciousness in the human brain—on the area that we believe controls our personality.

The most noticeable psychological effect is, as in sensory deprivation, one of the slowing down of time: second hands on clocks seem hardly to move. This sort of "eternal present" is very much like a prolonged version of the way time can stand still in moments of great personal danger. We have in our own physiology the capacity for producing this effect in emergencies, and LSD seems to carry that on a stage further, but it is no longer concerned with personal survival. The separation between self and non-self, the old, primeval haunt of the unconscious, very soon disappears, and ego boundaries dissolve. Cohen says, "The thin overlay of reason gives way to reverie, identity is submerged by oceanic feelings of unity, and seeing loses the conventional meanings imposed upon the object seen." (76)

It is important in this respect to realize that we normally perceive only what we can conceive. We fit sensations into our own view of the way things ought to be. The classic experiment of fitting people with glasses that invert everything proves this conclusively. Within a day or two the brain makes corrections to the visual field and these people see everything the "right" way up again, but when the glasses are removed, the whole world is once again inverted. Thus the world is seen not as it is but as it ought to be. Part of the problem is that we receive so many sensations, that we are forced to pick and choose and soon end up with a carefully selected and very narrow view of reality. LSD has the capacity to take the blinkers off and allow us to see things afresh, as though it were for the first time. In this condition we can begin to re-appreciate the sounds of colors, the scent of music, and the texture of mood. Bees and bats and deep-sea squid, without our range of competing sensitivities and interests, do these things all the time.

Children commonly see things with enormous clarity. It is possible that what we call hallucinations are a normal part of every child's psychic experience (their paintings seem to show this), but as we grow older our visions are dimmed and eventually suppressed altogether, because they come to have a negative social value. Each society lays down certain guide-lines of what constitutes sanity, and by a combination of these cultural pressures and our own needs for acceptance and conformity, most of us end up inside these prescribed limits. A few break out and are classified insane and deprived of their freedom on the ground that they need to be taken care of, but in fact their confinement is designed far more to pro-tect society than to save these individuals from themselves. The Soviet Union makes no bones about this and regularly certifies troublesome dissenters on the grounds that they must be mad if they don't agree with the State. A few in-dividuals manage to shake off the restrictions of sanity and get away with it, because they do so within the sphere of a religion in which such revolutionary activities are permissible because they have been labeled "divinely inspired." Far from being confined, many of the people who have had this kind of transcendental experience return to society with a new view of things and proceed to change their way of life and ours—not always for the best.

Some saints and prophets have undoubtedly been truly mad, but it makes no sense to classify all of them as insane. Their experiences are not unique. Almost everyone, at some time in his life, has a moment of rapture, bliss, or ecstasy brought on by a flash of beauty, love, sexual experience, or insight. These momentary visions of perfection and aesthetic delight are glimpses of a state that Christians know as "divine love," Zen Buddhists as "satori," the Hindus as "moksha," and the Vedanta as "samadhi." Such experiences are so little understood that they have come to be shrouded in mysticism and regarded as supernatural. In the sense that they do not fit into the formula of cultural "sanity," these states are "insane," but it helps a little to understand them if we avoid such a loaded label and refer to them instead as states of unsanity.

There is nothing supernatural about them, and the importance of chemicals such as LSD is that they show this very clearly and simply by peeling away the artificial layers of "sanity" and letting us once again be natural. One of the most common effects of psychedelic substances is that they heighten suggestibility and enable us to pick up environmental cues with exquisite sensitivity. In laboratory test situations the LSD subjects often seem to be reading the experimenter's mind, but it is clear from analysis that they are simply responding, in the way that most animals do, to the most minute changes in tone, facial expression, and posture. We are capable all the time of this kind of subliminal perception, which is indeed supernatural when compared to our normal levels of response, but in the broader biological arena these talents are commonplace and altogether very natural.

Our usual waking "sane" state is one of inhibition. Part of this is necessary to prevent overloading with incoming sensations, but the barriers erected by the reticular system also deprive us of so much that is full of magic and inspiration. This is absurd when we have now grown a brain that is for the first time capable of appreciating these wonders. I am not making a plea for mass dissociation and a world-wide escape into these areas of unsanity. Blake, Van Gogh, Verlaine,

Coleridge, and Baudelaire all lived and worked a lot of the time in a state of transcendental awareness, and they suffered terribly in their efforts to break back through the barriers of reason and reality. Now, perhaps more than at any other time in our evolution, we need to be clear and aware of the problems that beset us, but our endeavors become pointless unless we appreciate that we have become masters of our own destiny. We need to know where we are going and how we are going to get there. Already we have begun to make use of our conscious talents, but we have completely neglected those available on the other side of the mind. Nature has given us all the necessary equipment for our task in the space between our ears, and the techniques of hypnosis, autosuggestion, dreaming, and hallucination give us some idea of the powers we possess. All that remains is for us to use them wisely.

Chapter Eight:

The Cosmic Mind

PART OF LIFE'S strength lies in the fact that it is precarious. The protoplasm in every cell hangs in an unstable balance that can be tipped in either direction by even the most subtle stimulus. Every part of every organism is like a packet of explosive, primed for action and connected to a hair-trigger mechanism—even a solitary amoeba is poised in this way, ready to flow in any direction. There was a time when amoeboid movement was thought to be completely random, so species were given splendidly anarchic names such as *Chaos chaos*, but our notions about the physical basis of life have changed.

Amoebae still delight student naturalists; anyone who can draw a squiggly pencil line that at some point in its meanderings meets up with itself again can call this an accurate representation of an amoeba. But we now know that the amoeba's pseudopodia are thrust out with intent, sometimes so precise that they can entirely surround even rapidly moving prey in an embrace that engulfs them without touching at any point. This is possible because the amoeba responds to slight changes in its environment by rapid reciprocal changes in its structure. The social amoebae respond to each other in the same way, coming together for reproduction in response to a chemical signal between them. When acting in concert they probably broadcast chemical messages, and we must assume that congregations or other independent protozoa, such as those which get together to form a sponge, communicate in the same way. It is difficult, however, to understand how as many as half a million units can co-ordinate their activities without even the most rudimentary nervous system.

In later and more complex multicells, a miracle of organization takes place. Some of the components change their shape and stretch until their length is as much as one hundred thousand times their breadth—proportions unique in life—and these elongated cable cells become sensory links between the different areas of the animal. The nerves provide a mechanical basis for electrochemical communication and promote the joint activities that give most animals direction and purpose, but sponges have none of these advantages and yet manage to operate in a controlled and clearly non-random fashion that seems to be almost extrasensory. Even if torn to shreds and put through a sieve, their cells reassemble again, like an organism rising from the dead. Plants also lack a nervous system and show no transmission of impulse from cell to cell—and yet they, too, demonstrate concerted action. A touch on the end of one of the compound leaves of *Mimosa pudica* makes it fold up, and if the stimulus is strong enough, the response soon spreads to neighboring leaves until the whole plant seems to cringe in submission. The action of the Venus fly-trap is even more impressive, because the cells achieve a kind of battery fire, responding together in an explosive action that is fast enough to catch an intruding fly. The biochemistry of the contractions is clearly understood, but co-ordination of the separate cells is still a mystery. The answer to it may lie outside the bounds of normal sensory perception.

On a February morning in 1966 Cleve Backster made a discovery that changed his life and could have far-reaching effects on ours. Backster was at that time an interrogation specialist who left the CIA to operate a New York school for training policemen in the techniques of using the polygraph, or "lie detector." This instrument normally measures the electrical resistance of the human skin, but on that morning he extended its possibilities. Immediately after watering an office plant, he wondered if it would be possible to measure the rate at which water rose in the plant from the root to the leaf by recording the increase in leaf-moisture content on a polygraph tape. Backster placed the two psychogalvanic-reflex (PGR) electrodes on either side of a leaf of *Dracaena massangeana*, a potted rubber plant, and balanced the leaf into the circuitry before watering the plant again. There was no marked reaction to this stimulus, so Backster decided to try what he calls "the threat-to-well-being principle, a well-established method of triggering emotionality in humans." In other words he decided to torture the plant. First of all he dipped one of its leaves into a cup of hot coffee, but there was no reaction, so he decided to get a match and burn the leaf properly. "At the instant of this decision, at 13 minutes and 55 seconds of chart time, there was a dramatic change in the PGR tracing pattern in the form of an abrupt and prolonged upward sweep of the recording pen. I had not moved, or touched the plant, so the timing of the PGR pen activity suggested to me that the tracing might have been triggered by the mere thought of the harm I intended to inflict on the plant."

Backster went on to explore the possibility of such perception in the plant by bringing some live brine shrimp into his office and dropping them one by one into boiling water. Every time he killed a shrimp, the polygraph recording needle attached to the plant jumped violently. To eliminate the possibility of his own emotions producing this reaction, he completely automated the whole experiment so that an electronic randomizer chose odd moments to dump the shrimp into hot water when no human was in the laboratory at all. The plant continued to respond in sympathy to the death of every shrimp and failed to register any change when the machine dropped already dead shrimp into the water.

Impressed by the plant's apparent sensitivity to stress, Backster collected specimens of other species and discovered that a philodendron seemed to be particularly attached to him. He no longer handles this plant with anything but the greatest care, and whenever it is necessary to stimulate it in order to produce a reaction, his assistant, Bob Henson, "plays the heavy." Now the plant produces an agitated polygraph response every time Henson comes into the room, and seems to "relax" when Backster comes near or even speaks in an adjoining room. (10) Enclosing the plant in a Faraday screen or a lead container has no effect, and it seems that the signals to which it responds do not fall within the normal electromagnetic spectrum. In more recent experiments Backster has found that fresh fruit and vegetables, mold cultures, amoebae, paramecia, yeast, blood, and even scrapings from the roof of a man's mouth all show similar sensitivity to other life in distress.

This phenomenon, which Backster calls "primary perception," has been substantiated by repetition of his work in other laboratories. (86) It raises awesome biological and moral questions; since thinking about it, I for one have had to give up mowing lawns altogether, but if it were to be taken to its logical limits we would end up, like the community in Samuel Butler's *Erewhon,* eating nothing but cabbages that have been certified to have died a natural death. The answer to the moral problem lies in treating all life with respect, and killing, with real reluctance, only that which is necessary for survival —but the biological problems are not as easily resolved.

If dying cells send out a signal to which other life responds, why do they do so? And why should such signals be more important to a potted plant than they are to us? Alarm signals are common to all social vertebrates at least. Sea gulls have specific calls that warn their breeding colonies of the approach of predators; ground squirrels and prairie marmots have an early-warning system that alerts their colonies to the danger of air raids by birds of prey. The function of the signals is so clear that those of crows and gulls have been recorded and broadcast across airfields to frighten these birds off the run-ways just before a plane is due to land. Very often the alarm is interspecific—terns, starlings, and pigeons feeding with gulls all take to flight at the sound of the gull alarm call; and seals dive into the water when nearby colonies of cormorants give notice of approaching danger. (69)

Alarm calls obviously have high survival value and work well across the species line, but not all species function on the same frequencies or even with the same sense organs, so there would be a strong natural pressure toward the evolu-tion of a common signal—a sort of all-species SOS. Pressures of this kind seldom go unnoticed, and it would seem that Backster's discovery could be nature's answer to exactly this need. Presumably it would begin by a compromise signal be-ing developed among groups of closely related species in response to a common predator. Then it would be to the predator's advantage to be able to detect the signal and an-ticipate its effect on his prey, and finally both predators and prey would find the signal useful in giving warning of an avalanche or flood or some natural catastrophe that could affect them all.

The search for a signal accessible to all life would naturally narrow down to the lowest common denominator. All organisms consist of cells, and the existence of a system of communication among cells would provide the final answer. We have yet to prove conclusively that such a system exists, but the odds in favor of it get better all the time.

Man's exclusion from this warning may be only apparent. I am beginning to suspect that unconsciously we are every bit as aware of the alarm as every pigeon or potted plant. It is a well-established fact that even in sleep we respond to certain significant sounds: a mother will sleep through the roar of a passing train but wake as soon as her child cries softly in another room.

Many mothers claim to know when something is wrong even before the baby sounds his audible alarm. They may be right and tuning in to the universal alarm, but many senses are known to be particularly acute immediately after childbirth, so they could be responding to ordinary stimuli that are very subtle indeed.

The male ostrich *Struthio camelus* has several hens, and each of them, in strict hierarchical order starting with the dominant female, lays five or six eggs in the hollow he scrapes out on the ground. The last of a large clutch, of twenty eggs, may therefore he laid three weeks after the first one, but all hatch within a few hours of each other about six weeks later. (330) This wonderful synchronization is vital if the cock is to look after his brood effectively, and he ensures that it occurs by listening in to the eggs as they develop. By the sounds they make, he can assess their stage of development, and if one is too far advanced, he rolls it out of the nest and buries it for a while until the others catch up. Other eggs have parents less astute, and they synchronize themselves by listening to each other. Days before hatching, the chicks of most ground-living birds, which need to hatch and run off together almost immediately, break through the small shell membrane to gain access to the air space at the blunt end. They breathe this air, and the sound of their breathing can be heard by chicks in other eggs, who know by its rate how near to hatching their brood mates are. (91) In the Japanese quail *Coturnix coturnix* the rate builds up to three sounds a second, and it has been shown that an artificial click at this frequency accelerates the rate of hatching of all the eggs in a nest. The embryos in most eggs make little "pleasure" calls in response to a change in position when the egg is held in the hand. These can be heard with a sensitive stethoscope, but it seems certain that breeding parent birds hear these sounds quite clearly and make the appropriate response to them.

In the 1880s two French scientists discovered a boy who appeared to be able to guess correctly the page numbers of books chosen at random by another person. The condition under which the boy operated best was with the experimenter standing with the light behind him and the book open between himself and the child. It turned out that the boy was able to read the numbers from the minute back-to-front reflections on the cornea of the experimenter's eye. (221) These reflections were only one tenth of a millimeter high, but the child's sense of sight was so acute that this was enough to give him the information he needed. This kind of sensitivity is very rare; it is unusual for anyone to be able to see so well, but supernormal does not mean supernatural. The boy's sight was extraordinarily good, but a powerful sense of sight is a very natural phenomenon, and a vulture could probably do as well if it could be persuaded to try.

We have not yet been able to draw any hard and fast limits to the acuity of our senses of sight, sound, smell, taste, and touch. Every new probe into their potential seems to push the limits of receptivity further and further out, and new spheres of perception are continually being discovered. Many apparently supernatural abilities sooner or later turn out to be due to hyperacuity of an existing sense system and in no way extrasensory, but there is one phenomenon that keeps cropping up and has yet to be explained satisfactorily in terms of the established senses. This is "thought transference," or telepathy.

TELEPATHY

A recent definition of telepathy describes it in these terms: "If one individual has access to information not available to another, then under certain circumstances and with known sensory channels rigidly controlled, the second individual can demonstrate knowledge of this information at a higher level than that compatible with the alternative explanation of chance guessing." (222)

There are thousands of records of what seems to be communication of this kind between two people who already have strong emotional bonds. The evidence is largely anecdotal and deals usually with knowledge of crises affecting one member of a pair—husband/wife, parent/child, brother/sister—that is communicated at the time of the occurrence to the other member, somewhere else. Rapport is said to be most effective between identical twins, who suffer the same diseases at the same times and seem to lead very similar lives even when separated at birth. These accounts are interesting but almost impossible to assess in retrospect and offer no real clues as to the nature and origin of telepathy.

The most painstaking attempt to deliberately keep knowledge of a given fact from an individual to see if he could guess the target correctly is the work done by Rhine and his associates at Duke University. They took the public feeling that there was an area of human experience in which people seem to know, by "hunch" or "intuition," about things that are out of direct reach of eye or ear, and examined it under laboratory conditions, in which the odds against knowing by pure coincidence could be computed. This work began in the early 1930s, when Rhine first used the term extrasensory perception, or ESP, to describe the process and began a lengthy series of tests on card guessing.

Rhine used the Zener pack, which consists of twenty-five cards carrying five symbols: square, circle, cross, star, and wavy lines. In any test the chance score is five out of twenty-five, but in a variety of test situations with a number of subjects, Rhine found that many times scores were so high that they had odds of more than a million to one against chance. On one occasion a nine-year-old girl from an unhappy home scored twenty-three when tested at her school, and when brought into the Duke laboratory by an experimenter to whom she had become emotionally attached, succeeded in guessing all twenty-five cards correctly. A Duke student, Hubert Pearce, became very involved with the research and, when specifically challenged by Rhine to do well in an important test, identified every single card in the pack. These were exceptional results clearly influenced by the personalities involved, and in longer series of the basically monotonous tests both subjects continued to do better than chance, but at the level of only seven or eight out of twenty-five. So most of his research, which has now been going on for almost forty years, is providing telepathic evidence that shows up only in statistics. But even if the margin of success is small, it is so persistent, over tens of millions of tests, that it shows that something is taking place to produce this bias.

The statistical methods used at Duke have been criticized, but the president of the American Institute of Mathematical Statistics says, "If the Rhine investigation is to be fairly at-

tacked it must be on other than mathematical grounds."
(133) Spencer-Brown of Cambridge suggests that the deviation from chance may be real, but that it is caused not so
much by telepathy as by an as yet unrecognized factor that
affects randomness itself. To many other researchers the surprising thing about the statistics is that there should have
been any success at all in experiments of this kind. Gaither
Pratt describes the card tests as "a grossly inefficient instrument," which is "choking off the very function which it was
designed to measure." (257) And the Soviet worker Lutsia
Pavlova regards the Rhine tests, which involve transmitting a
great many bits of information in a short time, as the most
difficult way imaginable of trying to generate telepathy. She
says, "We find it best not to send signals too quickly. If different bits come too rapidly, the changes in the brain associated
with telepathy begin to blur and finally disappear." (233)

A series of card tests with less equivocal results was performed in London between 1936 and 1943 by Samuel Soal
and his subject Basil Shackleton. Soal grew weary of the
standard designs and made his own cards, portraying five
brightly colored animals. In one series with these images, on
which the unconscious could get some sort of grip, Shackleton
scored 1,101 out of 3,789, which provides odds against chance
so high that they become almost meaningless. One could not
get a result like this by chance even if the entire population of
the world had tried the experiment every day since the beginning of the Tertiary period, sixty million years ago. (307)
One of the most interesting things about this test situation is
the motivation of the subject. Soal described how the tests
began one day when his office door suddenly opened and a
tall, well-groomed man in his thirties appeared. "I have
come," he announced, "not to be tested, but to demonstrate
telepathy." This was Shackleton, and a firm belief in his own

ability undoubtedly played a major part in producing the exceptional results.

Official support may also help, because in Russia great strides in telepathy research have been made in state-supported projects during the past five years. The new era opened on 19 April 1966, when Karl Nikolaiev—an actor in Novosibirsk—managed to open telepathic contact with his friend Yuri Kamensky—a biophysicist in Moscow, 1,860 miles away. Both men were supervised by scientific teams, and at a prearranged time Kamensky was handed a sealed package selected at random from a number of similar boxes, and, on opening it, began to finger the object, examining it carefully and trying hard to see it through his friend's eyes. It was a metal spring consisting of seven tight spirals and, in Novosibirsk, Nikolaiev wrote his impressions as "round, metallic, gleaming, indented, looks like a coil." Ten minutes later, when Kamensky concentrated on a screwdriver with a black plastic handle, Nikolaiev recorded "long and thin, metal, plastic, black plastic." (345) The mathematical probability of being able to guess a single target out of all the possible objects in the world is too large to even consider as a possible explanation for Nikolaiev's success, so the authorities were suitably impressed and grants were readily provided for further research.

Soon the "Popov group" came into being. This is a panel of scientists known collectively and officially as "The Bio Information Section of the A. S. Popov All-Union Scientific and Technical Society of Radio Technology and Electrical Communications." Their first task was to try to detect the action of telepathy in the brain, so in March 1967 the group installed Kamensky in Moscow again and took Nikolaiev to a laboratory in Leningrad, where he was installed in an isolated, soundproof room and wired up to a series of physiological monitors. He spent a while getting himself into a receptive state, which he describes as "completely relaxed, but attentive," and when he indicated that he was ready, his brain was producing a steady alpha rhythm. Nikolaiev had no idea when the telepathic message from Kamensky would be transmitted, but just three seconds after the experimenters in Moscow gave the signal to begin sending, Nikolaiev's brain waves changed drastically as the alpha was suddenly blocked. For the first time in history, visible proof of the transmission of an impulse from one mind to another, across four hundred miles, had been obtained.

In later tests, EEG records showed similar dramatic changes in the brain patterns of the sender as well as the receiver, and the Popov group reported, "We detected this unusual activation of the brain within one to five seconds after the beginning of telepathic transmission. We always detected a few seconds before Nikolaiev was consciously aware of receiving a telepathic message. At first there is a general, non-specific activation of the front and mid sections of the brain. If Nikolaiev is going to get the telepathic message consciously, the brain activation quickly becomes specific and switches to the rear, afferent regions of the brain." (233) When receiving an image of something such as a cigarette box, the activity in Nikolaiev's brain was localized in the occipital region, associated with sight, and when the message consisted of a series of noises being heard by the sender, activity took place in the receiver's temporal area, which is normally involved with sound.

The connection between telepathy and the alpha rhythm is crucial. It seems certain that both telepathy and psychokinesis occur only under certain psychological conditions and that these are the ones marked by the production of brain waves of a particular frequency. In PK it seems to be the theta rhythm, but in telepathy it is the alpha pattern, between eight and twelve cycles per second. Subjects who score well in laboratory tests all say that they adopt a certain state of mind, which one described as "concentrating my attention on a single point of nothingness. I think about nothing at all, just looking at a fixed point and emptying the mind entirely if this is possible." (224) Another calls the telepathic state "concentrated passivity," and a third sees it as "relaxed attentiveness." The psychologist William James resolved this paradoxical state by recognizing two types of attention. One is the active type, which requires effort such as that shown "by one whom we might suppose at a dinner party resolutely listening to a neighbour giving him insipid and unwelcome advice in a low voice, whilst all around the guests were loudly laughing and talking about exciting and interesting things." (163) This kind of attention involves conflict and is quite distinct from the passive type, in which one responds almost instinctively to an exciting sense impression. An example of this could be the state of someone who wakes suddenly in the night thinking that something must have disturbed him and sits up watching, listening, and waiting for whatever it was to happen again.

The production of telepathic or of psychokinetic phenomena is still so rare as to be considered abnormal, and it seems that in many subjects the fear of being able to do this type of thing produces a state of conflict that actively prevents them from doing it again. Many successful performers, whose livelihood or prestige depends on producing the phenomena, resolve the conflict by dissociation. They enter a trance state in which their conscious minds can disclaim all responsibility for the events, or perhaps they even become "possessed by a spirit" of someone else, who can be blamed for the goings on. The success of these psychological gambits for avoiding conflict is indicated by the fact that many subjects seem to remember nothing at all of what happened during the performance. For some the dissociation is simple, but others appear to go through tremendous battles in the process. Hereward Carrington, one of the old "trouble shooters" of psychical research, described the condition of a psychokinetic subject at the end of her session as "weak, drawn, nauseated, hysterical, deeply lined about the face, physically and mentally ill—a broken shrivelled old woman." (65) He also noted that her expenditure of nervous energy was greatest when there were strangers present and her fear of failure, and therefore her degree of conflict, were also high.

The effortless attention that seems to accompany successful performances is very characteristic of the psychological state that goes with alpha rhythms. To produce the rhythm that turns on the light in a commercial "alphaphone," one has to achieve just this state of mind. It used to be thought that alpha was continuous as long as the eyes were closed and that it would automatically stop when they opened, but with practice one can keep the rhythm going with wide-open eyes by avoiding any kind of analytical or calculating thought. This means avoiding sensory activity and becoming as abstracted as possible, and probably explains why many psychic subjects prefer to work in the dark or at least in dim lighting, and all of them insist on quiet. An EEG analysis of Einstein showed that he maintained a fairly continuous alpha rhythm even while carrying out rather intricate mathematical calculations, but for him these were part of everyday life and required no great expenditure of effort. (243) So it seems that alpha need not be blocked by mental activities as long as these require no active attention and involve no conflict.

The meditation techniques of the East are specifically designed to promote relaxed attention. Zen texts carry the instruction to "think of not thinking of anything at all," (78) and master yoga teachers say, "When the mind becomes devoid of all the activities and remains changeless, then the yogi attains to the desired state." (23) The emphasis is on

the lack of conflict, and although an act of will is initially
required to reach this state, "once the habit is developed,
effort is replaced by spontaneity and, instead of having the
attention hold the object, the object holds the attention." (19)
A study of *kriya-yoga* adepts in Calcutta showed that their
normal rate of alpha activity was in the usual range of nine
to eleven cycles per second, but in deepest meditation they
produced prolonged alpha rhythm that was accelerated by
as much as three cycles. (83) Gray Walter tells of a study
in which he watched a Hindu doctor go into meditation:
". . . the alpha rhythm became more and more regular and
monotonous, until toward the end of the exercise, which lasted
about twenty minutes, the alpha rhythm was absolutely continuous, so that it looked like an artificial oscillation." (336)
These measurements show that meditation states are quite
unlike drowsiness, light sleep, dreaming, coma, or hibernation, but have much more in common with the patterns
observed during successful telepathy. It is quite possible
that the two states originate in the same way and are aspects
of a single biological condition.

The Popov group have built an automatic tuning device,
which is nothing more than an "alphaphone," to tell Karl
Nikolaiev when he is in the correct mood for receiving
telepathic messages. The presence of similar rhythms in both
sender and receiver seems to be one prerequisite for successful communication between them, and the Russian research
has shown that this is not just a passive and accidental
resemblance in brain patterns. In one of their experiments
Kamensky was exposed to a strobe light flashing at a set
frequency inside the alpha range, and naturally this stimulus
set up a corresponding rhythm in his brain. Nikolaiev, in
another building, prepared himself and settled down to receive communication by producing his own alpha rhythm,
and when the two thought they were in contact, it was

found that their patterns were perfectly synchronized. (286)
Not only that, but every time the frequency of the light
flashing at Kamensky was changed, Nikolaiev's rhythm
changed instantly to match it. Similar results have been
obtained at the Jefferson Medical College, in Philadelphia,
where two ophthalmologists showed that a change in brain
rhythm, such as the production of alpha waves, in one twin
could cause a matching shift in the brain of the other, identical twin some distance away. (153) This kind of contact is
apparently even more effective if a strong physical or emotional state is involved at the same time. (233) The Popov
group attached Kamensky to a binocular apparatus that provided light flashes at a different frequency for each eye. The
double stimulus set up conflicting patterns on either side of
his brain, and the result was instant nausea. The same
patterns appeared simultaneously in Nikolaiev's brain, each
on the appropriate side, and produced in him an attack of
"seasickness" so severe that the experiment broke up in
confusion. This is the most convincing demonstration of
telepathy to date, including, as it does, patterns in the brain
that could not be produced in any natural way.

Again, the evidence shows that the most effective telepathic
messages involve trauma and crisis and that no news travels
so well or so quickly as bad news. Biologically this makes
sense. There is no urgency attached to pleasure and well-
being; these are states that can be communicated in the
usual leisurely way by normal channels, such as greeting
cards, but if alarm signals are going to serve any useful
function, they must travel by the fastest possible telegraphic
or telepathic route.

In 1960 a French magazine splashed the news that the
United States Navy was using telepathy to solve the old
problem of communication between a submarine under water
and its base on the shore. They reported that the atomic

submarine *Nautilus* was in telepathic contact with trained receivers on the shore and that ESP had become a new secret weapon. The American authorities were quick to deny the reports, but the Russians were equally quick to point out that *they* had been using the system for years. The Soviet method involved rabbits instead of radio. They took newly born rabbits down in a submarine and kept the mother ashore in a laboratory with electrodes implanted deep in her brain. At intervals, the underwater rabbits were killed one by one, and at the precise time that each of her offspring died there were sharp electrical responses in the brain waves of the mother. There is no known physical way in which a submerged submarine can communicate with anyone on land, and yet even rabbits seem to be able to make contact of a kind in a moment of crisis.

The possibility of actually using telepathy as a means of communication to submarines and spaceships has been entertained by both the United States and the U.S.S.R., and in both countries scientists have used the ideas as an instrument to pry more money for research out of their governments. As far as we know, nothing really practical has emerged. The difficulty is that in deep-sea or outer-space exploration, reliability is essential, and nobody has yet managed to produce telepathic contact that works every time and on demand. Perhaps the closest so far is the Kamensky/Nikolaiev combination, in which EEG records show when contact is taking place and how long it lasts. Using a Morse signal in which a contact of forty-five seconds is read as a dash and a contact of less than ten seconds as a dot, they have succeeded in getting seven consecutive signals across space to spell out the Russian word *MIG*, which means "instant." (110) The test took twenty minutes, which is not exactly instantaneous, but even this would represent a saving in time when talking to a cosmonaut in the vicinity of Jupiter, where radio communications will lag by over an hour. The message, of course, would have to be very simple, and it is difficult to imagine any space project placing reliance on a system as unpredictable as this one still is, but it might be useful in an emergency.

Apart from influencing brain waves, telepathic contacts also seem to have an influence on blood pressure. Douglas Dean, an electrochemist at the Newark College of Engineering, has discovered that even those who are consciously unaware of receiving telepathy, might be doing so. (85) When someone concentrates on the name of a person with whom he has an emotional tie, the distant subject registers a measurable change in blood pressure and volume. Dean used a plethysmograph to show that about one in every four people have this kind of sensitivity. Using such loaded names and a system in which a response stands for a dot and a long period without stimulus represents a dash, he has managed to send simple messages from room to room, building to building, and, in one case, over twelve hundred miles, from New York to Florida. (178) This discovery ties in with Russian findings that individuals in apparently telepathic contact have a quicker heartbeat, greater cardiac noises, and in some cases perfect synchronization in pulse between sender and receiver. (227)

It has been suggested that this physical rapport could be enhanced by electromagnetic fields. A Washington electronics engineer reports that "working with high frequency machines, my colleagues and I have suddenly found that we are on occasion telepathic." (233) It is possible that the whole body is involved. One study shows that an increase in electrical activity and therefore a decrease in skin resistance takes place at the moment of contact, (236) but most indications point to the fact that physical relaxation and therefore a decrease in muscle tone and skin reaction is essential. Electromyographs attached to the arms of yogis in meditation show no response at all, even when the session lasts over two hours. (83) Relaxation produces a decrease in the rate of respiration and a corresponding increase in the pressure of carbon dioxide in the lungs. This in turn produces a rise in the carbon-dioxide tension of arterial blood, and when this comparatively poorly oxygenated blood reaches the brain, it starts a chain reaction in which the blood vessels dilate to increase the rate of flow and the brain rhythm accelerates as it battles to get the oxygen it needs. Usually this reaction produces fast alpha rhythms of exactly the frequency that seems to be conducive to telepathy. Accidental loss of blood produces the same deficiency with the same results, and it is interesting that people who lose blood often speak of being relaxed and detached, just watching the world go by and seeing other things and other people very clearly. Another, and more common, cause of oxygen deprivation is high altitude. Could it be purely coincidental that so many of the transcendental techniques have been perfected by people living at great heights in the Himalayas? A member of the first successful Everest expedition described his reactions above twenty-four thousand feet when he felt "the presence of one half of me soaring above, sublimely purposeful, aware of the beauty around. It chides, encourages, fortifies the other half, grinding dismally below." (232)

The correspondence between the conditions that seem to be best suited to telepathy and those which occur in meditation is so close that it is tempting to pursue the parallels even further. (224) All the groups that practice meditation also have very strict rules governing their diet. They are almost entirely vegetarian for ostensibly moral reasons, but there could also be a physiological basis for their food preferences. Meat has the direct effect of increasing the acidity of blood, and our bodies respond to this by lowering the amount of acidic carbon dioxide in compensation. A vegetable diet has the opposite effect: it reduces acidity, and compensation for this produces a rise in carbon-dioxide pressure in the lungs and a reduction in the amount of oxygen getting to the brain. So a vegetarian meal has roughly the same effect as an increase in altitude—and the yogis dining on rice and fruit down at sea level in India are making physiological excursions up into the mountains every day.

Many of the physical conditions that seem to be part of a state that encourages telepathy also occur in sleep. The muscle tone is reduced, respiration and carbon-dioxide pressure are decreased, and the brain is generally not concerned with analysis and calculation. At Maimonides Hospital, in New York, a "dream laboratory" has been established, primarily for research into sleep and dreaming but also to investigate the possibility of telepathy between a sender and a sleeping receiver. One of the team working there says, "Many persons who are incapable of effective communication in normal ways can communicate at a telepathic level and surprise the therapist with a dream of rich awareness even of the physician's problems." (309) The information included in these dreams could have been gained in a normal way during a psychoanalytic session, so they set up a series of experiments in which senders tried to communicate when EEG patterns showed that the receiver was dreaming. One of the targets was Dali's painting *The Sacrament of the Last Supper,* and on waking, the subject reported a dream of a group of people, a fishing boat, a glass of wine, and the feeding of the multitudes. On another occasion the senders were two thousand people at a pop concert in a nearby theater, and the target was a man meditating in the lotus position that they could see on the screen above the performers. The concert situation was chosen because "music appeals to a person's non-verbal nature, to levels of consciousness below the intellect." (79) It seemed to work because the subject had a dream of a holy man capturing the energy from the sun.

Several workers suggest that telepathy is masked by consciousness and that it takes place only when one's guard is down and it can slip by the active censor in our minds. There seem to be specific conditions in which telepathy can take place, and trying to examine it in a laboratory under controlled conditions is a little like trying to study the behavior of a dead animal. Sitting at a table hour by hour trying to guess the sequence of five meaningless symbols in someone else's pack of cards seems hardly likely to lay bare the unconscious areas where telepathic abilities may be latent. Our unconscious responds much more readily to emotional situations. This can be demonstrated very easily by an experiment such as that in which subjects were shown ten nonsense syllables, five of which were accompanied by an electric shock, until they became conditioned and produced electrical responses in their palms whenever they saw the "shocking" syllables. (160) The syllables were then flashed on the screen so fast that none of the subjects could consciously tell them apart, but their unconscious minds saw the patterns quite clearly and produced the reflex each time they were shown a brief glimpse of the syllables that had once been connected with the shocks. The unconscious is active all the time, but techniques like this are necessary to prompt or bully it into giving up its information.

The best instrument we possess for exploring the unconscious is hypnosis. The psychiatrist Stephen Black has said, "Hypnosis is not only the most simple and practical way of proving the existence of the unconscious—which is still in doubt in some circles—but is in fact the only way in which unconscious mechanisms can be manipulated under repeatable experimental conditions for purposes of investigation." (26) The induction of hypnosis depends on the establishment of a rapport between hypnotist and subject that is at first sight very much like one of the prerequisites for telepathy. There are, however, no EEG patterns unique to hypnosis, and there is no evidence at all to suggest that hypnotist and subject enter into physiological linkage like that of Kamensky and Nikolaiev, but there are reports of shared experience. The physicist Sir William Barrett carried out a series of tests with a young girl: "Standing behind the girl, whose eyes I had securely bandaged, I took up some salt and put it in my mouth; instantly she sputtered and exclaimed, 'What for are you putting salt in my mouth?' Then I tried sugar; she said 'That's better'; asked what it was like, she said 'Sweet.' Then mustard, pepper, ginger etc. were tried; each was named and apparently tasted by the girl when I put them in my own mouth, but when placed in her mouth she seemed to disregard them." (94)

This kind of communication has not been proved, but if it exists, it would lend strong support to Jung's notion of a collective unconscious, in which all experience is shared. Even Freud, though he himself had difficulty inducing hypnosis, believed that telepathy took place most easily in psychoanalytic situations, in which the unconscious was being exposed to scrutiny. His essay on *Psychoanalysis and Telepathy* was not published until after his death, but toward the end he wrote, "If I had my life to live over again, I should devote myself to psychical research rather than to psychoanalysis." (309)

It looks as if telepathy is regularly received by the unconscious and only occasionally breaks through to conscious levels. There seems to be a barrier that prevents it from surfacing in our conscious minds, and to overcome this blockage we, or those such as the psychoanalyst or the hypnotist who are assisting us, must find some way around or some subterfuge that circumvents it. The old mediumistic phenomena of "automatic talking" and "automatic writing" while in a state of trance may be ways in which the conscious mind "passes the buck" and surrenders its responsibilities. Dreams and hallucinations could be other ways around the repression. It is entirely possible that many of our everyday thoughts are telepathic, or at least partly telepathic, in origin and that we pass these off as our own simply because they have become mixed with much that is genuinely ours in crossing the threshold between the unconscious and full consciousness.

It seems to me that telepathy, defined as "access to information held by another without use of the normal sensory channels," is proved beyond reasonable doubt. It is too much a part both of common experience and of controlled investigation to be dismissed any longer. We now have a great many records of communication taking place outside the normal channels, but still very little idea of how it might operate.

We know a fair amount about how it does not work.

Leonid Vasiliev, physiologist at the University of Leningrad, has done a long and painstaking series of experiments in an attempt to track down the telepathic wavelength. He started with two hypnotic subjects that could be put into a trance from a distance by what can only be telepathic means. This provided him with a repeatable phenomenon that could be switched on and off at will and probed and pulled apart to reveal what he hoped would be the physical basis of transmission. He eliminated most of the normal electromagnetic possibilities by putting the subjects into a Faraday cage, but still they fell asleep on telepathic cue. He built a lead capsule with a lid that sealed itself in a groove filled with mercury, but still the message got through. Finally, when he found that it worked regardless of the distances involved, Vasiliev admitted defeat. (328)

The discovery that telepathy seems to be independent of distance has disturbed investigators, because most known physical forces diminish in proportion to the distance they travel—in accordance with a well-known law. In recent years, however, the law has been broken. Many metals, when cooled to the temperature of liquid helium, can be made to carry an electric current without any loss due to resistance or the distance involved. (121) In this condition they are known as superconductors, and what they do amounts almost to perpetual motion as long as the low temperatures are maintained. Now there are signs that new alloys can be made that will allow superconduction at much higher temperatures, perhaps even at room temperature, and the exciting thing about these new, layered materials is that the metal is sandwiched between bands of an organic compound. These new materials are also more directional than the old ones, allowing currents to flow only in certain channels. In this they are reminiscent of discoveries that under certain conditions radiations such as radio waves can be ducted so that they not only arrive at their destination undiminished in power but sometimes even gain in strength. Work on the sounds produced by whales shows that these mammals will deliberately seek out inversion layers deep in the ocean, where a band of warm water sometimes gets trapped between two layers of cooler water, and that they use these bands as submarine cables to communicate perhaps over thousands of miles across an entire ocean.

This raises the question of why, if such channels exist, have we not been able to detect them or deflect them in the space between two people in apparent telepathic contact? The answer to this could be that they depend on particles that are mathematically imaginary. Modern physics often uses virtual particles with imaginary energies and masses to describe functions in the physical world. An example is the "neutrino," which has no positive physical characteristics and is observable only by inference but plays a vital role in the interaction of other fundamental particles. The neutrino, and its counterpart the anti-neutrino, have never been directly discovered, but every competent physicist today is convinced that they exist, simply because he can see no way in which certain reactions could take place without them. The situation with telepathy is much the same. Certain phenomena have been observed regularly under a wide variety of conditions, and there is no reason to assume that a physical agent does not exist simply because we cannot yet see it.

Assuming that telepathy exists and acknowledging our failure to discover its mode of action, we are still left with the problem of what it means. Why did it evolve in the first place? And if it is not confined to man, what is its biological function?

Sir Alister Hardy, once Professor of Zoology at Oxford, has been disturbing his more orthodox colleagues since 1949 with the notion that telepathy may be the clue to a fundamental biological principle that has played a major part in evolution. He argues that the development of language, important as it was for man, is unlikely to have produced extrasensory kinds of perception as well, and suggests that it might have had the opposite effect. Language undoubtedly assisted the growth of reason, the exchange of ideas, the initiation and spread of new inventions, and the enlargement of our cerebral cortex, but it might also have repressed a more primitive form of knowing in favor of the more precise communication possible in a spoken system. Babies up to the age of about eighteen months seem to be very much like chimpanzees of the same age; they have similar interests and intellects and can communicate very effectively in the old, visual manner. Even adults, deprived of the advantages of language and linguistic clues, see, hear, feel, move, and explore in much the same way animals do. A man who cannot make notes or draw a map is no better at negotiating a maze than a trained white rat. In explicit knowledge, formulated in words and formulas and diagrams, we are unbeatable, but in tacit knowledge, which is concerned with what we are actually in the act of doing before it becomes expressed in words or symbols, we are not as good as many other species.

Hardy said, "Perhaps our idea on evolution may be altered if something akin to telepathy . . . was found to be a factor in moulding the patterns of behaviour among members of a species. If there was such a non-conscious group behaviour plan, distributed between, and linking, the individuals of the race, . . . it might operate through organic selection to modify the course of evolution." (134)

By "organic selection" he meant that the gene combinations best suited to the habits of an animal would tend to survive in preference to those which did not give full scope to the animal's patterns of behavior. For instance, if a bird that used to feed on insects from the surface of the bark of trees found that as man encroached and the insects became more scarce it could get more food by probing into the bark, then it might change its feeding habits in this direction. If all the members of the species adopted the new habit of probing, then those whose genes gave them the advantage of a slightly longer bill would have a better chance of survival. In time all the population would have longer beaks, and an evolutionary change in appearance would have taken place because of a simple change in behavior.

The blue tit, *Parus caeruleus,* in western Europe has recently learned to open the foil caps of milk bottles left on doorsteps and drink the cream off the top. This behavior pattern is spreading rapidly across the continent, apparently by imitation, and if the dairies continue to deliver their product in the same containers, it is possible that sooner or later these little birds will develop a bill better designed to exploit a valuable new source of food.

In both these cases the change in behavior was brought about by an environmental change. Most evolutionary developments are ones of this kind, occurring in response to external pressures of climate or the actions of predators or competitors. Plants evolve entirely in this way, developing in directions imposed on them by the selective forces of sun and rain, soil and shelter, competition with neighboring plants, and destruction by browsing herbivores. The fantastic carnival of flowers is one produced entirely for the benefit of those animals the plant needs to come and distribute its pollen. (133) The Australian orchid *Cryptosylia leptochila* has developed a flower that is a perfect replica, complete with spots in the proper places, of the abdomen of a female ichneumon fly, *Lissopimpla semipunctata*. The male is attracted to the flower, tries to mate with it, and in doing so, picks up pollen and carries this on to his next frustrating rendezvous. This is a clear example of the behavior of an animal acting as an evolutionary force on the shape of a plant. Animals are not entirely dependent on the external forces of selection in this way but can, by their exploratory nature, bring about changes in their own appearance by changing their behavior.

The importance of this distinction is that adaptations produced by external selection are generally limiting and negative in nature, shaping an organism to fit more easily into the environmental niche in which it occurs. Adaptations produced by the animal's own patterns of behavior are much less predetermined and can lead it out of the niche into the exploration and colonization of entirely new ways of life. Otters would never have developed their webbed feet, nor dolphins their flippers, if one of their entirely terrestrial ancestors had not deviated from its usual routine and gone paddling instead. And this is where telepathy comes in.

Some of these changes in behavior and body form took place in a comparatively short space of time, and it is difficult to see how this could have been achieved in every case just by the trial-and-error experiments of occasional adventurous individuals. New habits and ideas can spread by imitation, as

they seem to be doing in the milk-drinking tits and in a population of monkeys on one of the Japanese islands who have
learned to take sweet potatoes down to the sea and wash
them. Even here there are problems: the milk-bottle craze
has spread at a rate that alarms the dairies, and it seems that
a second group of monkeys, on a neighboring island, have recently and unaccountably also begun rinsing their food.

The existence of an unconscious telepathic link among members of the same species could be a great help in developing
and stabilizing new behavior patterns. Whately Carington,
who once experimented with the telepathic transmission of
drawings between people, put forth the idea that other patterns, such as the intricate webs of some spiders, might be
communicated in the same way. "I suggest that the instinctive
behaviour of this high order or elaborate type may be due to
the individual creature concerned being linked up into a
larger system (or common unconscious if you prefer it) in
which all the web-spinning experience of the species is stored
up." (64) It is nonsense to suggest that instinctive behavior is
governed by a collective unconscious; we know beyond doubt
that it is controlled by genetic inheritance, but it is possible
that telepathy could be useful before a habit becomes genetically fixed. A habit must become widespread before it can be
incorporated into the repertoire of a species, and it could be
spread and stabilized very effectively by some kind of telepathic system. Without telepathy it is difficult to see how an
elaborate instinctive pattern can develop at all in invertebrate animals that are highly unlikely to acquire new habits
by imitation or by tradition.

For a system of this kind to work, news of a new discovery
would have to be generally broadcast in the same way as an
alarm call and not confined to a cozy, two-ended telepathic
contact. Most human experiments have been of the single-
line type, but this does not mean that party lines are impossi-

ble. At one point in the long series of experiments between Kamensky and Nikolaiev, a third person was introduced. While Kamensky was in Leningrad transmitting to Nikolaiev in Moscow, unknown to either of them an interceptor, Victor Milodan, was installed in another building in Moscow. Five items were transmitted that evening, and Milodan managed to "eavesdrop" sufficiently well to identify two of them accurately. So even a very modern and sophisticated spy, specially trained in telepathic techniques, can still have trouble with "bugs."

Telepathy could also be useful for cohesion in complex societies such as those of bees and ants. We know that part of this function is played by chemicals, by pheromones that circulate in a hive and let everyone know that the queen still lives. Each worker bee and ant also has a complex of glands that release smells designed for special situations such as laying a trail to a food source or "scenting" an alarm. In ants the alarm smell is kept in the mandibular glands, and if discharged into still air, it forms a sphere that reaches a maximum diameter of about three inches in fifteen seconds; then it contracts again and fades out altogether after thirty-five seconds. (343) The alarm sphere therefore extends for only a short distance around the disturbance, say that caused by the intrusion of a foreign insect, and does not affect the rest of the nest. This is important, because there are so many minor disturbances each day that the colony would come to a complete standstill if each alarm were broadcast generally, but there are situations where more concerted action is necessary and where the local and short-lived effects of the smell alarm are inadequate. In those cases telepathy would be very useful and may in fact be employed.

Ivan Sanderson has studied harvester ants of the genus *Atta* in tropical America and reports remarkable communal activity. (291) These ants build a network of complex, well-cleared roads radiating out from their underground city for as much as half a mile to all the useful food sites in the vicinity. If one of these roads becomes blocked by a falling branch or other obstacle, traffic is disrupted until the special police ants arrive to direct the construction of a detour. Sanderson was impressed by the speed with which reinforcements arrived at a site, and arranged a number of roadblocks of his own where he and his associates were installed along the road at intervals with stop watches. They found that "a great phalanx of police came charging up the road from the nest, shoulder to shoulder, about fifty ants wide and rank after rank," almost instantaneously. There was not nearly enough time for word of the disaster to be carried by antenna-to-antenna touch all the way back, the wind was blowing away from the nest and would soon have dispersed any alarm scents, it was dark, and no sound seemed to be involved. It is certain that *Atta* have a telecommunication system, and it seems to be independent of known chemical and mechanical senses. They, and other species like them, could make good use of, and perhaps already use, some form of telepathy.

A colony of social insects is, in a very real sense, a single organism. The queen is the sex organ and master endocrine gland; the workers are reproductive tract, digestive canal, and regenerative organs; the police are regulatory activities; and the soldiers are the organs of defense. All are united by a set of instincts into a single self-supporting structure in which the interests of the parts are subordinate to the interests of the whole. It should not be surprising to find that such an organism has a rudimentary mind. After all, the functions of the human mind cannot be anchored to any one cell or even a group of cells. The brain is made up of far more parts than there are in an ant colony, and yet it manages to function as a whole, with more or less complete communication between its separate cells. Impressions are gathered from different areas and merged in the mind in exactly the same way I am suggesting that information from different sources may be merged in a telepathic union between apparently disparate individual animals in a community. This communion may even go a step further and involve all individuals belonging to the same species. There may be a sort of psychic blueprint for each species which involves an unconscious sharing of behavior patterns and perhaps even of form.

One of the major unexplained problems in biology is that of organization. In the fruit fly *Drosophila* there is a particular gene that governs formation of the eyes. If this is altered by mutation, a fly is produced without eyes and, bred with others like it, will produce a strain of sightless flies. But after a while the gene complex rearranges itself and some other gene steps in to deputize for the damaged one—and suddenly the flies have eyes again. If part of the eye of a frog is grafted in below the skin anywhere on its body, the epidermal cells in that area will form a perfect lens. So the structure of the eye in fly and frog is not dependent only on a special gene or on special cells. There seems to be some sort of organizer somewhere else, a master plan that knows what the animal should look like and that will make the necessary arrangements in times of need. Most of this organization is in the hands of DNA—the unique molecule that carries the heritage of every species—but this does not seem to be sufficient. The remarkable thing about life is not that it exists in such a variety of forms but that so many forms manage to maintain their basic shape and integrity for so long in the face of the multitude of environmental forces that never stop trying to disrupt it. Certainly the DNA code carries instructions that determine the general physical form, but perhaps there is another organizer, a sort of stream of shared experience that allows only the best copies of the species plan to survive.

Telepathy could do this.

INTUITION

Charles McCreery of the Institute of Psychophysical Research in Oxford is skeptical of the physiological changes some workers present as evidence for the occurrence of telepathy. He prefers to draw a fundamental distinction between "physiological apparatus as a means of determining the conscious ESP state and physiological apparatus as a detector of ESP." (224) This means that he is not sure about telepathy itself but believes it is possible to recognize the conditions in which it will occur. McCreery lists these as continuous alpha activity, which is often slightly accelerated; decreased muscle tone; and increased carbon-dioxide pressure.

If there is a clearly defined physiological state in which telepathy is most likely to occur, then it must be possible for someone to train himself to recognize this state in the same way that one can learn to produce alpha rhythms or decreased blood pressure at will. Perhaps this is what intuition is—simply an ability to recognize the telepathic state and use this knowledge to say, "I don't know why, but I just feel certain that . . ." This would mean that intuition is a vague conscious knowledge of the unconscious reception of telepathic information. In many of the telepathy tests, subjects do have a peculiar feeling about certain guesses or impressions and say that some "feel better" than the rest or that they "have a hunch" that things are going well. Often these hunches prove to be correct, but there is not nearly enough information available to prove that this correlation exists. Theoretically it should be possible to run tests designed so that the subject would withhold guesses until he felt this intuitive feeling of "rightness." But, so far, no tests of this kind have been done, and the connection between telepathy and intuition remains obscure.

It is possible that there is no correlation between them at all. One of the games played by the psychiatrist Eric Berne is to guess age, occupation, address, and family situation of people he meets. In this he often seems to be remarkably successful, and it has been suggested that he uses telepathy to get the information, but he feels that his intuition is based on normal sensory clues. He suggests that "things are being automatically arranged just below the level of consciousness; subconsciously perceived factors are being sorted out, fall automatically into place, and are integrated into the final impression, which is at length verbalized with some uncertainty." (24) Berne claims that he can tell when his intuition is working well and that the conditions necessary for successful guessing involve "a narrowed and concentrated contact with external reality." Which sounds similar to the "relaxed alert" state of good telepathy, but it is possible that both telepathic information and subliminal impressions are received when the mind is in this mood. We know that under hypnosis the unconscious can recall incredible things, such as the number of stairs climbed in visiting someone else's office last week or the number of lampposts in the street outside, but we have no idea why this sort of thing is collected and when.

It seems that far more environmental information gets into the unconscious than we suspected and that the barrier between unconscious and conscious processes is one of those vital filters that protect us from being swamped by sensations. If this is so, it is not surprising that we have trouble breaking through the barrier: our lives depend on its being maintained intact. A certain amount of seepage occurs in the form of dreams and hallucinations, and intuition may be another breach, perhaps one that takes place in emergencies when the information might be vital to our survival. Most often, intuitions are the product of past experience—memories, wishes, hopes, and fears that have been stored in the unconscious, but sometimes they may contain completely new information, perhaps obtained by telepathy.

The scant use we make of intuition may be a product of the complexity of our conscious lives. We see it as an alternative to the logical approach of the intellect and tend to divide people into those who operate more emotionally—on the basis of intuition—and those who adopt an intellectual attitude to all decisions. Folklore credits women with greater powers of intuition, but there is little evidence to justify this, although it is possible that women are forced to be more intuitive simply because they have been denied the chance of intellectual development. In species with lesser reasoning ability and a less active consciousness, the barriers seem to be much reduced and in most to be completely non-existent, but this does not mean that they lose sight of the distinction between "self" and "non-self."

Swallows sitting on a wire, space themselves out with almost exactly six inches between each two neighboring birds; for sea gulls the distance is twelve inches, and individual distance in flamingos is about two feet. Man draws the same kind of invisible circles around his body, and the diameter of these areas can be a good indication of his emotional state. The psychiatrist August Kinzel has discovered that the personal space surrounding a normal, well-balanced person is cylindrical and extends roughly eighteen inches in all directions. (176) Each of us apparently defends this area, and Kinzel has found that the space is very much larger for those of violent disposition. When he tried to approach prison inmates who had records of violence, he found that they stopped him at a distance of as much as three feet and showed markedly increasing tension and hostility as the distance shrank when he deliberately trespassed on their space. Their personal area also bulged out behind them to about four feet, and they regarded any approach from this direction as particularly menacing.

These zones are partly under conscious control. When tightly packed into an elevator or bus, we very carefully suppress hostility and arrange ourselves so that we are angled away from our nearest neighbors in a gesture that provides some reassurance for them. It is possible that we also avoid aggression in these circumstances by an intuitive grasp of the intentions of other individuals. This need not involve telepathy or any extrasensory receptivity but simply an unconscious awareness of others. The work of life fields suggests that a group of people together generate a composite field that has a distinctive character and that the addition of a new individual to a group does not just quantitatively add to the field but often changes its pattern altogether. Conversely, we all know the feeling of emptiness and loss that can arise when one person, who may not have been taking any active part in a discussion, leaves a group. The character of the group, its topic of conversation, and its activity can all change, and the party may even break up altogether.

This field of social awareness seems to be the one in which intuition plays its most active role. Whether or not it has anything to do with telepathy, it certainly provides a useful means of access to unconscious sources of information derived from our environment and other organisms in it.

There are a few situations in which it seems also to be possible to obtain information completely unknown to anyone else.

CLAIRVOYANCE

In the long series of card-guessing tests at Duke University most of the subjects were trying to guess the card being looked at by another person; these were genuine telepathy tests. But in a few, the subjects were aiming at a target nobody knew, such as the sequence in a shuffled deck. When these tests returned results better than chance, Rhine was forced to recognize a new phenomenon—clairvoyance. (272)

One of the most exhaustively tested subjects in the history of parapsychological research is a young Czechoslovakian student, Pavel Stepanek. He has produced phenomenal scores in all the classic card tests, but he has also introduced a variation of his own that has come to be known as the "focusing effect." (288) He scores particularly well with certain favorite cards and can find them when they are enclosed in envelopes and shuffled so that even the experimenter does not know which is which. After a while his focus comes to include the envelope too, and this has then to be placed in another wrapping. In his latest tests he is being offered a card in an envelope enclosed in a cover that is placed in another jacket, but still he gets them right. (258)

Most of these clairvoyance experiments provide evidence that becomes apparent only on statistical analysis, but two Dutch psychics offer much more dramatic demonstrations. (309) In 1964 Gerard Croiset of Utrecht was consulted by the police in the murder case of three civil-rights workers in Mississippi, and reports indicate that he was able to give accurate information and descriptions of the area in which the bodies were eventually found and to correctly implicate certain local policemen in the killings. In 1943 Peter Hurkos fell from a ladder, fractured his skull, and found that he had lost the power of concentration, but had gained a new faculty instead. When asked recently to assist the police of The Hague, he had only to hold the coat of a dead man to be able to describe the man's murderer in detail that included glasses, mustache, and wooden leg. When the police admitted that they already had such a man under arrest, Hurkos told them where to find the murder weapon. (157)

Strictly speaking, none of these examples can be recognized as true clairvoyance, because there was always someone involved somewhere who knew the vital information. Telepathy could have been taking place. Even in the cases of the card tests, there could have been flaws in the experimental design that allowed the experimenter to have an inkling, albeit unconscious, of where the hidden card was located. True clairvoyance must be concerned with the discovery of an object whose location is unknown to anyone, but then why not call it dowsing? The existence of clairvoyant abilities is so doubtful, and the possibility of such talents having any biological significance so remote, that it seems pointless to pursue them any further.

WITCHCRAFT

Milan Ryzl, a Czechoslovakian physician now working in the United States, tells of a series of telepathic experiments in which the sender tried to transmit bursts of emotion. When the sender concentrated on the anxiety of suffocation and conjured up racking attacks of asthma, the receiver several miles away suffered an intense choking fit. (287) When the sender concentrated on gloomy emotions and was given a depressant drug, the receiver showed the appropriate EEG response and began to experience strong head pains and a feeling of nausea that lasted for hours. This sheds an entirely new light on the old notion of black magic. There is no doubt that someone who believes that he has been bewitched can think himself into illness and even death, but this new work makes it look as though you don't necessarily have to think your own destructive thoughts. Someone else can think them up and point them at you.

William Seabrook lived for years among the Malinke people in old French West Africa and tells of a Belgian hunter who abused and murdered his local bearers until, as a matter of private justice, they arranged for a sorcerer to lay on a death-sending for him. In a clearing in the jungle the witch doctors set up the corpse of a man requisitioned from a nearby village, dressed it in one of the Belgian's shirts, combed some of his hair in among its own, fastened some of his nail parings to its fingers, and rebaptized the body with the hunter's name. Around this object of sympathetic magic, they chanted and drummed, focusing their malignant hatred on the white man miles away. A number of his employees, pretending sympathy for him, made certain that the Belgian knew that all this was going on and would continue until he died. He soon fell ill and did die, apparently from auto-suggestion. (302) The accepted explanation for events of this kind is that an unconscious belief in the power of the spell, even if one has not in fact been cast, can kill. But the discovery of what seems to be illness transmitted by telepathy suggests that the ceremony itself may be important. The frenzy of hate around the corpse in the jungle would certainly have a hypnotic effect on the participants and would produce exactly the conditions now known to be necessary for creating a telepathic state, the token doll in this case perhaps serving only as a focus for emotions that were in themselves doing damage at a distance.

A case can be made for considering all the trappings of magic in this light, as objects, like the altar in a church, on which attention can be focused and around which emotion can be generated. Spells producing sexual inhibition, possession, paralysis, and all forms of wasting disease undoubtedly rely on suggestion a great deal. Many work because the witches believe that they have these powers and because their subjects believe that they can use them, but the possibility of direct action on an unknowing person cannot be ignored.

There is not much doubt that the procedure of ritual magic

of every kind can cause hallucinations. Richard Cavendish describes the magician preparing himself for action by "abstinence and lack of sleep, or by drink, drugs and sex. He breathes in fumes which may affect his brain and senses. He performs mysterious rites which tug at the deepest, most emotional and unreasoning levels of his mind, and he is further intoxicated by the killing of an animal, the wounding of a human being and in some cases the approach to and achievement of orgasm." Which includes just about every emotion known to man. It is hardly surprising if after all this he, and those involved with him, see visions and conjure up terrifying personal demons.

A common adjunct of the sorcerer's and the witch's craft is a potion painstakingly prepared for a special effect. Witches were notorious poisoners—both the biblical and the Italian names for them refer specifically to this talent—and the poisons prepared were undoubtedly effective, but it is generally assumed that the elaborate rituals involved in collecting and mixing the ingredients were unnecessary and superstitious elaborations. This may not be true. There is an old idea that a remedy for cancer can be prepared from mistletoe, but that its effectiveness depends entirely on the time that the plant is picked. A cancer research institute in Switzerland tested this recently by doing seventy thousand experiments on parts of the plant picked at hourly intervals day and night. (112) They measured the degree of acidity, analyzed the constituents, and tested the effect of all the preparations on white mice. They have not yet found a cure for cancer, but they did discover that the properties of the plant were drastically affected not only by local time and weather conditions but by extraterrestrial factors such as the phase of the moon and the occurrence of an eclipse. (339) Nothing is the same from one moment to the next. The orientalist Du Lubicz described a medicine that worked almost miraculously if prepared according to the traditional Egyptian ritual, but which, prepared in any other way, was actually poisonous. The time and the place and the way in which something is done, do matter a great deal.

It was not many years ago that orthodox medicine completely dismissed psychosomatic causes. That has now changed, but I have the impression that in our new-found enthusiasm for things psychosomatic, we can go too far and attribute to them everything for which we can find no other reasonable explanation. Our future lies in the mind and in our understanding of it, but the intricate rituals and ceremonies that once surrounded occult practices associated with the powers of the mind may surprise us and turn out to have direct effects of their own.

Matter, mind, and magic are all one in the cosmos.

PART FOUR

TIME

"If only I had known, I should have become a watchmaker."

ALBERT EINSTEIN, in *New Statesman*, 16 April 1965.

TIME IS A RHYTHM. It comes and goes like the crackle of electricity in the brain or the gush of blood through the heart or the flood of the tide up the beach. All these things are governed by cosmic clocks, and our measurements are nothing but bookkeeping conveniences. Seconds and minutes have nothing to do with nature. Every organism interprets the universal rhythms in its own way. A cattle tick may sit on the end of a twig for months waiting for a passing mammal; a larval cicada lives for years in the ground at the base of a tree waiting for conditions that will be exactly right for its one day of life as an adult. For them these periods pass as a single moment, of no more consequence in their lives than the interval between two of our heartbeats.

Manipulations of time can give us some idea of how little we understand these differences. A time-lapse film of bean shoots growing in the dark, with one frame exposed each hour, shows a scene of unbridled ferocity as each of the plants thrashes and claws at its neighbors in an attempt to get to the light. Slow-motion films of moths in flight shows them picking up the sonar signal of an approaching bat, calculating its strength and source, and taking the appropriate avoiding action, all in the space of one tenth of a second. Each species lives in its own way and its own time, seeing only one section of the environment through the narrow slit of its own sense system. Real space and time exist outside of individual awareness.

In this section I want to relate some of the phenomena in our experience to the flow of time and to put the evolution of nature and Supernature into temporal perspective.

Chapter Nine:

New Dimensions

THREE HUNDRED YEARS AGO scientists thought they knew what weight was, that it had some fixed and absolute meaning. Then Isaac Newton showed that things weigh less on the top of a mountain and that weight is affected by gravity. Today any child who has seen an astronaut waltzing ponderously on the moon, knows that despite all his equipment the man weighs less there than he does on earth. After Newton, science turned to mass as its anchor, but then came Albert Einstein, who showed that mass is also variable; he demonstrated that the faster a thing moves, the more its mass increases. His findings prompted scientists to wonder: if speed is more important than mass, could time be used as a dependable basis of measurement?

The answer came, again, from Einstein. No, he said, time has no absolute meaning and will also be affected by gravity. He was right. When you travel very fast, time slows down, so the moon walkers have aged a fraction of a second less than we. But even those of us who stayed behind were not standing still; we are all moving rapidly through space and growing old less quickly than we would be if the earth were standing still. Everything is relative, and the basis of the theory of relativity is that space and time are inextricably tangled together.

Nothing is what it seems. We see two things happen and we say that one took place before the other; we can even measure the time interval between the two with one of our artificial timekeepers, but this may not be what took place at all. If the two events were sufficiently distant from us and from each other, information about them would come to us at different times. Someone watching from another vantage point might see them taking place simultaneously, and for a third person, in yet another position, the order of events could be completely reversed. So even when we are concerned with a single sense, based on the perception of visible light, the information carried by the medium can be distorted. The problem becomes even more complex when more than one sense is involved. When watching a man chopping wood in the distance, we see the ax raised again before we hear the sound of its last impact with the log. If we knew nothing about the process or were ignorant of the relative speeds of sound and light, we might very easily assume that axes were instruments that made loud sounds when held up above the head.

I feel sure that many of the apparently supernatural events in our experience are due to misinterpretation of this kind, and that at the root of all the problems lies the paradox of time.

TIME

Time has very little to do with sundials, sandglasses, pendulum clocks, and spring watches. Even atoms of cesium in atomic timepieces are nothing more than devices for measuring time. Perhaps the best definition is, "Time is a function of the occurrence of events." (62) Between any two events that do not happen at the same time, there is a lapse, an interval, that can be measured. All the instruments of measurement are based on one assumption: implicit in their pinpointing the moment of "now" is the notion that the rest of time may be divided into "before" and "after" this moment. Like the concepts of weight and mass, this one is now open to question.

The old distinction between space and time is based on the fact that space seems to be presented to us in one piece, whereas time comes to us bit by bit. The future seems to be hidden, the past is dimly visible through memory and its aids, and only the present is revealed directly. It is as though we sat in a railway carriage looking out sideways at the present as time flows by. But as it becomes possible to measure the passage of time in smaller units, it becomes increasingly difficult to decide just what the present is and when it starts and stops. No matter how fast the train is going, we can see at a single glance everything outlined by the window. The fellow in the seat opposite us has his blind partly drawn and sees less. But at the same instant, someone in a carriage nearer the engine looks out his window and sees a slightly different view. While, riding illegally up on the roof, is someone else, whose vision is not at all restricted by the size of the carriage windows and, while looking out sideways in the same way as all the paying passengers, he sees a much wider field including the line a little way ahead. Which person is seeing the present? The answer seems to be that all are and that the differences in their views of it are imposed only by the limitations of their viewpoint. The rider on the roof is not looking into the future; he just has a better view of the present and is using his sense system more fully.

Hindu philosophy has always included the idea of an ever-moving present, and modern physics is now coming to accept this pattern. In the realms of subatomic mathematics it even considers the possibility of the train traveling in the opposite direction, reversing the passage of time. Everything else in the universe is undirectional; it becomes increasingly difficult to accept, and impossible to prove, that time should be the sole exception. Biologists have hardly begun to think about it. The notion of time as an arrow, as a long straight line, is a part of all evolutionary thinking. Palaeontologists draw charts to show the linear descent of the modern horse from a little marsh-living mini-horse with more than one digit on the end of every leg. Geneticists trace more complex but still linear patterns of inheritance from generation to generation, all neatly numbered in sequence. Embryologists follow the development of a complex organism through every division from a single fertilized egg. Only ecologists and ethologists work with substantially different shapes, because they cannot help but notice that life is basically cyclical.

The freshwater eel *Anguilla anguilla* spends most of its life in the rivers of western Europe, but it is not born there. Young elvers suddenly appear in the coastal waters each year, and their origin was a complete mystery until Johann Schmidt made his classic study in the 1930s. (276) He compiled data on the size of eel larvae found at different places in the Atlantic and, plotting these on a map, traced their point of origin to a spot where the smallest ones most often occurred. This proved to be the Sargasso Sea, midway between the Caribbean and the bulge of equatorial Africa, three thousand miles from Europe. It seems that eels spawn at a great depth in these waters in the spring, and the tiny, transparent, leaflike larvae float up nearer to the surface in the summer. They are wafted away by the North Equatorial Current and into the Gulf Stream, in which they spend three years slowly drifting toward Europe and growing until they are about three inches in length. As soon as they reach coastal waters, the leaf larvae undergo a remarkable transformation into little, pearly-white, cylindrical elvers that avoid salt water and invade the river estuaries. They make their way relentlessly inland, wriggling up waterfalls, slithering across meadows on rainy nights, and even climbing up to the mountain streams ten thousand feet high in the Alps. In chosen backwaters and pools they settle down to a quiet life that may last until the males are fourteen and the females over twenty years old. Then, suddenly they are struck by an urgent need to return to salt water; their whole hormonal system undergoes a tremendous change and they become fat and silvery, with mucus on their skin. These powerful silver eels abandon their lakes and pools, often striking out over land in the dark, resting up in damp holes during the day, where they breathe through the water retained in their gill chambers until it is possible to continue their compulsive flight to the sea. When they reach the ocean, they disappear.

Schmidt assumed that they travel deep under water in a countercurrent, swimming in the dark for a year on their epic journey back to the spawning grounds in the Sargasso. But Denys Tucker has discovered that the moment the eels enter salt water, their anuses close up and they are therefore unable to feed and must live entirely on their internal stores of fat. (324) These resources are not enough for the vast effort needed to swim three thousand miles, so Tucker believes that they die without ever breeding. He calls the European eel "only a useless waste product of the American eel," which was once assumed to be a different species, *Anguilla rostrata*, but could be just a variation of the same form produced by a different environment. Both American and European forms come from the Sargasso Sea as larvae, and it could be true

that only the American adults are close enough to the breeding grounds to be able to return and lay new eggs.

It has been suggested that the Sargasso Sea was once the
site of an inland sea on the lost continent of Atlantis and
that the eels are simply trying to return to their ancestral
breeding ground. It is certain that the eels are intent on
breeding when they leave the European rivers; their gonads
are fully developed, but no adult has yet been found in
the deep Atlantic, and no eel marked in Europe has ever
been recovered from the Sargasso Sea. A more likely explanation is that the journey was once much shorter, but the
continents have drifted apart and the European adults are
now just a "waste product" and destined to die of exhaustion
in their impossible attempt to return to the place where they
hatched. There is no biological reason why they should not
stop and breed somewhere closer, perhaps in the waters off
the Azores, but the response to a situation that existed millions
of years ago still persists and drives them to destruction.

We are seeing in the behavior of each generation of living
eels the shadow of something that happened a long time
ago. It is like looking out at a star that we can see exploding,
knowing that it actually happened a billion years ago and that
we are looking at something that long ago ceased to exist.
We witness, in both eel and star, an event of the remote past
taking place in our present. Space and time become insepara-
ble, and when we cannot think of one without the other,
time ceases to be the old, one-dimensional unit of classical
physics, and the combination space-time becomes a new factor
—the four-dimensional continuum.

The idea of a dimension that no one, not even the mathematician, has been able to imagine, let alone see, is difficult
to grasp. It is uncomfortable to think of the here-and-now
as the past, but it seems to be true. Space-time is a continuum, and it is impossible to draw distinctions between

past and present and perhaps even future. In biological terms
the fourth dimension represents continuity. A wheat seed that
germinates after four thousand years in the tomb of an Egyptian pharaoh is no different from the other seeds in that husk
that sprouted the year after they were first grown on the
banks of the Nile. Bacteria normally divide every twenty
minutes, but under unfavorable circumstances they can become resistant spores that are sometimes entombed in rock
and wait for millions of years to be released and continue
multiplying as though nothing had happened. Life conquers
time by suspending it in a way that is almost as good as
having a time machine. It may deal with space in the same
way.

The busiest and most bizarre organisms in any drop of
pond water are tiny, transparent, highly sculptured things
with crowns or wheels of cilia that serve them equally well
for both gathering food and gaining momentum. Seventeen
hundred species have been described, and all are included
in a distinct phylum of their own—the Rotifera, meaning the
"wheel-bearers"—but no two biologists can agree about where
this group belongs on our evolutionary tree. Rotifers are so
peculiar in almost every aspect of their structure and behavior,
that suspicions are beginning to grow that they do not belong
in our system at all. Geography means nothing to rotifers;
similar pools of fresh water in Mongolia or Monrovia or
Massachusetts all have the same species of rotifer in them.
And changes in environmental conditions simply send them
into a wrinkled, desiccated state that looks like a minute
speck of dust, which can survive prolonged drying, freezing,
or almost anything else that can happen. For instant rotifers,
just add water. These encapsulated specks have even been
recovered from the air at fifty thousand feet, and there is no
reason why they should not be found at even greater
heights, perhaps even propelled by freak atmospheric events

out of the atmosphere and into orbit or on into space. In laboratory experiments dormant rotifers have survived in space vacuum conditions, and it has been suggested that they might leave earth in this way and wait indefinitely for other sources of water. It is even possible that they could have arrived here from somewhere else, extending the normal gap between generations from days to light-years, turning time into space and becoming part of the space-time system.

Space is everywhere all at once, and if the mathematics of space-time are correct, then time may have the same properties. In this view, time is not propagated like light waves but appears immediately everywhere and links everything. If it is indeed continuous, then any alteration in its properties anywhere will be instantly noticeable everywhere, phenomena such as telepathy or any other communication that seems to be independent of distance will be much easier to understand. At the principal observatory of the Soviet Academy of Sciences, Nikolai Kozyrev is doing experiments that seem to manipulate time.

Kozyrev is Russia's most respected astrophysicist, a man who predicted gas emissions on the moon ten years before the Americans discovered them. He has recently invented a complex assembly of precision gyroscopes, asymmetrical pendulums, and torsion balances that he uses to measure something he thinks may be time. In one, simple experiment he stretches a long elastic with a machine that consists of a fixed point, or effect, and a moving part, or cause. His instruments show that something is taking place in the vicinity of the elastic and that, whatever it is, it is greater at the effect end than at the cause end. This gradation is detectable even when the instruments are masked from all normal force fields and shielded by a wall one yard thick. Kozyrev believes that time itself is being altered and "that time is thin around the cause and dense around the effect." (233)

He is also intrigued by the fact that all life is basically asymmetrical. He has found that an organic substance made of molecules that turn to the left, such as turpentine, produces a stronger response on his equipment when placed near the stretched elastic, and that the presence of a right-handed molecule, such as sugar, produces a lesser response. In his view, our planet is a left-handed system and therefore adds energy to the galaxy. Kozyrev came to these conclusions following an intensive study of double stars, which, though separated from each other by considerable distances in space, gradually come to be very much alike. He found that resemblance in brightness, radius, and spectral type was so great that it could not be produced by the action of force fields alone. He compares the communion between two stars with the telepathic contact between two people and suggests, "It is possible that all the processes in the material systems of the universe are the sources, feeding the general current of time, which in its turn can influence the material system." (183)

Kozyrev is not alone in this mystic view of the energy of time. Charles Muses, one of the leading theoretical physicists in the United States, agrees that time may have its own pattern of energy. He says, "We shall eventually see that time may be defined as the ultimate causal pattern of all energy release," and he even predicts that the energy put out by time will be found to be oscillating. (220)

Cosmological theories seldom have any direct relevance for life here on earth, but this is one that could affect us profoundly. The idea that time affects matter is familiar to everyone who has ever seen a field in erosion or watched himself grow older, but the possibility that there might be a reciprocal action, in which matter affects time, is revolutionary. It means that nothing happens without effect and that, whatever happens, all of us are touched by it, because we live in the continuum of space-time. John Donne said, "any man's death diminishes me," (89) and he could have been right not because he knew or cared about the man, but because he and the man were part of the same ecological system—part of Supernature.

PRECOGNITION

Every conditioned reflex is a sort of travel in time. When the bell rang, Pavlov's dogs salivated, because they were re-living the last time when the bell rang and it was followed immediately by food. Many animals learn to function in this way, because their lives are specialized and confined within limits where the one kind of stimulus is invariably followed by the other. The reflex has survival value for many species, but in man the picture changes. We are exploratory and con-stantly running into new situations, where old responses would be inappropriate. We are confronted with uncertainty and sometimes respond to it with superstitions based on simi-lar experiences in which we came to no harm. Soldiers often jealously guard a certain item of clothing or equipment that is closely associated with past experience of escape from danger. But most often we respond to uncertainty with some pattern of behavior that seems to lessen the doubt by making the future known to us. We set up some system of prophecy or divination. These systems take many forms and, surpris-ingly, some of them work.

An American anthropologist with the magnificent name of Omar Khayyam Moore examined divination techniques used by the Indians in Labrador. These people are hunters, and failure to find food means hunger and possible death, so when meat is short they consult an oracle to determine in which di-rection they should hunt. They hold the shoulder bone of a caribou over hot coals, and the cracks and spots caused by the heat are then interpreted like a map. The directions indicated by this oracle are random, but the system continues to be used, because it works. Moore reasons that, if they did not use the bone oracle, the Indians would return to where they had last hunted with success or where cover was good or water plentiful. This could lead to overhunting of certain areas, but the use of the oracle means that their forays are randomized; the regular pattern is broken up, and they make a better and more balanced use of the land, which means in the end that they are more successful. Some kinds of magic work. The very fact that they continue to be used in communities whose existence depends on them, shows that divination of this kind works often enough to have survival value. As Moore says, "Some practices which have been classified as magic may well be directly efficacious as techniques for attaining the ends envisaged by their practitioners." (216)

We survive by controlling our environment, and control is made possible by information. So lack of information quickly breeds insecurity and a situation in which any information is regarded as better than none. Even white rats seem to feel this way about it. An elegant experiment was set up in which the inevitable maze, leading to food in one of two boxes, was modified so that on one path the rat was provided with information about whether there would be food in the box at the end or not. (259) The chances of food being in either box were even, but after some days of training, all the rats developed a distinct preference for the side where they obtained advance information, even though the food rewards were no greater. Humans show the same sort of preference for knowledge about an uncertain but unavoidable outcome. Time and again we show that, regardless of the nature of the news and in spite of the fact that we get no advantage from it other than learning what was going to happen in any case, we would prefer to know and thereby reduce our insecurity. This anxiety about the future can be so great that bad news is preferable to an absence of information; it may even come as a relief, because it frees us to adjust to a situation. (162) Studies on prisoners have shown that those with the possibility of parole are under considerably greater strain than those who are reconciled to the fact that they have a life sentence to serve. There can hardly be a maxim more inaccurate than the one that claims, "No news is good news."

And yet we do not demand a state of complete certainty. A good part of our success as a species is based on our ability to cope with environmental variation and our tendency to seek out new sources of stimulation. The popularity of risky pastimes such as mountaineering and motor racing is evidence of man's need for a certain amount of uncertainty and risk, a certain quantity of adrenalin in the system. But this can be too high, and in threatening situations anxiety is very intense and there is a strong desire for both information and some means of control. Any activity that involves some feeling of participation in the turn of events is welcome, and this need to know what is in store helps to account for the current tremendous popularity of do-it-yourself systems of divination and prophecy.

Precognition means "knowing in advance," and systems of knowing cover just about every possible source of variation. They include aeromancy (divination by cloud shapes), alectryomancy (in which a bird is allowed to peck grains of corn from letters of the alphabet), apantomancy (chance meetings with animals), capnomancy (the patterns of smoke rising from a fire), causimomancy (the study of objects placed in the fire), cromniomancy (finding significance in onion sprouts), hippomancy (based on the stamping of horses), onychomancy (the patterns of fingernails in sunlight), phyllorhodomancy (consisting of the sounds made by slapping rose petals against the hand), and tiromancy (a system of divination involving cheese). None of these need be taken seriously, because the phenomena all involve events that can only be random and in no way reflect any kind of biological principle, though I must admit to a certain weakness for the charming system involving rose petals, which we owe to those magnificent ancient Greeks.

Some of the more complex systems of divination are not as easily dismissed. Certainly the most impressive is the *Book of Changes*, or *I Ching*. This began as a series of oracles written more than three thousand years ago, which has been expanded and annotated so that, complete with commentaries, it now constitutes a formidable body of material. But the value of the *I Ching* lies in its simplicity. It is basically a binary system built up on a series of simple alternatives. To form each of the traditional patterns, the person consulting the oracle divides a number of yarrow stalks or tosses coins to get what amounts to a yes or a no answer. This is done six times in succession, so that the final result is a hexagram, or pattern composed of six horizontal lines, which are either intact or broken, according to the results of the draw. There are sixty-four possible combinations of the two types of line, and each of these hexagrams has a name and a traditional interpretation. In casting the stalks or the coins, the character of each line is determined on a majority basis, but if all the stalks or all the coins indicate the same choice, then this line in the hexagram is given special significance and opens the way for further possibilities of interpretation.

As with all methods of divination, a great deal depends on the person who interprets the results. In most systems success is possible only due to the intuition and psychological awareness of the "seer," who literally sees what people need or want to know by observing them very carefully. But the *I Ching* has a character of its own, a sort of inner consistency that almost defies description. Carl Jung noticed this and, I think, put his finger right on the answer. He was at that time interested in his idea of synchronicity and the theory of coincidences, and suspected that the unconscious might have something to do with the way the patterns came out. I feel certain that he was right and that the power of psychokinesis has a great deal to do with the weird accuracy of the *I Ching*.

All commentaries on the *Book of Changes* say something like, "The more familiar one becomes with the personality of the I Ching, the more one understands what this wise gentlestern friend is trying to say to you." (327) And this is absolutely true. As soon as one becomes familiar with each of the hexagrams and comes to know that a solid line in a certain position has special significance, then the patterns begin to come out right and give the kind of advice one consciously or unconsciously expects to hear. Colin Wilson describes this relationship well: "We know, theoretically, that we possess a subconscious mind, yet as I sit here, in this room on a sunny morning, I am not in any way aware of it; I can't see it or feel it. It is like an arm upon which I have been lying in my sleep, and which has become completely dead and feelingless. The real purpose of works such as the I Ching . . . is to restore circulation to these areas of the mind." (342) Consulting the *Book of Changes* at a time of personal crisis amounts almost to a session with your favorite psychoanalyst. There is nothing in the fall of the coins or in the text of the book that is not already in you; all the *I Ching* does with its beautifully organized patterns is to draw the necessary information and decisions out and to absolve the conscious mind of the burden of responsibility for these decisions.

Symbols have a great appeal for the unconscious mind. It uses them to squeeze its ideas past the censor of the conscious in the *I Ching,* in dreams, and in the somewhat less benign system of divination that involves the tarot. (260) The tarot pack consists of seventy-eight cards, most of which are similar to ordinary playing cards, but twenty-two carry color-ful symbols that were popular in the Middle Ages. There are emperors, popes, hermits, jugglers, fools, and devils—all characters with a high emotional content for someone who lived at that time. They still provide a sort of alphabet by means of which the "seer" can work out his interpretation or the questioner can cross-examine his unconscious, but they lack the elegant precision of the *I Ching*. And it is more difficult to see how the unconscious can organize the order of cards in a shuffle than it is to assume that mind offers something to the momentum of a falling coin. With its ominous symbols and its emphasis on violence, the tarot undoubtedly crashes into unconscious areas, but it looks like a coarse bludgeon in comparison to the subtle probe of the *I Ching*.

So even the most popular systems of divination are largely concerned with expanding present potential and seem to have very little to do with actually forecasting the future. Mechanical systems such as these are often manipulated by professionals on behalf of their clients, or they may be abandoned in favor of purely mental prophecies that are given with or without props such as crystal balls. But no matter how the divination takes place, the method of operation is the same. Symbols are used to open up the present or the past in such a way that one seems to get a glimpse of the future. A client is drawn into providing information about himself that ends up looking as though it came from the seer. No hypnosis need be involved, but the technique is very similar. The subject is induced to do things to himself under the impression that someone else is responsible and must therefore be exercising supernatural powers. Even the best known prophets show up in a poor light when stripped of these subjective impressions. Mental sleight of hand, usually practiced by ourselves on ourselves, conceals the limited success most performers really enjoy.

Oracular double talk is as old as Delphi. If anyone were

really able to predict the future with any accuracy, he would need only a year or two to become absolute ruler of the world. I have looked as carefully as one can at the case histories of some of the world's most wealthy and influential people and can find there no evidence of supernatural abilities. They achieve their success through application and some luck, but all make mistakes, often very elementary ones, and none have taken gambles that were not based largely on experience. Full precognition seems to be non-existent, but there is some evidence that some people sometimes have access to snippets of information that cannot be explained in any other way.

William Cox, an American mathematician, has recently completed an interesting survey in an attempt to discover whether people really do avoid traveling on trains that were going to be involved in an accident. Cox collected information on the total number of people on each train at the time of the accident and compared these with the number of passengers who traveled on the same train during each of the preceding seven days and on the fourteenth, twenty-first and twenty-eighth day before the accident. (309) His results, which cover several years of operation with the same equipment at the same station, show that people did in fact avoid accident-bound trains. There were always fewer passengers in the damaged and derailed coaches than would have been expected for that train at that time. The difference between expected and actual number of passengers was so great that the odds against its occurring by chance were over a hundred to one.

It would be fascinating to make further investigations of this kind. So much of the material dealing with prophecy and prediction is anecdotal and impossible to analyze or view objectively, but statistical surveys could show that some of the other "hunches" so popular in folklore are indeed mathematical realities and that there is some kind of collective awareness of things to come. Survival in a biological sense depends almost entirely on avoiding disaster by being able to see it coming. An antelope turns away from the water hole where a lion is lying in wait, because it catches a trace of smell on the wind or hears a bird making sounds that show it is disturbed. An otter flees from its stream because a minute change in vibration warned it of an approaching flash flood. In assessing examples of apparent precognition, we need to be aware of life's receptivity to very subtle stimuli that tell us that the future has already started. They enable living organisms to anticipate the future by expanding the present. In the unconscious areas that respond to subliminal signals from the environment, the future already exists. We cannot change it; if we could, it wouldn't be the future, but we can alter the extent to which we will be involved in it. In a very real sense this is tampering with time, but it is made possible by entirely natural extensions of our normal senses, which give us a more than usually acute view of distant things.

In biological terms precognition therefore means knowing not what will happen but what could happen if . . .

GHOSTS

At the University of Colorado, Nicholas Seeds has taken mouse brains and teased them apart into their component cells. (303) These he put into a culture solution in a test tube and shook gently for several days. At the end of this time the separate cells reaggregated and formed pieces of brain in which cells were connected by normal synapses, showed the usual biochemical reactions, and grew a natural myelin protective sheath. Somehow cells are capable of recreating past patterns; they have a molecular memory, which is passed on from one cell to another so that a new one can reproduce the behavior of its parents. If a change, or mutation, occurs, this, too, is faithfully duplicated by the descendants. The dead live again in defiance of time.

The cyclical patterns of life mean that matter is never destroyed but goes back into the system to re-emerge sometime later. Living organic matter rises again in the same form with the same behavior patterns in a process of reincarnation. Each new generation is a reincarnation of the species, but this does not mean that individuals reappear. The Greeks believed in metempsychosis—the transmigration of the soul into a new body—and similar ideas are so widespread among all cultures that they can be considered almost universal. But despite some sensational stories, there is little real evidence that anything of the sort occurs. It is difficult enough to prove that we have souls in the first place. While apparent knowledge of other times and places can be attributed to telepathic contact with someone still alive, it seems unnecessary to assume that the phenomena are produced by an eternal spirit.

Souls or spirits that occur without benefit of body are a separate kind of phenomenon, but can be considered in much the same way. For the sake of argument, it is worth considering the possibility that man can produce an "astral projection," or part of himself that can exist without his normal physical body and perhaps even survive his death. These spirits are said to wander at will, and there are countless records of their having been seen, in whole or in part, in a great variety of situations. In England, one person in six believes in ghosts and one person in fourteen thinks that he has actually seen one. (123) These are enormous numbers of people, and I have no intention of suggesting that they must all have been mistaken, but to me there is one very strange and significant thing in all their sightings. All the ghosts of which I have ever heard, wore clothes. While I am prepared in principle to concede the possible existence of an astral body, I cannot bring myself to believe in astral shoes and shirts and hats. The fact that people see ghosts as they or somebody else remembers them, fully dressed in period costume, seems to indicate that the visions are part of a mental rather than a supernatural process. In those cases in which several people see the same apparition, it could be broadcast telepathically by one of them. And where a similar ghost is seen by separate people on separate occasions, I assume that the mental picture is held by someone associated with the site.

George Owen, a Cambridge biologist who has done pioneer work in scientific parapsychology, says, "The assumption of an actual astral body present in the vicinity of the percipient is, however, somewhat gratuitous and unnecessary if we are prepared to accept an explanation in terms of telepathy." (238) As another biologist I say, "Hear, hear!" The explanation of an unknown in terms of another phenomenon still in dispute might seem labored and tortuous, but it is good science and better logic to settle for the more plausible of two explanations. Colin Wilson picked out another aspect of hauntings that fits this mental hypothesis. (342) He suggests that the chief characteristic of ghosts appears to be a certain stupidity, "since a tendency to hang around places they knew in life would appear to be the spirit-world's equivalent of feeble-mindedness; . . . one feels that they ought to have something better to do." Wilson thinks that the state of mind of ghosts may be similar to that of someone with a high fever or delirium, someone unable to distinguish between reality and dreams. This description can apply equally well to the state of mind of someone seeing the ghost. Delirium is not necessary, but a certain amount of dissociation brought about by conflict between conscious and unconscious states, perhaps as a result of receiving a powerful telepathic communication, could be present.

Communications with the dead are similarly suspect. I cannot help wondering why, out of the billions who once walked the earth, it should always be Napoleon, Shakespeare, Tolstoy, Chopin, Cleopatra, Robert Browning, and Alexander the Great who just happen to be on hand when a spirit medium summons up someone from the past. Rhine sums up the problem by saying, "The outcome of the scientific investigation of mediumship is best described as a draw." (309) In seventy-five years of research no incontestable proof of survival has been found, but neither has it been possible to prove that some sort of survival after death could not occur.

The most interesting evidence ever gathered in this respect has been published recently by Konstantin Raudive, a Latvian psychologist now living in Germany. Raudive has discovered that tapes made by speaking directly into a microphone, by recording from a radio tuned to random "white noise" interference, or by connecting the recorder to a crystal diode set with a very short aerial, all include soft extraneous voices. The voices speak with a strange rhythm in many languages, sometimes so softly that it is necessary to amplify them by electronic means. Raudive says, "The sentence construction obeys rules that differ radically from those of ordinary speech and, although the voices seem to speak in the same way as we do, the anatomy of their speech apparatus must be different from our own." The strangest thing about these recorded voices is that they seem to respond to questions put by Raudive and his collaborators by producing more of their Esperanto-style comments that often look like direct answers.

In the past six years Raudive has recorded more than seventy thousand conversations of this kind. (263) The speech content of the recordings is exhaustively recounted and analyzed in a book that includes testimonials from very well-known and reputable scientists who were either present when the tapes were made or who were able to examine the equipment involved. There can be no doubt about the reality of the sounds; they are on the tapes and can be broken down into phonemes and analyzed by voice-print machinery, but their source is open to question. Raudive believes that man "carries within himself the ability to contact his friends on earth when he has passed through the transition of death." In other words he is certain that the voices are those of the dead, and he confidently identifies some of them as Goethe, Mayakovsky, Hitler, and his own mother. It is difficult to argue with this, because rigidly controlled experiments have been unable to account for the presence of the voices by any normal method.

On 24 March 1971 a test was made at the studios of a major recording company in England. Engineers used their own equipment and installed instruments to exclude freak pickups from radio stations and both high- and low-frequency transmitters. Raudive was not allowed to handle any of the equipment at any time, and a separate, synchronized recording was made of every sound taking place in the studio. During the eighteen-minute recording, both tapes were monitored constantly and nothing untoward could be heard, but on playback it was discovered that there were more than two hundred voices on the experimental tape and that some were so clear that they could be heard by everyone present. (264)

I am struck by the similarity between this phenomenon and the thought pictures of Ted Serios. In both cases recording apparatus is picking up a signal that appears not to originate in the immediate environment, but both pictures and sounds are produced only in the presence of a particular person. The voices on Raudive's tapes speak only in the seven languages familiar to him. In neither case could the signals be detected or blocked by physical apparatus—Raudive has worked inside a Faraday cage—but the testimony of witnesses of the highest possible caliber makes it impossible to doubt that the results are obtained without conscious fraud. Like the Raudive voices, the Serios pictures were at first attributed to spirit sources, but the connection between their content and the psychology of the man involved is in both cases too great to ignore. I think that both phenomena will be found to be produced by the same means and that it will originate in the mind of the living man and have nothing whatsoever to do with the dead.

It is possible that the voices have a perfectly normal physical explanation. We still know so little about things around us that it might not be long before we can build machines that will recapture the sights and sounds of the past. Film and recordings do just that, for our immediate past anyway. Now there is a suggestion that there could be similar records that we have just overlooked. A pot revolving on a wheel with a pointer just touching the clay could be a primitive sort of phonograph. All we need to do is rotate the pot again at the same speed, find the appropriate stylus, and we may be able to recapture the sounds being made in the pottery on the day the clay was thrown. Work already in progress on unvarnished pottery from the Middle East has produced some results that are encouraging.

EXOBIOLOGY

In this look at other worlds around us, I cannot exclude the possibility that a part may be played by beings from other worlds altogether. Biology has lately given rise to a new discipline: exobiology, the study of extraterrestrial life. Ever since 1959, when analysis of a piece of meteor substance showed traces of organic compounds, a controversy has raged as to whether these compounds came into the atmosphere with the meteorite or whether they originate on earth. The dispute has never been satisfactorily resolved, and discussions about life elsewhere have had to continue to be based on inference and conjecture. Astronomical calculations based on the fraction of stars with planets, the number of these planets suitable for life, the fraction of such suitable planets on which life actually appears, and the number of these on which life reaches consciousness and the desire to communicate—arrive at the conclusion that perhaps one in one hundred thousand stars has an advanced society in orbit around it. That means that there could be as many as a million intelligent life forms in our galaxy alone. But our success in establishing contact with any of them depends also on the longevity of each of us. It is possible that the acquisition of nuclear technology is a consequence that no species can control for long, and that all the beings that do manage to get this far only succeed in destroying themselves with it rather quickly.

Assuming that they do not succumb, the chances seem to be quite high that sooner or later we will meet one or more of them. Erich von Daniken thinks that we are one of them. (333) He has collected a scrapbook of loose ends in archaeology and anthropology, such as the map found in Istanbul that shows the continents as they would look from space, distorted by the curvature of the globe; an iron pillar in India that does not rust; patterns on the plains of Peru that can be appreciated only from the air; descriptions in sacred manuscripts of gods coming down to earth in chariots with wheels of fire; and ancient paintings and etchings that portray figures wearing what look like space helmets. From all this he deduces that God was an astronaut and that we are partly the product of an extraterrestrial intelligence. It is a provocative idea, but as a biologist with a belief in our own still largely unexploited ability, I find it unattractive and unnecessary to give credit for our achievements to some transient aliens.

Ivan Sanderson has the same idea, but expresses it in biological terms: He suggests that earth was seeded by an egg of life from somewhere else and that this eventually hatched and grew into a complex larva that embodies all life as we know it.

He sees us as part of this larva, reaching the stage where we begin to think of metamorphosis and start spinning the web of intellect around us, encysting our minds in the cocoons of machines, the pupae, where they undergo essential changes and emerge eventually as adult forms to fly off to other worlds and start the whole process again by laying eggs there. The adult into which we will ultimately develop is, he suggests, nothing more than a flying saucer, or UFO. (293)

This bloodcurdling idea makes quite good biology; it could all be true. It is quite possible that the next step in our evolution is the development of an electronic intelligence and that the only way this could be produced from a lifeless planet was through the intermediate stages of organic life. The first generation of machine minds are already with us. They are based on printed circuits with electrons moving about through wires, and they depend on us. But the next step after that could be into pure energy fields, which would leave us and live either in space or in those parts of the universe where exploding stars and novae provide an active environment of the sort of intense radiation that this superelectronic mind would need to nourish it.

I hope that it is not true. I am impressed by our inefficiency, by our vast, as yet untapped potential, and by the progress we have already made using only one small corner of our minds. We are indeed larvae, eating our way through earth's resources in a mindless, caterpillar fashion, but I believe that the imago is already beginning to stir within. When the climate is right, it will break out not as some sort of supercomputer but as an organic being that will embody all of Supernature and look back on technology as a childhood toy.

Conclusion

LIFE SURVIVES in the chaos of the cosmos by picking order out of the winds. Death is certain, but life becomes possible by following patterns that lead like paths of firmer ground through the swamps of time. Cycles of light and dark, of heat and cold, of magnetism, radioactivity, and gravity all provide vital guides, and life learns to respond to even their most subtle signs. The emergence of a fruit fly is tuned by a spark lasting one thousandth of a second; the breeding of a bristle worm is co-ordinated on the ocean floor by a glimmer of light reflected from the moon; the development of the eggs of a quail is synchronized by a soft conversation between the embryos; conception in a woman waits for that phase of the moon under which she was born. Nothing happens in isolation. We breathe and bleed, we laugh and cry, we crash and die in time with cosmic cues.

Inorganic matter got together in the right way to create a self-perpetuating organism that started a system of elaboration that has now produced a pattern with several million pieces. This is Supernature, and man sits at the center of its web, tugging at the strands that interest him, following some through to useful conclusions and snapping others in his impatience. Man is the spearhead of evolution, vital, creative, and immensely talented, but still young enough to wreak havoc in his first flush of enthusiasm. Hopefully this period of awkward adolescence is coming to an end as he begins to realize that he cannot possibly survive alone, that the web of Supernature is supported by the combined strength of a vast number of individually fragile fragments, that life on earth is united into what amounts to a single superorganism, and that this in turn is only part of the cosmic community.

At first sight, the process of evolution looks extremely wasteful, with most developments running into the dead ends of extinction, but even in their failure these contribute something to the few species that do succeed. It is imperative that there should be a multitude of participants so that life can move on a broad front, testing all possibilities in a search for the right ones. Even those that die have not lived in vain, because news of their failure is broadcast and becomes part of the inheritance of Supernature. This communion is possible because life shares a mutual sensitivity to the cosmos, has a common origin, and speaks the same organic language.

The alphabet is written in chemical symbols shared by all protoplasm. The most common word is water, which has the property of instability that makes it a most sensitive, reliable receiver of subtle signals. Simple formulas in an aqueous solution make it possible for information to pass from cell to cell as long as there is direct contact between them. The same information can jump across space provided with an overlap of electrical fields or where two communicants are sufficiently alike to resonate in sympathy with each other. And at the highest levels, messages are carried across gaps in time.

In the vanguard of evolution comes a development that is confined to a few species and seems to play no part in making them better fitted for survival in this system. Biology is usually very parsimonious and entirely utilitarian, but men—and possibly chimpanzees and dolphins—have acquired a need for things that satisfy none of the normal, natural hungers. We have developed a taste for the mysterious. We have become aware of ourselves, of our life, and of the fact that we must die. We have opened a door on forethought and imagination and discovered anxiety as well. The fact that even a potted plant responds to the death of an animal nearby, means that life has always been aware of the phenomenon of death, but with consciousness comes a more complete awareness of our relation to this state—of the fact that we can cause it, or prevent it, or in trying to prevent it even bring about our own death. And with this kind of consciousness comes guilt and conflict and the development of a mental barrier behind which we can hide things away from ourselves.

The origin of this new awareness in biological terms is still obscure, but we are beginning to get some idea of its implications. Cosmic evolution produced our solar system and this habitable planet; inorganic evolution put together the right ingredients to produce life; organic evolution shaped and molded that life into its kaleidoscope of forms; cultural evolution took just one group and pushed them rapidly through intelligence and awareness to a position where they could manipulate the rest of evolution for themselves. So we have arrived at the moment of control with a new and growing consciousness both of the enormity of the task and of the breadth of our own ability to cope with it. In this situation two things stand out above all others: One is that our greatest strength lies in unity with all of Supernature here on earth, and the other is that this unity could give us the impetus we need to transcend the system altogether.

Supernature could become something really supernatural.

Bibliography

1. ADDERLEY, E. E. & BOWEN, E. G. "Lunar Component in Precipitation Data," *Science 137:* 749, 1962.
2. ADDEY, J. M. "The Search for a Scientific Starting Point," *Astrology 32:* 3.
3. ———. "The Discovery of a Scientific Starting Point," *Astrological Journal 3:* 2, 1967.
4. ———. *Astrological Journal 5: 1, 1969.*
5. AMOORE, J. E., PALMIERI, G. & WANKE, E. "Molecular Shape and Odour," *Nature 216:* 1084, 1967.
6. ANAND, B. K., CHHINA, G. S. & SINGH, B. "Some Aspects of Electroencephalographic Studies in Yogis," *Electroencephalographic and Clinical Neurophysiology 13:* 452, 1961.
7. ANDERSON, R. & KOOPMANS, H. "Harmonic Analysis of Varve Time Series," *Journal of Geophysical Research 68:* 877, 1963.
8. ANDREWS, D. H. *The Symphony of Life.* Lee's Summit, Missouri: Unity Books, 1966.
9. ARRHENIUS, S. "Die Einwirkung kosmischer Einflusse auf physiologische Verhältnisse," *Skand. Arch. Physiol. 8:* 367, 1898.
10. BACKSTER, C. "Evidence of a Primary Perception in Plant Life," *International Journal of Parapsychology 10:* 4, 1968.
11. BACON, T. "The Man Who Reads Nature's Secret Signals," *National Wildlife 5:* February 1969.

12. BAGNALL, O. *The Origin and Properties of the Human Aura.* New York: University Books, 1970.

13. BARBER, T. X. "Physiological Effects of Hypnosis," *Psychological Bulletin 58:* 390, 1961.

14. ———. *Hypnosis—a Scientific Approach.* New York: Van Nostrand Insight Series, 1969.

15. BARNETT, A. *The Human Species.* London: Penguin Books, 1968.

16. BARRETT, W. & BESTERMAN, T. *The Divining Rod.* London, 1926.

17. BARRY, J. "General and Comparative Study of the Psychokinetic Effect on a Fungus Culture," *Journal of Parapsychology 32:* 237, 1968.

18. BECK, S. D. *Animal Photoperiodism.* New York: Holt, Rinehart & Winston, 1963.

19. BEHANAN, T. *Yoga; a Scientific Evaluation.* New York: Dover Publications, 1959.

20. BELL, A. H. *Practical Dowsing—a Symposium.* London: G. Bell & Sons, 1965.

21. BELOFF, J. & EVANS, L. "A Radioactivity Test of Psychokinesis," *Journal of the Society for Psychical Research 41:* 41, 1961.

22. BENSON, H. & WALLACE, R. K. "The Physiology of Meditation," *American Journal of Physiology 221:* 795, 1971.

23. BERNARD, T. *Hatha Yoga.* London: Arrow Books, 1960.

24. BERNE, E. "The Nature of Intuition," *The Psychiatric Quarterly 23:* 203, 1949.

25. BINSKI, S. R. "Report on Two Exploratory PK Series," *Journal of Parapsychology 21:* 284, 1957.

26. BLACK, S. *Mind and Body.* London: William Kimber, 1969.

27. BLACK, S., HUMPHREY, J. H. & NIVEN, J. "Inhibition of the Mantoux Reaction by Direct Suggestion Under Hypnosis." *British Medical Journal 1:* 1649, 1961.

28. BLACK, S. & WIGAN, E. R. "An Investigation of Selective Deafness by Direct Suggestion Under Hypnosis," *British Medical Journal 2:* 736, 1963.

29. BLEIBTREU, J. N. *Parable of the Beast.* London: Victor Gollancz, 1968.

30. BOISCHOT, A. *Le Soleil et la terre.* Paris: Presses Universitaires, 1966.

31. BONNER, J. T. "Evidence for the Sorting Out of Cells in the Development of the Cellular Slime Molds," *Proceedings of the National Academy of Sciences 45:* 379, 1959.

32. BORDI, S. & VANNEL, F. "Variazione Giornaliera di Grandezze Chimicofisiche," *Geofis. e Meteorol. 14: 28, 1965.*

33. BORISSAVLIETCH, M. *The Golden Number.* London: Tiranti, 1958.

34. BOWEN, E. G. "A Lunar Effect on the Incoming Meteor Rate," *Journal of Geophysical Research 68: 1401, 1963.*

35. ———. "Lunar and Planetary Tails in the Solar Wind," *Journal of Geophysical Research 69: 4969, 1964.*

36. BRADLEY, D., WOODBURY, M. & BRIER, G. "Lunar Synodical Period and Widespread Precipitation," *Science 137: 748, 1962.*

37. BRAID, J. A. *Neurypnology or the Rationale of Nervous Sleep Considered in Relation with Animal Magnetism.* London: Churchill, 1843.

38. BRAUN, R. "Der Lichtsinn augenloser Tiere," *Umschau 58: 306, 1958.*

39. BREDER, C. M. "Vortices and Fish Schools," *Zoologica 50: 97, 1965.*

40. BRIERLEY, D. & DAVIES, J. "Lunar Influence on Meteor Rates," *Journal of Geophysical Research 68: 6213, 1963.*

41. BRILLOUIN, L. *Science and Information Theory.* New York: Academic Press, 1956.

42. BROWN, F. A. "Persistent Activity Rhythms in the Oyster," *American Journal of Physiology 178: 510, 1954.*

43. ———. "Response of a Living Organism, Under Constant Conditions Including Pressure, to a Barometric-Pressure-Correlated Cyclic External Variable," *Biological Bulletin 112: 285, 1957.*

44. ———. "An Orientational Response to Weak Gamma Radiation," *Biological Bulletin 125: 206, 1963.*

45. ———. "How Animals Respond to Magnetism," *Discovery,* November 1963.

46. BROWN, F. A., BENNETT, M. F. & WEBB, H. M. "A Magnetic Compass Response of an Organism," *Biological Bulletin 119: 65, 1960.*

47. BROWN, F. A., PARK, Y. H. & ZENO, J. R. "Diurnal Variation in Organismic Response to Very Weak Gamma Radiation," *Nature 211: 830, 1966.*

48. BULLEN, K. E. *Introduction to the Theory of Seismology.* Cambridge: University Press, 1962.

49. BURR, H. S. "Biological Organization and the Cancer Problem," *Yale Journal of Biology and Medicine 12: 281, 1940.*

50. ———. "Field Properties of the Developing Frog's Egg," *Pro-

ceedings of the National Academy of Sciences 27: 276, 1941.

51. ——. "Electric Correlates of Pure and Hybrid Strains of Corn," *Proceedings of the National Academy of Sciences* 29: 163, 1943.

52. ——. "Diurnal Potentials in Maple Tree," *Yale Journal of Biology and Medicine* 17: 727, 1945.

53. ——. "Effect of Severe Storms on Electrical Properties of a Tree and the Earth," *Science* 124: 1204, 1956.

54. ——. "Tree Potential and Sunspots," *Cycles* 243: October 1964.

55. BURR, H. S., HARVEY, S. C. & TAFFEL, M. "Bio-electric Correlates of Wound Healing," *Yale Journal of Biology and Medicine* 12: 483, 1940.

56. BURR. H. S., HILL, R. T. & ALLEN, E. "Detection of Ovulation in the Intact Rabbit," *Proceedings of the Society for Experimental Biology and Medicine* 33: 109, 1935.

57. BURR, H. S., LANE, L. T. & NIMS, L. F. "A Vacuum-tube Microvoltmeter for the Measurement of Bio-electric Phenomena," *Yale Journal of Biology and Medicine* 9: 65, 1936.

58. BURR, H. S. & LANGMAN, L. "Electrometric Timing of Human Ovulation," *American Journal of Obstetrics and Gynecology* 44: 223, 1942.

59. ——. "Electromagnetic Studies in Women with Malignancy of Cervix Uteri," *Science* 105: 209, 1947.

60. BURR, H. S. & MUSSELMAN, L. K. "Bio-electric Phenomena Associated with Menstruation," *Yale Journal of Biology and Medicine* 9: 2, 1936.

61. BURR, H. S. & NORTHROP, F. S. C. "The Electrodynamic Theory of Life," *Quarterly Review of Biology* 10: 322, 1935.

62. CALDER, R. *Man and the Cosmos.* London: Penguin Books, 1970.

63. CAPEL-BOUTE, C. *Observations sur les tests chimiques de Piccardi.* Brussels: Presses Académiques Européennes, 1960.

64. CARINGTON, W. *Telepathy.* London: Methuen, 1954.

65. CARRINGTON, H. *Modern Psychical Phenomena.* London: Kegan Paul, 1919.

66. CARSON, R. *The Sea Around Us.* London: Staples Press, 1951.

67. CASTANEDA, C. *The Teachings of Don Juan.* Berkeley: University of California Press, 1968.

68. CASTANEDA, C. *A Separate Reality*. London: Bodley Head, 1971.

69. CHAUVIN, R. *Animal Societies*. London: Victor Gollancz, 1968.

70. CHAUVIN, R. & GENTHON, J. P. "Eine Untersuchung über die Möglichkeit psychokinetischer Experimente mit Uranium und Geiger-zähler," *Zeitschrift für Parapsychologie und Grenzbegiete der Psychologie 8:* 140, 1965.

71. CHEDD, G. "Mental Medicine," *New Scientist 51:* 560, 1971.

72. CHERTOK, L. "The Evolution of Research into Hypnosis." In *Psychophysiological Mechanisms of Hypnosis*. New York: Springer-Verlag, 1969.

73. CHRISTOPHER, M. *Seers, Psychics and ESP*. London: Cassell, 1971.

74. CLARK, L. B. "Observations on the Palolo," Carnegie Institution of Washington Year Book *37*, 1938.

75. CLARK, V. In WEST & TOONDER.

76. COHEN, S. *Drugs of Hallucination*. London: Paladin, 1971.

77. COLE, L. C. "Biological Clock in the Unicorn," *Science 125:* 874, 1957.

78. CONZE, E. *Buddhist Scriptures*. London: Penguin Books, 1959.

79. COTT, J. "The Extrasensory Perception Man," *Rolling Stone*, January 6, 1972.

80. COX, W. E. "The Effect of PK on Electrochemical Systems," *Journal of Parapsychology 29:* 165, 1965.

81. CRASILNECK, H. B. & HALL, J. A. "Physiological Changes Associated with Hypnosis," *Journal of Clinical and Experimental Hypnosis, 7:* 9, 1959.

82. DARWIN, C. *The Expression of Emotions in Man and Animals*. London: Murray, 1873.

83. DAS, N. N. & GASTAUT, H. "Variations de l'activité électrique du cerveau, du coeur et des muscles squelettiques au cours de la méditation et de l'extase yogique," *Electroencephalographic and Clinical Neurophysiology 6:* 211, 1955.

84. DAVID-NEEL, A. *Magic and Mystery in Tibet*. London: Souvenir Press, 1967.

85. DEAN, E. D. "Plethysmograph Recordings As ESP Responses," *International Journal of Neuro-psychiatry 2:* October 1966.

86. DE LA WARR, G. "Do Plants Feel Emotion?" *Electro Technology*, April 1969.

87. DESMEDT, J. E. *Neurophysiological Mechanisms Controlling Acoustic Input.* Springfield, Ill.: Thomas, 1960.
88. DEWAN, E. M. & ROCK, J. *American Journal of Obstetrics and Gynecology.*
89. DONNE, J. *Devotions.* Part 13, 1620.
90. DRAVNIEK, A. "Identifying People by Their Smell," *New Scientists* 28: 630, 1965.
91. DRIVER, P. M. "Notes on the clicking of Avian Egg Young, with Comments on Its Mechanism and Function," *Ibis 109:* 434, 1967.
92. ECCLES, J. C. *The Neurophysiological Basis of Mind.* Oxford: The Clarendon Press, 1953.
93. EDMONDSTON, W. E. & PESSIN, M. "Hypnosis as Related to Learning and Electrodermal Measures," *American Journal of Clinical Hypnosis* 9: 31, 1966.
94. EDMUNDS, S. *Hypnotism and the Supernormal.* London: Aquarian Press, 1967.
95. EDWARDS, F. "People Who Saw Without Eyes." In *Strange People.* London: Pan Books, 1970.
96. EISENBUD, J. *The World of Ted Serios.* London: Jonathan Cape, 1968.
97. ERICKSON, M. H. "The Induction of Color Blindness by a Technique of Hypnotic Suggestion," *Journal of General Psychology* 20: 61, 1939.
98. EYSENCK, H. "Is Beauty Absolute?" *Perceptual and Motor Skills* 32: 817, 1971.
99. FABRE, I. M. & KAFKA, G. *Einführung in die Tierpsychologie.* Leipzig: Barth, 1913.
100. FAST, J. *Body Language.* London: Souvenir Press, 1971.
101. FISHER, S. "The Role of Expectancy in the Performance of Posthypnotic Behavior," *Journal of Abnormal and Sociological Psychology* 49: 503, 1954.
102. FISHER, W., STURDY, G., RYAN, M. & PUGH, R. "Some Laboratory Studies of Fluctuating Phenomena," In GAUQUELIN, *The Cosmic Clocks.*
103. FODOR, N. In STEIGER.
104. FORWALD, H. "An Approach to Instrumental Investigation of Psychokinesis," *Journal of Parapsychology* 18: 219, 1954.
105. ———. "An Experimental Study Suggesting a Relationship Between Psychokinesis and Nuclear Conditions of Matter," *Journal of Parapsychology* 23: 97, 1959.
106. FRANKLIN, K. L. "Radio Waves from Jupiter," *Scientific American* 211: 35, 1964.

107. FRANCQ, E. "Feigned Death in the Opossum," *Dissertation Abstracts 28B:* 2665, 1968.

108. FRENCH, J. D. "The Reticular Formation." In *Handbook of Physiology 1:* 1281, 1960.

109. FRIEDMAN, H., BECKER, R. & BACHMAN, C. "Geomagnetic Parameters and Psychiatric Hospital Admissions," *Nature 200:* 626, 1963.

110. FRNM. "Psi Developments in the USSR," *Bulletin of the Foundation for Research on the Nature of Man 6:* 1967.

111. FUKURAI, T. *Clairvoyance and Thoughtography.* London: Rider & Company, 1931.

112. FYFE, A. *Moon and Plant.* London: Society for Cancer Research, 1968.

113. GARRETT, E. *Adventures in the Supernormal.* New York: Garrett Publishers, 1959.

114. GATLING, W. & RHINE, J. B. "Two Groups of PK Subjects Compared," *Journal of Parapsychology 10:* 120, 1946.

115. GAUQUELIN, M. *L'Influence des astres.* Paris: Dauphin, 1955.

116. ———. *Les Hommes et les astres.* Paris: Denoël, 1960.

117. ———. "Note sur le rythme journalier du début du travail de l'accouchement," *Gynécologie et Obstétrique 66:* 231, 1967.

118. ———. "Contribution à l'étude de la variation saisonnière du poids des enfants a la naissance," *Population 3:* 544, 1967.

119. ———. *The Cosmic Clocks.* London: Peter Owen, 1969.

120. GAUQUELIN, M. & GAUQUELIN, F. *Méthodes pour étudier la répartition des astres dans le mouvement diurne.* Paris: 1957.

121. GEBALLE, T. H. "New Superconductors," *Scientific American,* November 1971.

122. GEIGY, J. R. "Animals Asleep," Documenta Geigy, Basel, 1955.

123. GORER, G. *Exploring English Character.* London: Cresset, 1955.

124. GRAD, B. "A Telekinetic Effect on Plant Growth," *International Journal of Parapsychology 6:* 473, 1964.

125. ———. "Some Biological Effects of the Laying-on-of-Hands," *Journal of the American Society for Psychical Research 59:* 2, 1965.

126. ———. "The Laying-on-of-Hands: Implications for Psychotherapy, Gentling and the Placebo Effect," *Journal of the American Society for Psychical Research 61:* 286, 1967.

324 BIBLIOGRAPHY

127. GRAD, B., CADORET, R. J. & PAUL, G. I. "The Influence of an Unorthodox Method of Treatment on Wound Healing of Mice," *International Journal of Parapsychology* 3: 5, 1961.

128. GREPPIN, L. "Naturwissenschaftliche Betrachtungen über die geistigen Fähigkeiten des Menschen und der Tiere," *Biol. Zentralbl. 31:* 1911.

129. GULYAIEV, P. "Cerebral Electromagnetic Fluids," *International Journal of Parapsychology* 7: 4, 1965.

130. HABER, R. N. "Eidetic images," *Scientific American 220:* 36, 1969.

131. HAECKERT, H. *Lunationsrhythmen des menschlichen Organismus.* Leipzig: Geest und Portig, 1961.

132. HALBERG, F. "The 24 Hour Scale: A Time Dimension of Adaptive Functional Organization," *Perspectives in Biology and Medicine 3:* 491, 1960.

133. HARDY, A. *The Living Stream.* London: Collins, 1965.

134. ———. "Biology and ESP." In *Science and ESP.* London: Routledge & Kegan Paul, 1967.

135. HARKER, J. E. "Diurnal Rhythms in *Periplaneta americana* L.," *Nature 173:* 689, 1954.

136. ———. "Factors Controlling the Diurnal Rhythms of Activity in *Periplaneta americana* L.," *Journal of Experimental Biology 33:* 224, 1956.

137. ———. "Diurnal Rhythms in the Animal Kingdom," *Biological Reviews 33:* 1, 1958.

138. HARTLAND-ROWE, R. "The Biology of a Tropical Mayfly *Povilla adusta* with Special Reference to the Lunar Rhythm of Emergence," *Rev. Zool. et Botan. Afric. 58:* 185, 1958.

139. HASLER, A. D. "Wegweiser für Zugfische," *Naturwissenschaftliche Rundschau 15:* 302, 1962.

140. HAUENSCHILD, C. "Neue experimentelle Untersuchungen zum Problem der Lunarperiodizität," *Naturwiss. 43:* 361, 1956.

141. HAWKING, F. "The Clock of the Malarial Parasite," *Scientific American 222:* 123, 1970.

142. HAZELWOOD, J. In STEIGER (309).

143. HEATWOLFE, H., DAVIS, D. M. & WENNER, A. M. "The Behaviour of Megarhyssa," *Zeitschrift für Tierpsychologie 19:* 653, 1962.

144. HEBB, D. O. *The Organization of Behavior.* New York: Wiley, 1949.

145. HEDIGER, H. *The Psychology and Behavior of Animals in Zoos.* New York: Dover Publications, 1968.

146. HEIRTZLER, J. R. "The Longest Electromagnetic Waves," *Scientific American* 206: 128, 1962.

147. HESS, E. H. "Attitude and Pupil Size," *Scientific American,* April 1965.

148. HESS, W. R. *The Functional Organization of the Diencephalon.* New York: Grune & Stratton, 1957.

149. HILGARD, E. R. "The Psychophysiology of Pain Reduction Through Hypnosis." *In Psychophysiological Mechanisms of Hypnosis.* New York: Springer-Verlag, 1969.

150. HILLMAN, W. S. "Injury of Tomato Plants by Continuous Light and Unfavorable Photoperiodic Cycles," *American Journal of Botany 43:* 89, 1956.

151. HILTON, H., BAER, G. & RHINE, J. B. "A Comparison of Three Sizes of Dice in PK Tests," *Journal of Parapsychology* 7: 172, 1943.

152. HITTLEMAN, R. *Guide to Yoga Meditation.* New York: Bantam Books, 1969.

153. HIXSON, J. "Twins Prove Electronic ESP," *New York Herald Tribune,* October 25, 1965.

154. HOSEMANN, H. "Bestehen solare und lunare Einflusse auf die Nativität und den Menstruationszyklus," *Zeitschrift für Geburtshilfe und Gynäkologie 133:* 263, 1950.

155. HUFF, D. *Cycles in Your Life.* London: Victor Gollancz, 1965.

156. HUNTINGTON, E. *Season of Birth, Its Relation to Human Abilities.* New York: John Wiley, 1938.

157. HURKOS, P. *Psychic.* London: Barker, 1962.

158. HUTCHINSON, B. *Your Life in Your Hands.* London: Neville Spearman, 1967.

159. IKEMI, Y. & NAKAGAWA, S. "A Psychosomatic Study of Contagious Dermatitis," *Kyushu Journal of Medical Science 13:* 335, 1962.

160. INGLIS, J. "Abnormalities of Motivation and Ego Functions." In *Handbook of Abnormal Psychology.* London: Pitman Medical, 1960.

161. IVANOV, A. "Soviet Experiments in Eyeless Vision," *International Journal of Parapsychology 6:* 1964.

162. JAHODA, G. *The Psychology of Superstition.* London: Penguin Books, 1970.

163. JAMES, W. *The Principles of Psychology.* New York: Dover Publications, 1950.

164. JEANS, J. *The Mysterious Universe*. New York: Dover Publications, 1968.
165. JEFFRIES, M. "World of Science," London *Evening Standard*, 10 December 1971.
166. JENNY, H. *Cymatics*. Basel: Basilius Press, 1966.
167. ———. "Visualising Sound," *Science Journal*, June 1968.
168. JONAS, E. "Predetermining the Sex of a Child." In OSTRANDER & SCHROEDER.
169. KAISER, I & HALBERG, F. "Circadian Periodic Aspects of Birth," *Annals of the New York Academy of Science* 98: 1056, 1962.
170. KALMUS, H. "Tagesperiodische verlaufende Vorgänge an der Stabheuschrecke und ihre experimentelle Beeinflussung," *Zeitschrift für Vergleichende Physiologie* 25: 494, 1938.
171. KAMMERER, P. *Das Gesetz der Serie*. Stuttgart: Dtsch. Verl-Anst., 1919.
172. KASAMATSU, A. & HIRAI, T. "An Electroencephalographic Study of the Zen Meditation," *Folia Psychiatr. Neurol. Japan.* 20: 4, 1966.
173. KELLEY, C. R. "Psychological Factors in Myopia," *Proceedings of the American Psychological Association*, 31 August 1961.
174. KILNER, W. J. *The Human Atmosphere*. London: Rebman, 1911.
175. KINGDON-WARD, F. D. R. Bates, ed., In *The Planet Earth*. London: Pergamon, 1964.
176. KINZEL, A. F. "The Inner Circle," *Time* magazine, 6 June 1969.
177. KIRCHOFF, H. "Umweltfaktoren und Genitalfunktionen," *Geburtsh. u. Frauenh.* 6: 377, 1939.
178. KIRKBRIDE, K. "ESP Communication for the Space Age," *Science and Mechanics*, August 1969.
179. KNOBLOCH, H. & PASAMANICK, B. "Seasonal Variation in the Birth of the Mentally Deficient," *American Journal of Public Health* 48: 1201, 1958.
180. KNOWLES, E. A. G. "Reports on an Experiment Concerning the Influence of Mind over Matter," *Journal of Parapsychology* 13: 186, 1949.
181. KOLODNY, L. "When Apples Fall," *Pravda* (Moscow), 17 March 1968.
182. KONIG, H. & ANKERMULLER, F. "Ueber den Einfluss besonders niederfrequenter elektrischer Vorgänge in der Atmosphäre auf den Menschen," *Naturwiss.* 21: 483, 1960.

183. KOZYREV, N. "Possibility of Experimental Study of the Properties of Time," JPRS, U. S. Dept. of Commerce 45238, 2 May 1968.

184. KRAUT, J. "Nature's Way," *Time* magazine, 29 November 1971.

185. KRUEGER, A. & SMITH, R. "The Physiological Significance of Positive and Negative Ionization of the Atmosphere." In *Mans Dependence on the Earthly Atmosphere.* New York: Macmillan, 1962.

186. KULLENBERG, B. "Field experiments with Chemical Sex Attractants," *J. Zool. Bidr. fran.* 31: 253, 1956.

187. LANGEN, D. "Peripheral Changes in Blood Circulation During Autogenic Training and Hypnosis." In *Psychophysiological Mechanisms of Hypnosis.* New York: Springer-Verlag, 1969.

188. LAWSON-WOOD, D. & LAWSON-WOOD, J. *Judo Revival Points, Athletes' Points and Posture.* Sussex: Health Science Press, 1965.

189. ——. *Five Elements of Acupuncture and Chinese Massage.* Sussex: Health Science Press, 1966.

190. LEATON, MALIN & FINCH. "The Solar and Luni-solar Variation of the Geomagnetic Field at Greenwich and Abinger," *Observatory Bulletin of Great Britain* 53: 273, 1962.

191. LEES, A. D. "The Role of Photoperiod and Temperature in the Determination of Parthenogenetic and Sexual Forms in the Aphid *Megoura Viciae,*" *Journal of Insect Physiology* 3: 92, 1959.

192. LEONIDOV, I. "Signals of What?" *Soviet Union 145:* 1962.

193. LETHBRIDGE, T. C. *Ghost and Divining Rod.* London: Routledge & Kegan Paul, 1963.

194. ——. *A Step in the Dark.* London: Routledge & Kegan Paul, 1967.

195. LEWIN, I. *The Effect of Reward on the Experience of Pain.* Detroit: Wayne State University Press, 1965.

196. LEWIS, J. H. & SARBIN, T. R. "Studies in Psychosomatics," *Psychosomatic Medicine 5:* 125, 1943.

197. LEWIS, P. R. & LOBBAN, M. C. "Dissociation of Diurnal Rhythms in Human Subjects on Abnormal Time Routines," *Quarterly Journal of Experimental Physiology* 42: 371, 1957.

198. LINGEMANN, O. "Tuberkulöses lungenbluten und meteorbiologische Einflusse," *Der Tuberkulösarzt* 9: 261, 1955.

199. LISSMANN, H. W. "Electric Location by Fishes," *Scientific American,* March 1963.

200. LISSMANN, H. W. & MACHIN, K. E. "The Mechanism of Object Location in *Gymnarchus Niloticus* and Similar Fish," *Journal of Experimental Biology* 35: 451, 1958.

201. LIVINGSTONE, D. *Missionary Travels and Researches in Southern Africa*. London: Murray, 1865.

202. LOOMIS, A. L., HARVEY, E. N. & HOBART, G. "Electrical Potentials of the Human Brain," *Journal of Experimental Psychology* 19: 249, 1936.

203. LORENZ, K. *On Aggression*. London: Methuen, 1966.

204. MABY, J. C. & FRANKLIN, B. T. *The Physics of the Divining Rod*. London: G. Bell & Sons, 1939.

205. MAGAT, M. "Change of Properties of Water Around 40° C," *Journal of Physical Radiom*. 6: 108, 1936.

206. MALEK, J., GLEICH, J. & MALY, V. "Characteristics of the Daily Rhythm of Menstruation and Labor," *Annals of the New York Academy of Science* 98: 1042, 1962.

207. MARTINI, R. "Der Einfluss der Sonnentätigkeit auf die Haufung von Umfallen," *Zentral bl. Arbeitsmedizin* 2: 98, 1952.

208. MASHKOVA, V. "Sharpsighted Fingers," *International Journal of Parapsychology* 7: 4, 1965.

209. MAXWELL, N. "The Laughing Man with a Hole in His Chest," London *Sunday Times*, 3 October 1971.

210. MENAKER, W. & A. "Lunar Periodicity in Human Reproduction," *American Journal of Obstetrical Gynecology* 78: 905, 1959.

211. MILECHNIN, A. *Hypnosis*. Bristol: John Wright, 1967.

212. MILES, S. "The Accident Syndrome," *Science Journal* 6: 3, 1970.

213. MINKH, A. A. "Biological and Hygienic Significance of Air Ionization," *Biometeorology Two* 2: 1016, 1967.

214. MIRONOVITCH, V. "Sur l'évolution séculaire de l'activité solaire et ses liaisons avec la circulation générale," *Meteorol. Abhandlungen* 9: 3, 1960.

215. MIRONOVITCH, V. & VIART, R. "Interruption du courant zonal en Europe Occidentale et sa liaison avec l'activité solaire," *Meteorol. Abhandlungen* 7: 3, 1958.

216. MOORE, O. K. "Divination—a New Perspective," *American Anthropologist* 59: 69, 1957.

217. MOORE-ROBINSON, M. "And Puppy Dog Tails," *New Scientist*, 13 November 1969.

218. MORRIS, D. *The Naked Ape*. London: Jonathan Cape, 1967.

219. ———. *Intimate Behaviour*. London: Jonathan Cape, 1971.

220. MUSES, C. A. Introduction to *Communication, Organization, and Science*, by J. Rothstein. New York: Falcon's Wing Press, 1958.

221. MYERS, F. W. H. *Human Personality*. London: Longmans, Green & Company, 1963.

222. McBAIN, W. N. "Quasi-sensory Communication," *Journal of Personality and Social Psychology 14*: 281, 1970.

223. McCONNELL, R. A. "Wishing with Dice," *Journal of Experimental Psychology 50*: 269, 1955.

224. McCREERY, C. *Science, Philosophy and ESP*. London: Faber & Faber, 1967.

225. NASA. *Initial Results of the IMP-1 Magnetic Field Experiment*. Greenbelt, Md.: Goddard Space Flight Center, 1964.

226. NATHAN, P. *The Nervous System*. London: Penguin, 1969.

227. NAUMOV, E. "From Telepathy to Telekinesis," *Journal of Paraphysics 2*: 2, 1966.

228. NELSON, J. H. "Shortwave Radio Propagation Correlation with Planetary Positions," *RCA Review 12*: 26, 1951.

229. ———. "Planetary Position Effect on Short Wave Signal Quality," *Electrical Engineering 71*: 421, 1952.

230. NORTON, A. C., BERAN, A. U. & MISZAHY, G. A. "Electroencephalography During Feigned Sleep in the Opossum," *Nature 204*: 162, 1964.

231. NOVOMEISKY, A. "The Nature of the Dermo-optic Response," *International Journal of Parapsychology 7*: 4, 1965.

232. NOYCE, W. "The Art of Surviving," London *Sunday Times*, March 1960.

233. OSTRANDER, S. & SCHROEDER, L. *Psychic Discoveries Behind the Iron Curtain*. Englewood Cliffs, N.J.: Prentice-Hall, 1971.

234. OSWALD, I. *Sleep*. London: Penguin Books, 1970.

235. OSWALD, I., TAYLOR, A. M. & TREISMAN, M. "Cortical Function During Human Sleep," *CIBA Symposium on Sleep*. Boston: Little, Brown, 1961.

236. OTANI, S. "A Possible Relationship Between Skin Resistance and ESP Response Patterns." In *Parapsychology Today*, by J. B. Rhine & R. Brier. New York: Citadel, 1968.

237. OWEN, A. R. G. *Can We Explain the Poltergeist?* New York: Garrett Publications, 1964.

238. OWEN, A. R. G. & SIMS, V. *Science and the Spook*. London: Dennis Dobson, 1971.

239. PALMER, J. D. "Organismic Spatial Orientation in Very Weak Magnetic Fields," *Nature 198*: 1061, 1963.

240. PAUWELS, L. & BERGIER, J. *"The Morning of the Magicians.* New York: Stein & Day, 1964.

241. PAVLOV, I. P. *Über die sogenannte Tierhypnose.* Berlin: Akad. Verlag, 1953.

242. PEI, M. *The Story of Language.* London: Allen & Unwin, 1966.

243. PENFIELD, W. & JASPER, H. H. *Epilepsy and the Functional Anatomy of the Human Brain.* London: J. & A. Churchill, 1965.

244. PENGELLEY, E. T. & ASMUNDSEN, S. J. "Annual Biological Clocks," *Scientific American 224:* 72, 1971.

245. PETERSEN, W. *Man, Weather, Sun.* Springfield, Ill.: Thomas, 1947.

246. PICCARDI, G. "Exposé introductif," *Symposium Intern. sur les Rel. Phen. Sol et Terre.* Brussels: Presses Académiques Européennes, 1960.

247. ——. *The Chemical Basis of Medical Climatology.* Springfield, Ill.: Thomas, 1962.

248. PITTENDRIGH, C. S. & BRUCE, V. G. "Daily Rhythms As Coupled Oscillator Systems," *Photoperiodism and Related Phenomena in Plants and Animals.* Washington, D.C.: A.A.A.S., 1959.

249. PODSHIBYAKIN, A. K. "Solar Flares and Road Accidents," *New Scientist,* 25 April 1968.

250. POHL, R. "Tagesrhythmik im phototaktischen Verhalten der *Euglena gracilis," Zeitschr. für Naturf. 36:* 367, 1948.

251. POPE, A. *An Essay on Man.* Part I. New York: Macmillan, 1966.

252. POPLE, J. "A Theory on the Structure of Water," *Proceedings of the Royal Society A202:* 323, 1950.

253. POUMAILLOUX, J. & VIART, R. "Correlations possibles entre l'incidence des infarctus du myocarde et l'augmentation des activités solaires et géomagnétiques," *Bull. Acad. Méd. 143:* 167, 1959.

254. PRATT, J. G. "A Reinvestigation of the Quarter Distribution of the PK," *Journal of Parapsychology 8:* 61, 1944.

255. ——. "Lawfulness of the Position Effects in the Gibson Cup Series," *Journal of Parapsychology 10:* 243, 1946.

256. ——. "Target Preference in PK Tests with Dice," *Journal of Parapsychology 11:* 26, 1947.

257. ——. "Rhythms of Success in PK Test Data," *Journal of Parapsychology 11:* 90, 1947.

258. PRATT, J. G. & JACOBSEN, N. "Prediction of ESP Performance on Selected Focusing Effect Targets," *Journal of*

the American Society for Parapsychological Research 63,
1969.

259. PROKASKY, W. F. "The Acquisition of Observing Responses in the Absence of Differential External Reinforcement," *Journal of Comparative Physiological Psychology 49:* 131, 1956.

260. PUSHONG, C. A. *The Tarot of the Magi.* London: Regency, 1970.

261. RAIMA, R. A. "The Peculiar Distribution of First Digits," *Scientific American 221:* 109, 1969.

262. RAND CORPORATION. *A Million Random Digits with 100,000 Normal Deviates.* Chicago: Free Press, 1946.

263. RAUDIVE, K. *Breakthrough.* New York: Taplinger, 1971.

264. ——. "Voices from Nowhere," *Man, Myth & Magic 87:* 2453, 1971.

265. RAVITZ, L. J. "How Electricity Measures Hypnosis," *Tomorrow 6:* 49, 1958.

266. ——. "Periodic Changes in Electromagnetic Fields," *Annals of the New York Academy of Science 96:* 1181, 1960.

267. ——. "History, Measurement and Applicability of Periodic Changes in the Electromagnetic Field in Health and Disease," *Annals of the New York Academy of Science 98:* 144, 1962.

268. REEVES, M. P. & RHINE, J. B. "The Psychokinetic Effect: A Study in Declines," *Journal of Parapsychology 7:* 76, 1943.

269. REINBERG, A. & GHATA, J. *Rythmes et cycles biologiques.* Paris: Presses Universitaires, 1957.

270. REITER, R. "Wetter und Zahl der Geburten," *Dtch. Med. Wochenschr. 77:* 1606, 1952.

271. REJDAK, Z. "The Kulagina Cine Film," *Journal of Paraphysics 3:* 3, 1969.

272. RHINE, J. B. *Extrasensory Perception.* Boston: Bruce Humphries, 1934.

273. ——. "Dice Thrown by Cup and Machine in PK Tests," *Journal of Parapsychology 7:* 207, 1943.

274. RHINE, J. B. & HUMPHREY, B. M. "The PK Effect with Sixty Dice per Throw," *Journal of Parapsychology 9:* 203, 1945.

275. RHINE, L. E. *Mind over Matter.* London: Macmillan, 1970.

276. RICARD, M. *The Mystery of Animal Migration.* London: Paladin, 1971.

277. RICHMOND, N. "Two Series of PK Tests on Paramecia," *Journal of the Society for Psychical Research 36*: 577, 1952.

278. ROBERTS, J. A. "Radio Emission from the Planets," *Planetary Space Science Research 11*: 221, 1963.

279. ROCARD, Y. *New Scientist*, 1966.

280. ROMENSKY, N. V. *Recueil des travaux scientifiques de l'administration des stations thermales et climatériques.* Sotchi, 1960.

281. ROSENFELD, A. "Seeing Colors with the Fingers," *Life*, 12 June 1964.

282. ROSENTHAL, R. *Experimenter Effects in Behavioral Research.* New York: Appleton-Century-Crofts, 1966.

283. ROUGE ET NOIR (a periodical). *Winning at Casino Gaming.* Glen Head, N.Y.: Rouge et Noir, 1966.

284. RUBIN, F. "The Lunar Cycle in Relation to Human Conception and the Sex of Offspring," *Astrological Journal 9*: 4, 1968.

285. RUSSELL, E. W. *Design for Destiny.* London: Neville Spearman, 1971.

286. RYZL, M. "Parapsychology in Communist Countries of Europe," *International Journal of Parapsychology 10*: 3, 1968.

287. ——. "New Discoveries in ESP," *Grenzgebiete der Wissenschaft 1*: 1968.

288. RYZL, M. & PRATT, J. G. "The Focusing of ESP upon Particular Targets," *Journal of Parapsychology 27*: 4, 1963.

289. SALISBURY, H. E. *The Soviet Union.* New York: Harcourt Brace Jovanovitch, 1967.

290. SANDERSON, I. T. "Could Ancient Sculptors Soften Stone?" *Fate Magazine*, February 1963.

291. ——. "Atta, the Telepathic, Teleporting Ant," *Fate Magazine*, May 1963.

292. ——. "Let's Investigate Flying Rocks," *Fate Magazine*, September 1963.

293. ——. *Uninvited Visitors.* London: Neville Spearman, 1969.

294. SCHAFER, W. "Further Development of the Field Effect Monitor," *Life Sciences: General Dynamics* A67-41582: 125, 1968.

295. SCHMIDT, H. "Mental Influence on Random Events," *New Scientist 50*: 757, 1971.

296. SCHNEIDER, F. "Die Beeinflussung der ultraoptischen Orientierung der Maikäfer durch Veranderung des lokalen Massenverteilungsmusters," *Revue Suisse de Zoologie 71*: 632, 1964.

297. SCHNELLE, F. "Hundert Jahre phänologische Beobachtungen im Rhein-Main Gebiet," *Meteorol. Rundschau* 7, 1950.

298. SCHULTZ, J. H. & LUTHE, W. *Autogenic Training.* New York: Grune & Stratton, 1959.

299. SCHULZ, N. "Les globules blancs des sujets bien portants et les taches solaires," *Toulouse Médical* 10: 741, 1960.

300. ———. "Lymphocytoses relatives et activité solaire," *Revue Médicale de Nancy*, June 1961.

301. SCOTT, I. A. *The Lüscher Colour Test.* London: Jonathan Cape, 1970.

302. SEABROOK, W. *Witchcraft.* London: Sphere Books. 1970.

303. SEEDS, N. "A Brain Rewires Itself in a Test Tube," *New Scientist*, 6 January 1972.

304. SHAPIRO, D., TURSKY, B., GERSOHN, E. & STERN, M. "Effects of Feedback and Reinforcement on the Control of Human Systolic Blood Pressure," *Science* 163: 588, 1969.

305. SINCLAIR-GIEBEN, A. H. C. & CHALMERS, D. "Evaluation of Treatment of Warts by Hypnosis," *Lancet* 2: 480, 1959.

306. SMITH, A. *The Body.* London: Allen & Unwin, 1968.

307. SOAL, S. G. & BATEMAN, F. *Modern Experiments in Telepathy.* London: Faber & Faber, 1954.

308. SOCHUREK, H. "Hot Stuff," *Observer Magazine*, 5 December 1971.

309. STEIGER, B. *ESP: Your Sixth Sense.* New York: Award Books, 1966.

310. STEWARD, F. C. "From Cultured Cells to Whole Plants: The Induction and Control of Their Growth and Morphogenesis," *Proceedings of the Royal Society B175*: 1, 1970.

311. SULLIVAN, W. *We Are Not Alone.* London: Penguin, 1970.

312. TAKATA, M. "Über eine neue biologisch wirksame Komponente der Sonnenstrahlung," *Archiv Met. Geophys. Bioklimat.* 486, 1951.

313. TAKATA, M. & MURASUGI, T. "Flockungszahlstörungen im gesunden menschlichen Serum, kosmoterrestrischer Sympathismus," *Bioklimat. Beibl.* 8: 17, 1941.

314. TAUGHER, V. J. "Hypno-anesthesia," *Wisconsin Medical Journal* 57: 95, 1958.

315. TAYLOR, R. L. "Habitual Short-term Expectancies and Luck," *Journal of General Psychology* 76: 81, 1967.

316. TCHIJEVSKY, A. L. "L'Action de l'activité périodique solaire sur les épidémies," *Traité de climatologie biologique et médicale.* Paris: Masson, 1934.

317. TEICHMANN, H. "Das Riechvermögen des Aales," *Naturwiss. 44:* 242, 1957.

318. TEMPEST, W. "Noise Makes Drivers Drunk," London *Observer,* 28 November 1971.

319. TERRY, K. D. & TUCKER, W. H. "Biological Effects of Supernovae," *Science 159:* 421.

320. THOMSON, D. "Force Field Detector," *Maclean's Magazine,* September 1968.

321. TINBERGEN, N. *The Study of Instinct.* Oxford University Press, 1951.

322. TRINDER, W. H. *Dowsing.* London: G. Bell & Sons, 1967.

323. TROMP, S. "Review of the Possible Physiological Causes of Dowsing," *International Journal of Parapsychology 10:* 4, 1968.

324. TUCKER, D. W. "A New Solution to the Atlantic Eel Problem," *Nature 183:* 495, 1959.

325. TUNSTALL, J. "Pharaoh's Curse," London *Times,* 14 July 1969.

326. VAN LENNEP, D. J. "Why Some Succeed and Others Fail," *Progress 48:* 270, 1962.

327. VAN OVER, R. (ed.). *I Ching.* New York: New American Library, 1971.

328. VASILIEV, L. L. *Experiments in Mental Suggestion.* Hampshire: Galley Hill Press, 1963.

329. VERNON, J. A. *Inside the Black Room.* London: Penguin, 1966.

330. VINCE, M. A. "Embryonic Communication, Respiration and the Synchronisation of Hatching." In *Bird Vocalisations.* Cambridge, Eng.: Cambridge University Press, 1969.

331. VOGRALIK, V. G. "Pinpricks for Health," *Sputnik* (Moscow), July 1969.

332. VOLGYESI, F. A. *Hypnosis in Man and Animals.* London: Baillière, 1966.

333. VON DANIKEN, E. *Chariots of the Gods.* London: Souvenir Press, 1969.

334. WADDINGTON, C. H. *The Strategy of Genes.* London: Allen & Unwin, 1957.

335. WALTER, W. G. *The Living Brain.* London: Penguin, 1961.

336. ———. "Voluntary Heart and Pulse Control by Yoga Methods," *International Journal of Parapsychology 5:* 25, 1963.

337. WATSON, L. *The Omnivorous Ape*. New York: Coward-McCann & Geoghegan, 1971.

338. WEBER, J. "The Detection of Gravitational Waves," *Scientific American 224: 22*, 1971.

339. WEST, J. A. & TOONDER, J. G. *The Case for Astrology*. London: Macdonald, 1970.

340. WHITFIELD, G. & BRAMWELL, C. "Palaeoengineering: Birth of a New Science," *New Scientist 52: 202*, 1971.

341. WILLIAMS, H. L., LUBIN, A. & GOODNOW, J. J. "Impaired Performance with Acute Sleep Loss," *Psychological Monographs 73: 14*, 1959.

342. WILSON, C. *The Occult*. London: Hodder & Stoughton, 1971.

343. WILSON, E. D. "Pheromones," *Scientific American*, May 1963.

344. WOOD JONES, F. *The Principles of Anatomy As Seen in the Hand*. London: Braillière, 1946.

345. YAKOLEV, B. "Telepathy Session, Moscow-Novosibirsk," *Sputnik* (Moscow), February 1968.

346. YOUNG, J. Z. *An Introduction to the Study of Man*. London: Oxford University Press, 1971.

347. ZEUNER, F. E. *Dating the Past*. London: Methuen, 1950.

Appendix

1. BARBER, T. X. et al. (editors). *Biofeedback and Self-Control*.
Aldine Annuals. Chicago: Aldine-Atherton, 1971.
A collection of thirty-eight scientific articles drawn mainly from medical journals dealing with psychosomatic and psychophysiological research.

2. BURR, H. S. *Blueprint for Immortality*.
London: Neville Spearman, 1972.
Burr's personal record of his discovery and exploration of the Electro-dynamic, or Life, Field. Including full bibliography.

3. FREEDLAND, N. *The Occult Explosion*.
London: Michael Joseph, 1972.
An up-to-date review of contemporary manifestations of occult interest.

4. KARLINS, M. & ANDREWS, L. M. *Biofeedback*.
New York: J. B. Lippincott, 1972.
A summary of the latest research into regulation of bodily processes and consciousness. With full bibliography.

INDEX

Acupuncture, 147–49

Addey, John, 73–74

Alarm calls and signals, survival value of, 249–50, 274

Alchemy, 175–80

Allergies, as responsive to hypnotic suggestion, 217–18

Alpha activities and rhythms in brain waves, 223, 224, 259; and sleep, 213; and telepathy, 256–57, 259, 263

"Alphaphone," 223, 258

American Federation of Astrologers, 71

American Institute of Mathematical Statistics, 253–54

American Institute of Medical Climatology, 50

American Society of Geneticists, 71

Amino acids, as units of protein construction, 3

Amoebae: multiplication of, 198–99; pseudopodia of, 245–46

Andrews, Donald, 105, 106

Andrews, Dr. Edson, 49, 50

Animal communication, 186

Animal hypnosis, 213–14

Animals, cold-blooded, effects of temperature fluctuations on, 19–20

Animals, dreams of, 235–36

Animals, higher, sleep habits of, 231

Animals, land: moon's influence on, 26, 30, 31; sensitivity of, to water, 110–11, 118; behavior patterns of; 195–96; immobilization of, how induced, and survival value of, 209–10, 211–13; sleep habits of, 231

Animals, sound vibrations and, 106–7

Animals, tidal, reaction of, to moon's influence, 22

Animals, warm-blooded, and sleep, 230–31

Annual cycle, heat and light sensitivity to, 17–20

Aquatic mammals, and appearance of sleep, 231

Astral: bodies, 146–47; projection, 306, 307

Astrological predictions, based on position of planets at time of birth, 54–60

Astrology, and horoscope construction, 61–76

Atoms: arrangement of, in a molecule, 5; behavior of water's atoms, 35; of life, 123–24; infrared rays generated by, 142–43

Aura surrounding the body, 141–50; and thermographic technique, 142–43

Aurora borealis, as related to magnetic storms, sunspots, and other phenomena, 32, 53

Automatic talking and writing, 266

Autosuggestion, 219–29, 282. *See also* Hypnotism, mass

Axis of earth, and yearly cycle of changes in circadian rhythm, 16–17

Baby identification, and palm-printing, 191

Backster, Cleve, 247, 248, 249

Bagnall, Oscar, 144

Baldo, Camillo, 194

Barber, Theodore, 219

Barley seeds, experiments with, 163–64

Behavior, patterns of: and the mind, 183, 184; learned patterns of animals, 195–96; assessment of, by functional requirements, 197

Beloff, John, 134, 135

Bengali sect, and state of ecstasy, 224

Berger, Hans, 89

Berne, Eric, 277

Biochemical systems, and exchange of matter, 4

"Biophysical Effects Method, The," 113

Birds: heat and light experiments on, 17–19; sleep patterns of, 230

Birth: time of, as affecting human height, weight, and IQ, 46–47; and position of the planets, giving rise to astrological predictions, 54–60; birth control and lunar rhythms, 69–70

Black, Stephen, 175, 214, 217

Blind, ability to "see" by the, 167–73

Blood pressure, control of, at will, 222–23

Blushing, 207

Body, language, 186, 187; shape and proportion, 202–3; dominated by brain, 209

Book of Changes, 301, 302

Boyle, Robert, 175

Braid, James, 213

Brain: and electrical impulses, 126–28; signals from, determining use of hand, 194; domination of body by, 209; records of experience stored by, 219–20; and sleep, 231–32; and drugs, 237–43

Brain and mind, relationship between, 150

Brain patterns and rhythms, 90–91, 152–55

Brain waves: and electrophysiology, 89, 152–53; and PK effects, 152–55; and theta rhythms in, 153–55, 256; of a hypnotized subject, 215; alpha rhythms in, 223, 224, 231, 259; and telepathic transmission, 256–57, 259, 262, 263

Brain waves of birds and small animals, 213

Bramwell, Cherrie, 199–200

British Acoustical Society, 92

British Society of Dowsers, 112

Brown, Frank, 22, 23, 28, 29, 30, 31, 35, 40–41

Burr, Harold, 81–87